MY KOREAN DELI

MY KOREAN DELI

RISKING IT ALL FOR A CONVENIENCE STORE

BEN RYDER HOWE

HENRY HOLT AND COMPANY
NEW YORK

Henry Holt and Company, LLC
Publishers since 1866
175 Fifth Avenue
New York, New York 10010
www.henryholt.com

Henry Holt ® and 🔲 ® are registered trademarks of Henry Holt and Company, LLC.

Library of Congress Cataloging-in-Publication Data

Howe, Ben Ryder.
  My Korean deli: risking it all for a convenience store / Ben Ryder Howe.
    p.   cm.
  ISBN 978-0-8050-9343-8
  1. Howe, Ben Ryder. 2. Convenience stores—New York (State)—New York.
3. Delicatessens—New York (State)—New York. 4. Korean American business
enterprises—New York (State)—New York.   5. Businesspeople—New York (State)—
New York.   I. Title.
  HF5469.55.U63N4946 2010
  381'.147092—dc22
  [B]

                                                                    2010024962

Henry Holt books are available for special promotions and premiums.
For details contact: Director, Special Markets.

First Edition 2010

Designed by Meryl Sussman Levavi

Printed in the United States of America

10 9 8 7 6 5 4 3 2 1

For Dwayne Wright

1968–2009

"Most guys from the projects has Wizard of Oz
disease: they can't go nowhere unless they got three
other people with them. They're like, 'I'm the Tin
Man and I don't have a heart. Will you come with
me to look for one? Cuz I'm afraid to leave Brooklyn
alone.'"

MY KOREAN DELI

PART ONE

STEAM TABLE

FALL 2002

Last summer my wife's family and I decided to buy a deli. By fall, with loans from three different relatives, two new credit cards, and a sad kiss good-bye to thirty thousand dollars my wife and I had saved while living in my mother-in-law's Staten Island basement, we had rounded up the money. Now it is November, and we are searching New York City for a place to buy.

We have different ideas about what our store should look like. My mother-in-law, Kay, the Mike Tyson of Korean grandmothers, wants a deli with a steam table, one of those stainless steel, cafeteria-style salad bars that heat the food to just below the temperature that kills bacteria—the zone in which bacteria thrive. She wants to serve food that is either sticky and sweet, or too salty, or somehow all of the above, and that roasts in the dusty air of New York City all day, while roiling crowds examine it at close distance—pushing it around, sampling it, breathing on it. Kay's reason for wanting a deli of this kind is that steam tables bring in a lot of money, up to a few thousand dollars per hour at lunchtime. She also wants a store that is open twenty-four hours and stays open on Christmas and Labor Day. She'd like it to be in the thick of Manhattan, on a street jammed with tourists and office workers.

I don't know what I want, but an all-night deli in midtown with a steam table isn't it. I'm the sort of person who loses my appetite if I walk past an establishment with a steam table. I get palpitations and the sweats just being around sparerib tips. Of course, I don't have to eat the food if we buy a deli with a steam table. I just have to sell it. That's what Kay says she plans to do. But Kay has an unfair advantage: years ago, after she came to America, she lost her sense of smell, and now she can't detect the difference between a bouquet of freesias and a bathroom at the bus station. My nose, on the other hand, is fully functional.

Luckily, I'm in charge of the real estate search, and so far I have successfully steered us from any delis serving hot food. As a result, Kay's frustration is starting to become lethal.

"What's the matter?" she asked me the other day. "You not like money? Why you make us poor?"

These are not unfair questions. I would say that one of my biggest faults as a human being is that I do not love money, which makes me lazy and spoiled. Like finding us a store, for example. Call me a snob, but somehow a deli *grocery*—a traditional fruit and vegetable market—seems more dignified than a deli dishing out slop by the pound in Styrofoam trays. Is that practical? We are, after all, talking about the acquisition of a deli, not a summer home or a car. If dignity is so important, why not buy a bookstore or a bakery? Why not spend it on a business where I have to dress up for work?

Don't get me wrong: I'm not insecure about becoming a deli owner. I even sort of like the idea. Aside from a few "gentleman farmers," no one can remember the last person in my family who worked with their hands. After blowing off law school and graduate school, after barely getting through college and even more narrowly escaping high school, why would I suddenly get snobbish?

But the truth is, I'm still young (thirty-one is young, right?) and can afford to be blasé. It's like the job I had as a seventeen-year-old pumping gas outside Boston, a gig I remember as brainless heaven. I enjoyed coming home smelly. I enjoyed looking inside people's cars while scraping the crud off their windows. I enjoyed flirting with women drivers twice my age.

Who knows how I would have felt if seventeen were just the beginning, and I could look forward to fifty more years of taking orders from strangers.

TODAY WE ARE looking at a deli with a steam table. This morning I was informed of the news by a fire-breathing giant, a creature escaped from a horror movie about mutants spawned by an industrial accident, who hovered at my bedside until I awoke with a start, upon which the creature said: *For two weeks you be in charge of finding our store, and you not come up with anything. So starting today we do it my way.* Then the creature exited, accompanied, it seemed to my half-asleep ears, by the sound of dragging chains.

For the rest of the morning I lie there under the sheets as a form of protest, not intending to get out, until my wife, Gab, sits down on the bed next to me with a cup of coffee.

"I want you and my mother to go together," Gab says. "I can't come because I have things to do at home."

The store is near Times Square and has a name like Luxury Farm or Delicious Mountain. Its Korean owners claim to be making eight thousand dollars a day, a preposterous sum that nevertheless has Kay all excited.

"Don't be afraid of steam table," she says as we drive to the store. "If smelling something stranger, close nose and think of biiig money."

I exhale deeply and try to follow her advice, but instead of fistfuls of cash all I can think of are slabs of desiccated meat loaf slathered in congealed gravy and the smell of boiled ham. So I focus on the drive into midtown—the glowering skyscrapers, the silhouettes of bankers and lawyers behind tinted windows a few stories above the traffic, the gigantic television screens featuring high-cheekboned models talking on cell phones, and at street level my future comrades among the peonage: the restaurant deliverymen, the tarot readers, the no-gun security guards and the DVD bootleggers.

The owner of the deli is a distressingly perky woman named Mrs. Yu. She's frizzy-haired and victimized by an excess of teeth, and she's wearing the Korean deli owner's official uniform: a puffy vest and a Yankees cap settled snugly over her Asianfro. Her age—approximately mid-fifties—is the same as Kay's, which makes her part of the generation of Koreans who came to America in the 1980s and became the most successful immigrant group ever—ever: the people who took over the deli industry from the Greeks and the Italians, the people who drove the Chinese out of the dry-cleaning trade, the people who took away nail polishing from African-Americans, and the people whose children made it impossible for underachievers like me to get into the same colleges our parents had attended.

"My name Gloria Yu," she says when we walk in. "My store make you rich." She winks at me. "Cost only half million dollar."

It seems hard to imagine how any convenience store, even one that can get away with charging twelve dollars for a six-pack of Bud Ice, could be worth half a million dollars, but Gloria Yu's store probably deserves it if any of them do. Like a ship squeezed inside a bottle, a full-sized supermarket has somehow been folded into the space meant for a restaurant or a flower shop. Thousands of items line the shelves, seemingly one of everything. In my general state of paranoia, it occurs to me that if I were to be trapped in this place by some sort of prolonged emergency, such as a flood or a toxic cloud, I could survive for months, maybe even a year, and find something new to eat each day.

"So," Gloria Yu says to me, her voice quivering with excitement, "this your first store?"

"Yes, it is," I confess guiltily.

"I knew it!" she says, practically jumping up and down with excitement. "I knew it! I knew it! You not look like *normal* deli owner." A few customers glance nervously our way.

"So where you from?" Gloria Yu asks me.

"Um, Boston."

"Boston? Like the Boston, Massachusetts? No, no, no. No, no, no."

"What do you mean, 'no, no, no'?" I ask impatiently. "That's where I grew up."

"Not where you grow up, where your *family* from?" Gloria Yu says.

"Oh, you mean originally? Like where are my ancestors from? Here, I suppose. Here as much as anywhere else."

"Hmm . . ." says Gloria Yu, massaging her chin thoughtfully. "Very interesting. Okay, time to show deli!"

Now Gloria Yu thinks I am some sort of freak. Hopefully it will prevent her from selling us her store.

"You two go ahead," I say. "I'm going to wander around alone."

Am I a freak? Why does the steam table scare me so much?

On an even deeper level, though, I wonder, Is fear of the steam table a fear of commitment? A fear of going all the way? Maybe I just need to get it over with and eat a plateful of American chop suey.

"Hey you!" a voice says.

I look around, but there's no one. Kay and Gloria have moved several paces ahead. I'm standing in the drink section, an area filled with glass-doored refrigerators and a rainbow assortment of fluids.

"Hey mister!" the voice commands.

Still nothing.

"Over here," the voice says. "Look inside." And now I see. Next to me, apparently imprisoned within a soda refrigerator, is a balding Korean man in a puffy vest.

"I'm you," the man says, banging meekly on the glass.

"I'm sorry?" I say, yanking the door open. The prisoner stands behind a rack of soft drinks, only his right hand poking through.

"I'm Yu," he says. "Mr. Yu. Store owner. You come to buy store, right?"

"Oh," I say. "Nice to meet . . . you." I speak these words, as far as anyone watching is concerned, to nothing but a rack of soda. (The refrigerator is one of those models that open up from behind, so you can stock the shelves from back to front. Except for his hand, Mr. Yu remains hidden.)

"This store very good," Mr. Yu says cheerily, his hand gesturing dramatically and at one point seeming to lunge straight for my crotch. "Eight thousand a day no problem. You like something to drink?" The hand starts pointing at different flavors. "Which one your favorite? Have any one. Try many different color."

"Thank you," I say to the hand, while taking out a bottle of Code Red. "It's a nice store." Mr. Yu wants to continue the conversation, but before he can, I gently close the door. Then, in an unplanned gesture, I bow solemnly to the walk-in refrigerator.

"Okay, Mr. Original American," says Gloria Yu, coming up behind me with Kay. "You ready to buy my deli?" She winks at me again and says something to Kay in Korean—something evidently quite hilarious, as they both erupt in hysterical laughter.

"What's so funny?" I ask.

"Don't be worrying," says Gloria Yu, adding mysteriously, "You'll be making successful again soon."

"What? Excuse me?"

"Don't be worrying, I said. Success coming! But first, I want to show you something." A devious smile lights up her lips. "I want you and your mother-in-law to come with me so I can show you where *this*"—she gestures expansively at the steam-table spread, like a game show model unveiling a new car—"is made."

We follow Gloria Yu to the store's basement, where things get dingy pretty fast. The space is cramped, the light dim, and as the temperature starts to climb, the smell of American chop suey becomes as overpowering as a trash can full of baby diapers. In the basement we find a gang of six Mexicans dressed in thick fire-retardant gloves and steel-toed boots—work gear more appropriate to a steelworks than a kitchen. Evidently you don't cook the food that gets served at a steam table. You attack it with extreme bursts of heat from an oven that looks like a smelter. And you don't prepare it, either. You buy it premade from an offsite mass producer of cafeteria and hospital fare somewhere in Connecticut.

The whole experience is rather shocking, and I think Kay feels bad for me. On our way home, I expect the usual barrage of scorn, like sitting too close to a nuclear reactor, but instead she's quiet. And then as we drive over the Verrazano-Narrows Bridge, the gateway to Staten Island and the traditional summing-up point for any of our family's journeys, she tells me she's changed her mind.

"We need small place, for family only. That one too big. Besides, I'm not really trusting that woman anyway. If store be making eight thousand dollars every day, how come she and her husband still working there?"

A few minutes later we pull into the driveway of our home and find Gab outside. Instead of having just snubbed out a cigarette, which is what she was really doing, she pretends to have been waiting for us. She does have news, after all.

She bends over and sticks her head through the passenger window, maintaining just enough distance so that we won't smell the smoke on her breath.

"I found the perfect store," she says.

IT WASN'T MY idea to buy a deli. The idea came to my wife at the time of her thirtieth birthday. Thirty can be an uncomfortable turning point for those inclined to measure their own accomplishments against those of their parents. Gab took it especially hard.

"What have I done with my life?" she asked me.

I reminded her that she had graduated from one of the best colleges in the world (the University of Chicago, where we met almost ten years ago) and obtained both a master's degree and a law degree. She'd even had a burgeoning career as a corporate attorney at a Manhattan law firm, until she'd decided to chuck it all so she could open this deli for her mother.

"And?" she retorted angrily. "Do you know what my mother had accomplished by the time she was thirty? She had three kids who she had raised with no help from my father. She had her own business, which she ran by herself. And she was about to immigrate to America, a country she knew nothing about. All by thirty!"

I thought of reminding Gab that her mom never finished

college—Gab was beating her three to none in the degree category—but it didn't seem like what she wanted to hear.

Over the course of the next few months, Gab's thirtieth-birthday paranoia transformed into an obsession with repaying her mother's sacrifice. Mistakenly, I had thought that she had already done that by being successful herself. But as the year went on, it became clear that Gab would not be satisfied without a sacrifice of her own. So her goal became to give back some of what Kay had given up in coming to America.

She was going to give her back her business.

And sacrifice her husband.

Kay's old business had been a bakery serving typical Korean desserts. She spoke of it so lovingly one wondered how she had ever coped with its loss. However, unless Americans suddenly developed a taste for mung bean balls and glutinous rice cakes, doing the same kind of business was not going to be an option. Kay knew how to run a deli, having twenty years of experience clerking at 7-Elevens and Stop'n Gos across America. Yet she was no longer the same person she had been in her twenties. Though still frighteningly strong at the age of fifty-five (her one weakness being an inability to say no to relatives requesting favors), she was now prone to thunderous physical breakdowns that left her bedridden for days. And the breakdowns were getting longer and more thunderous. She still smoked, she ate terribly, and she invariably found ways to get out of the doctors' appointments her children tried making for her.

Moreover, physical health was not the only issue. America had wrought some mysterious changes, like the loss of her sense of smell. And there was the question of why she'd never returned to owning her own business. Was she scared? Intimidated? Had she lost her nerve? Or had she lost the desire and the drive? Was she possibly depressed? No one knew, because Kay would no more discuss her feelings than she would go to a doctor. (She had no trouble exhibiting them, but discussing them was out of the question.) Due to her complex psychology, it was possible, of course, that she was all of those things. However, the only obvious reason why she hadn't opened a store was money.

You need money to start a business, and Gab and I, around the time of her thirtieth birthday, were enjoying, for the first time in our married lives, having just a little money in our bank account. It was money we guarded with insane desperation, not even telling each other how much was in the account. The very act of saving was new to us, like a magic power we couldn't quite believe we had acquired. But even more important, it was that money and that money alone that would eventually buy our freedom from Kay's house on Staten Island.

We had moved into the basement nine months before, after the lease on our Brooklyn apartment expired. After living in Brooklyn for three years, we had tired of paying rent to our landlord, a former ad executive from Parsippany who had miswired our brownstone so that everything blew up in our faces. We wanted to own our own space and there were thoughts of starting a family, and when the lease ran out we decided it was time. Kay's house was to serve as a temporary refuge while we house-hunted.

Deep shame attended our moving into Gab's mother's household, but it was not as bad as moving to Staten Island, New York City's pariah borough, a place where once-hot trends like Hummers and spitting go to die, a place so forsaken that not even Starbucks would set up a store there, nor even the most enterprising Thai restaurant owner—only immigrants from the former Soviet bloc, people fleeing environmental disasters and the most involuted economies on earth. (Perhaps they found something homelike in the smoldering industrial landscape, a familiar scent in the air.) As Gab and I quickly discovered, friends were uneasy about visiting us in our new borough. "Can you smell the dump where you live?" they would ask. "How long does it take to develop a Staten Island accent?" We promised they wouldn't have to go back to Park Slope wearing velour sweat suits or smelling like garbage, but still they wouldn't visit us.

Our bedroom was in a basement. It had exactly one window, a shoe box–sized portal at ground level that occasionally allowed us a clean, unobstructed view of an ankle. One of our neighbors had a bored old house cat who used to come and sit in the one window and watch us undress. Probably he wondered what kind of deranged animal chose to live its life underground, watching people's ankles. Above our heads, clomping around day and night, were relatives of Gab's who'd recently made the trip from Korea and were as surprised to see us as we them. "We can understand living with your parents in Korea," they said, "but America is a very big country." Some of them stayed with us for months, squeezing three at a time into beds made for one. Some of them were new immigrants who spoke no English at all, but it didn't matter in Kay's house because the television was forever playing Korean soap operas, and the radio was constantly tuned to Korean talk radio, and the refrigerator was filled with bean sprout soup, sea slugs and fermented cabbage. I was the only one for whom it mattered, because I did not eat Korean food and could not speak a word of Korean.

Gab and I had no sex at all for the first three months. Too dangerous. In an Asian household no one wears shoes indoors, so you never hear anyone coming. And since the general rule in the Paks' house was that an unworn shirt was your shirt, an uneaten chicken leg your chicken leg, people were always barging into the basement hoping to get into *our* bed.

From the day we moved in, we were dying to get out, which gave us the power to save thirty thousand dollars in less than a year.

But then came Gab's thirtieth birthday, and suddenly our misery didn't matter anymore—in fact, the greater our misery, the better Gab felt. "Don't worry," she said to me. "We'll still be able to move out." She had a plan. At first, she and I would be the owners of whatever store we bought, and Kay would be the manager. During this period, we would keep the store's profits and use them to replenish our bank account. Later on, within the six months or so it would take for the business to stabilize, we would transfer ownership to Kay and resume our old lives.

This plan was so foolhardy, so pregnant with the seeds of its own destruction, that it was almost as if it had come from me, not Gab.

GAB'S "PERFECT" STORE is in Brooklyn, a borough that, while beloved by many, stirs nothing in the heart of Kay, or that of anyone else in my wife's family, for that matter. For the Paks, Brooklyn is nothing but a sprawling, dirty, dangerous place with no Korean restaurants or supermarkets and none of the prestige or business opportunities of Manhattan. Except to go the airport or endure a passage on the Brooklyn-Queens Expressway, the borough has no place in their lives.

"The store is owned by North Koreans," Gab reports gleefully. This is excellent news because training in the Kim Il Sung school of neo-Stalinist entrepreneurship tends to put one at a fairly severe competitive disadvantage, and we have hopes that the store will be undervalued.

Nothing, however, could have prepared us for the spectacle we were about to witness. While the store is in a trendy neighborhood surrounded by restaurants with one-word names and menus offering eleven-dollar desserts, the store itself—well, I've seen hunting cabins in the woods that were better stocked. The shelves are all but empty, and the place looks like it has been bombed, judging by the rubble swept into the corners and the tattered awning fluttering in the stiff November wind.

The owners, an older couple and their two silent daughters, are extremely friendly, but things only get weirder after we meet. "Country people," Kay whispers to me as they lead us on a tour. They are like human beings from a different century, and they have funny accents and use words that Kay and Gab don't understand. Both have numerous missing teeth and haircuts they've obviously given themselves.

The store embarrasses them, and they apologize for it, offering to feed us as compensation. "Come," they say, leading us to the kitchen, where a mysterious crimson broth burbles and seethes inside a blackened pot. "No, thank you," we all say. Next to the stove I see a box of broken-down fruit crates, tree branches and other bits of scrap wood. Gab goes off to use the bathroom and returns wearing an alarmed scowl, having peed in a makeshift closet with only duct-taped cardboard for walls. This place has secrets. I begin to feel like an intruder. And then we ask to be shown the basement.

The owners look at each other nervously. "Okay," says the husband. "Follow me."

It's nothing to be ashamed of, really—just violently at odds with the city health code. The owners (or somebody; we don't ask) turn out to live in the basement, where there are beds, dressers and clotheslines hung with wet laundry. Being basement dwellers ourselves, Gab and I withhold judgment, but Kay is appalled. It looks like the power has been cut off recently, judging by all the candles, and I assume that the kindling I saw by the stove is what they've been using to heat themselves. Then suddenly a loud noise fills the basement, vibrating like an earthquake, and a subway car goes by right on the other side of the basement wall.

"Bet that keeps you up at night," I say to the male owner.

"Bet what does?" he replies.

We go back upstairs and take another look. The store is a full-blown disaster—during the twenty minutes we've been visiting, not one customer has come in—but with work it can be turned around, and outside waits a fancy neighborhood filled with big spenders. The owners want seventy-five thousand dollars, which we offer them; then we wait for their response. Nothing happens for several days. We have now been looking for a store for three months, and patience in the Pak family has truly all but run out.

"How hard can it be?" Gab exclaims. "Is New York City not filled with delis? We aren't looking to open a whole supermarket. All we want is our own little space."

"Maybe it's a message," Kay says. "Buying store is mistake."

But we've already considered the alternatives, such as a Subway or a twenty-four-hour photo shop or a fishmonger's, and ruled out each one, because the Pak family's expertise lies in convenience stores.

Then the owners of the Brooklyn store call. They tell Gab they've decided not to sell after all and, in keeping with their mysterious ways, offer us no explanation. Perfectly polite and friendly, but perfectly strange at the same time. In a month or so we will drive by their business, just to see if they were telling us the truth, and we will confirm that indeed it has not been sold, but neither is it open. The place is dark and shuttered. A little after that Kay will hear through the Korean grapevine that the old man had suffered a heart attack and the family had moved to parts unknown.

"Now what we do?" Kay says in disgust. "I'm not be having energy anymore. This drive me to be the crazy person."

We all look to Gab, who is slumped on the living room couch and seems in fact to be sinking into it, sucked down by some depressive force emanating from below the house. She says nothing for a while, but then:

"I can look at one more store," she says. "Just one. After that I'm finished."

Kay gets the Korean newspaper, and there in the classifieds it is: *"Busy street, bright store, new refrigerators—Brooklyn. $170K."*

That was how we found out about Salim's store.

SLUSH PILE

AS I PREPARE TO BECOME NEW YORK'S NEWEST DELI OWNER, I take comfort in still having my job at the *Paris Review,* where I've worked for five years. Being an editor at America's premier literary journal is like an anchor, holding me fast no matter how far I drift. Yet I've been free in how I talk about the deli—too free. I've told too many people, when the truth is that you never know how people are going to respond. In professional baseball they say that when a player gets sent to the minors, an invisible wall forms around him in the locker room; one second he's a teammate and then *poof!* Suddenly he's a ghost, a leper, a virus. I'm afraid that when people hear about the deli, they'll say the right things ("That's wonderful!

I'll be sure to stop by when you're working!") but be afraid to go near me for fear of catching the curse and ending up the manager of an I Can't Believe It's Yogurt at the mall.

I didn't tell everyone, just some friends and people in the office. But maybe that's too many, for the one person I haven't told—my boss, the famed writer, editor and bon vivant George Plimpton—is the one person whose reaction I fear most. George isn't an ogre or anything. Far from it. Basically he's a kindly, lovable old man who likes to walk around the office in his boxer shorts and rarely fires anyone. He's certainly not one of those pathological magazine editors who overworks their staff until they slump over their desk dead of a heart attack at age thirty-six. If you're going to slump over your desk at the *Paris Review*, it had better be dead drunk, not dead dead. But there is one issue that would cause George to fire his own family, and that's loyalty. When it comes to allegiance to the cause, he's like a Mafia boss. And while a deli is not exactly competition for the next Lorrie Moore story or a National Magazine Award, it might be construed as competition for a certain senior editor's passion and commitment.

What's worse is that lately I have taken a lot of time off, and I suspect George has noticed. Now, it's hard to take off too much time at the *Paris Review*, where editors have been known to not report to work for up to an entire year.

"Where were you?" says George sternly upon their return.

"I had to go to Europe to find myself," says the editor.

"Very well then," says George. "Carry on." Other valid excuses included skiing, finishing my novel, and working off a brutal hangover.

My excuse isn't something I want to share with George, however. It's called burnout, and call me paranoid, but that seems like the kind of thing you soldier through rather than confess to your boss. Admitting to your boss that you've lost the passion for work would be sort of like admitting to your wife that you've lost the passion for, well, *her*, would it not? ("Now, honey, don't take this *personally* . . .") Doesn't seem like a good idea.

I started feeling burned out about a year ago, I think. There was no single moment when it began, no crummy experience that set it off, just a deadening feeling that what had motivated me to become an editor no longer did the trick. The most worrisome change was that at some point I noticed that I wasn't all that interested in what we published. I didn't care what went in the magazine. Sometimes I read it, sometimes I didn't. If it was a story or an interview I brought in, I took it as a professional responsibility to back it as vigorously as I could through publication. But otherwise I had a hard time caring. And this is weird because like everyone else at the *Review*, I supposedly do what I do *because* I care, not for the money, which there isn't any of. People at the *Review* care enough not only to accept measly little salaries but to work at tiny little desks with ten-year-old computers in the basement of George's townhouse. They care enough to reject superlative, wondrous stories by the most famous authors in the world because they have a single lousy sentence or half-assed scene, or because *it's not his or her best work*. They care enough to get into shouting matches over the serial comma, em dashes and whether you can begin a sentence with "And" or "But." But now I can no longer experience outrage upon seeing a ho-hum story accepted or *The Chicago Manual of Style*'s guidelines on the italicization of familiar foreign words flouted. Little things that used to make me crazy don't anymore. This isn't the material's fault, incidentally: the *Paris Review* is famous for having introduced the work of Philip Roth and Jack Kerouac, among others, and it continues to publish the great writing of the day. Maybe the problem is that there's no risk involved.

Risk—what would that even entail? I'm not sure I know. Not simulated risk, not managed risk, not the sort of risk you get whizzing down a zip line in Outward Bound. (Wheeee!) I'm talking about the real world, dog-eat-dog, kill-or-be-killed. Not that literary publishing doesn't entail risk on an individual level—you might start a new magazine and end up publishing only two issues, or you might write a book and get an embarrassing review. You might lose your job. These are obviously real and painful outcomes, and greatly to be avoided. But fear of getting fired or embarrassed doesn't always get you out of bed in the morning (or if it does, it doesn't do much more), and on a larger level, since publishing is a losing enterprise so much of the time and failure is almost expected (Donald Barthelme: "What an artist does, is fail. . . . There is no such thing as a successful artist."), "risk" becomes a relative concept. (Possibility of failure versus the possibility of ruining one's life, having to flee the country, etc.) Moreover, some might say that publishing is insulated, even rigged; everyone comes from the same upper-middle-class background, and it's all very social, very dependent on things other than sheer talent, like networking and personality. When those are the kinds of skills that matter, you can never really be sure of your successes, or your failures.

Disaster—have I ever faced disaster? No one to catch you if you fall? No safety net? What would that be like?

Don't get me wrong: I certainly don't want to take any foolish risks. Nothing rash, nothing imprudent. And I feel fairly certain that this funk, or whatever it is, will eventually pass. I can't even conceive of quitting the *Review* or letting myself get fired by George. Which is why this deli business has me worried.

TODAY IS MY day off, and at the end of the afternoon I get a call at home from Tom, George Plimpton's assistant.

"George is looking for you," Tom says.

"Me?" I blurt out. "Why me?"

"I don't know. But I think you should come to the office as soon as possible."

I look at the clock, trying to decide how quickly I can make it to the Upper East Side. It's the end of the afternoon and I am sitting in Kay's basement in my pajamas. I tell Tom it'll have to be tomorrow. "By the way, did George say what he wanted?" I ask.

"Nope," says Tom.

"How did he seem?"

"Agitated."

"Agitated? Really?" This isn't good. "Can you describe the agitation?"

Tom sighs. "He came in the office and asked, 'Where's Ben?' three times. Does that seem agitated enough?"

"Okay, okay," I say. This isn't good at all, so I make plans to visit the office the next day, screwing up plans I had already made with Gab to see the new store, which agitates *her* greatly. Lately a tone of desperation has entered Gab's voice. She's been taking our inability to find a store awfully hard.

"There are fourteen thousand delis in New York City," she says, shaking her head. "We can't even find one to buy, let alone fail at owning. What kind of immigrants are we? Maybe we've been in this country too long."

I have no answers. All I can say is "Let me sort out this business at the *Review* and find out what's wrong with George." We decide that I should drive to the *Review* in Kay's Honda (normally I would take the ferry and the subway, a two-hour trip) so that I can return to Staten Island as quickly as possible.

ON MY WAY to the Upper East Side I practice groveling for my job. "Please, George, don't fire me. I'll do anything to avoid this right now. You don't know how low I'm sinking." Or maybe he does know, and that's the problem. In any case, whether it's because someone told him about the deli or because my desk has been unoccupied for too many days, I intend to make it up with a dramatic offer: to read the slush pile again, the monstrous heap of unsolicited, occasionally brilliant but for the most part punishingly unreadable stories that arrive at the *Paris Review* each day by the duffel bag. That will impress him. Reading the slush is like getting lobotomized with a giant magnet. It's something only interns can handle.

On my way I duck into a store, a deli, to get change to put in the meter.

"Can I help?" the owner says. It's a closet deli, one of those stores that make you feel like you've accidentally fallen into a coffin. It's a deli I've tended to avoid over the years while working a few blocks away, largely because of the cat hair (one hoped it was cat hair) that the store owner gave as a bonus with every purchase of fresh fruit or a pastry. There was also the owner's off-putting demeanor, which could best be described as funereal.

"Just a minute," I say. I wasn't planning on buying anything, just getting a few quarters and biding my time before the confrontation with George, but the store is empty of customers (as usual) and to just walk out would be rude. The owner goes back to watching a black-and-white television the size of a toaster.

Just pick something and get out of here, I think.

"Here," I exclaim, grabbing the item nearest to the register, a packet of harmless-looking energy pills.

"And a Red Bull," I add. The owner retrieves one from a little refrigerator behind the counter.

Energy will be good, I think as I leave the store. For this performance I need to be on my toes. In top form, so I can charm George's socks off. Only after I have consumed the contents of the package and started to feel a disconcertingly pleasant buzz in my lower abdomen do I realize that in addition to the Red Bull I have just swallowed the Men's 4-Pac, a "natural" male performance enhancer.

✳ ✳ ✳

GEORGE PLIMPTON IS seventy-five years old, as tall as an NBA small forward, as pale as New England fog, and usually covered with gashes and scrapes, as if he's just emerged from a rosebush. Some of the wounds result from being old and having unfortunate Wasp skin, which I share, but beyond that George lives in a tall man's goofy world and is constantly crashing into things, tripping over them, or causing them to fall on him simply by being in their presence. Once, after those of us who work for him thought we had seen all of him there was to be seen (I wasn't kidding when I said he liked to walk around the office in his boxers, although usually only after hours), he took the opportunity to show the office an MRI of his testicles, which had been injured at a writers' conference in a late-night collision with a golden retriever.

Lest I create the image of a clown, however, let me be clear in saying that George is anything but. Funny, yes. Refreshingly juvenile for a seventy-five-year-old—that too. But George also has a formidable side. You don't become a bestselling author, friend to numerous presidents, real-life action hero (it was George who tackled Sirhan Sirhan in the kitchen of the Ambassador Hotel after the assassination of Robert Kennedy), and remain in the public eye for fifty years without a certain amount of gravitas. George can be goofy, but you never know if the tree branches in his hair and the giant rip in the seat of his pants are the result of an accident or a ploy to put people at ease. He's wily—plus, he can drink anyone under the solid mahogany pool table in his living room. He still plays tennis to the death with men one-third his age.

After letting myself into the Plimpton townhouse I go upstairs and knock on the door.

"George?" I call out. The door is open, but the Plimpton apartment seems empty. "Anybody home?" No answer. I check the kitchen and living room and, finding no one, decide to rest a moment on the couch. *Jesus, what do they put in the Men's 4-Pac?* I am feeling strangely . . . handsome, which doesn't seem at all appropriate to the occasion.

I take a moment to savor being in the Plimpton apartment, with its astounding 180-degree panoramic view of the East River (seen from the same distance and height as a passenger on a luxury liner), its de Kooning and Warhol posters, its trophy kills from safaris in Kenya. Many times since Gab and I moved to Staten Island and our year of sharing bathrooms and eating in front of the television began, I have come up here to remind myself how it's possible to live. Not to be a jerk, but it's a nice change every once in a while to be in a house where food isn't stored on the front porch. Coming to George's from Kay's is like going from the set of a Korean *Married with Children* to one of those three-page foldout magazine advertisements for Ralph Lauren.

Suddenly I hear a noise from the far end of the apartment—a snort or a roar, like a wild animal coming out of the bush.

"Hello, George?" I get up from the couch in a hurry, not wanting to be seen taking my leisure as an uninvited guest in the home. It's bad enough that if I ever come back here it's likely to be as a delivery boy with a sandwich order.

"*Snuphuluphuluph!!*" The beast erupts again, sounding this time more like a sleeping bear. I creep (it's hard to creep in the Plimpton apartment because it has old oak floorboards that groan underfoot like the mast of an ancient schooner) through the second living room, around the pool table, under the glare of a mounted African water buffalo, past the temptation of a quick shot of Tanqueray from the open bar, and into George's office, where I find the old man dead asleep, passed out in a swivel chair in his boxers and a misbuttoned oxford while watching *SportsCenter*.

"George!" I blurt out.

George makes a noise like a vacuum cleaner that just inhaled a gerbil. Then his eyes pop open like two window shades with their drawstrings plucked.

"Who's there?" he commands, bleary-eyed. "I say: reveal yourself."

"George, it's me, Ben."

For a split second his eyes narrow and his brow deepens in an expression of what appears to be fury, but then I realize that he's only trying to get his bearings, which he does, gradually, while remaining splayed out in a pose that would be sexy if George were, say, female and half a century younger.

"Ben . . ."

"George, is this a bad time? I can come back."

". . . late night, with Norman at Elaine's, too many . . ."

"I see."

"*Snuphuluphuluph!!*" He gives himself a good vigorous scratch on the belly, which seems to wake him up.

"Okay," he says finally. "Shall we have our little discussion?"

"Sure." I take a breath. George pulls close a chair and rotates it to face me, interrogation-style. I feel like I'm back in boarding school— the sense of guilt, the illicit chemicals flowing in my blood—only this time the headmaster isn't wearing any pants.

"Ben—"

"George—"

"I—"

"You—"

"The Vollmann—"

"The what?!"

The Vollmann—a piece by the acclaimed novelist William S. Vollmann—was something I had recently brought to the magazine and was scheduled to run in an upcoming issue.

"It's a fine story," George says, "but it needs work. Let's go through it line by line."

So that's what this is about? Here I am fearing for my job, my sense of self-worth as a human being, and all he wants is to do a little line editing? I almost want to howl with relief: a reprieve, a reprieve! I'm still an editor! For the next half hour George and I huddle over the manuscript together, and honestly it's just as much of a thrill as it was when I first came to New York after college, as ready to be dazzled as a Nebraska farm girl stepping off a Greyhound bus in Hollywood. (The detour into porn would come soon enough.) George is a brilliant line editor, especially of dialogue, and rather mysterious in his methods. Sometimes the cuts are obvious, and sometimes not, but the results are almost always an improvement.

"You're a genius, George," I tell him after we finish. "Can I go now?"

He looks at me solemnly. "Actually, there's something else."

Uh-oh.

"As you know," he continues, "I do not aspire to be the sort of boss who arouses fear or intrudes on personal lives, so when I say this, don't think of me as an elder but rather as a pal, a concerned pal. I hope you will not mind my saying that for a while now you have not seemed your usual lively, intense, if somewhat too anxious self. You've been a bit, how shall I say, *blue*. Down in the dumps. And I wanted to ask, Is everything okay?"

Startled by the question, not to mention the exceedingly gentle way in which it is asked, my initial reaction is to answer it honestly. But then, knowing that the worst thing I can do is to admit that I'm burned out, I dissemble again:

"I'm fine, George, really, there's nothing—"

"THEN WHY HAVEN'T YOU BEEN COMING TO WORK?" he thunders, and at that point I realize I must tell him something, and it better not be a promise to read the slush, so I begin by describing my life on Staten Island, the indignity of our new surroundings, the basement, the extended family from Korea wanting to share beds and clothes, and George, to whom all of this is news, listens raptly, inert, his jaw dropping lower and lower until he says:

"You poor, poor chap. What a wretched existence. I had no idea. Is there any prospect of an exit?"

So I tell him about Gab's fast-fading hopes for a business that, in addition to repaying her parents, would provide the income necessary for regaining our independence. George's reaction is curious. His ears prick up, his eyes brighten and he leans forward:

"Did you say a deli?" he asks.

I nod.

"As in a corner store, selling lottery tickets and the like?"

"Yes, I'm afraid so."

"Marvelous."

"I'm sorry?" I cannot have heard that right.

"I said marvelous. Wonderful. Enchanting."

I almost swallow my tongue.

"Incidentally, can I work there? I've always wanted to be a stocker."

"Stocker?"

"Yes, a stocker—one who puts stock on the shelves. You can't tell me you don't know this—it's your line of business, for Pete's sake!"

"You mean *stockboy*."

"Oh, is that what they're called? Whatever. Let me be your stocker. Just for a day."

"Okay," I say, "it's a deal." And I think to myself, *How could I have ever misjudged this man so harshly? He's a saint.* After that George and I go into the living room, where he mixes us a pair of drinks and we watch the barges drift by on the East River in the late afternoon. It is a favorite pastime of mine, watching the barges at the end of the day, when they always seem to be fighting against the fierce East River tide, as if in a struggle against the very immensity of city life.

"We're hosting a party tonight, in case you weren't aware," George says. "It's going to be a grand occasion. You'll be staying, won't you?"

Glumly, I tell George I have to get home. I'm not sure if Gab managed to schedule a visit to Salim's tonight, but I promised to bring her the car.

"Ah, I see," says George, "reporting for duty. It begins already, your double life." He smiles and drains his cocktail.

"That is what you're proposing, you realize?" he continues. "A double life. A divided existence, schismatic even. Let me give you a bit of advice about such endeavors: they are even trickier than they look. You must be careful. One half is always threatening to swallow the other, to consume it, to wipe it out. Sometimes a double existence is more than impractical; it is fundamentally an impossible feat—a folly—and in the end you may have to give one side up."

"Yes, George."

I wait for him to express hope that it will be the deli I relinquish and not the *Paris Review,* but he doesn't. Then he puts down his drink and goes off to get ready for the party, leaving me to watch the barges.

LOCATION IS EVERYTHING

IN THE RETAIL WORLD, LOCATION IS EVERYTHING—UNLESS you're a Korean deli owner. "Location who care?" my mother-in-law often says. "If owner work hard, what difference make? All store same."

I can't tell if this attitude is what makes Koreans so successful or what keeps them from taking over the world. Indifference to risk is admirable, but it can also get you in trouble. Gab once told me that the best way to understand Korean national character was through Korean Air, which at one point held the distinction of being one of the most accident-prone airlines in the world. Korean Air pilots frequently crashed because, according to Gab, they didn't see little things like mountains and cockpit emergency lights. "The company was so hell-bent on success," she said, "they became oblivious to safety. Their attitude was 'Get this plane in the air! I don't care if it's missing a wing. Start flying!'"

This may explain the preponderance of Korean-run businesses in high-crime districts. After all, if your attitude is that all businesses are the same and only the owner's work ethic determines success, why would you pay more rent to sell oranges in a fancy neighborhood?

Most of Gab's relatives have spent significant time working in bad neighborhoods, and many have been assaulted, robbed and threatened more times than they can remember. Strangely, when they're not working, they're the most security-obsessed people I know. They fortify their houses with trip wires, moats and floodlights and practically dead-bolt the doors when they go out to get the mail. When it comes to business, though, the Paks seem willing to go anywhere.

Of course, as much as any suburban kid raised on Ice Cube and Snoop, I love the ghetto. Yet as much as I want Gab to fulfill her dream of buying a store for her mother, I don't want to die for it.

There is something that scares me even more than us getting a store in East New York or Brownsville, and that's the possibility of ending up in a perfectly safe part of the city, on a perfectly okay block, in a decent building even, but in the local loser store. The loser store—every neighborhood has one—is the store in your neighborhood that inexorably fails year after year under different owners, first as a sports memorabilia shop, then as a florist, then as a Pan-Asian bistro or "wrapperia." Sometimes the source of bad luck is straightforward and obvious, such as being next to the local methadone clinic or probation check-in center, but often you have to wonder if there's an abandoned cemetery under the basement or if in a previous incarnation the property held an orphanage that went up in a fire.

After our failure to get the North Korean deli, a kind of gloom settles over Kay's normally frenetic household. Over the previous few months we'd seen thirty or forty stores; now we stopped looking, except for Salim's deli.

Gab and Kay go into Brooklyn one day and come back from looking at Salim's store with mixed feelings.

"It was the size of a two-car garage, yet inside it seemed even smaller," says Gab.

"It was very dirty, very bad condition, but it had lots of customers," says Kay.

Was it a loser store? Judging by their reports, I'm not sure. Boerum Hill, the neighborhood Salim's deli is in, is becoming one of the trendiest places to live in the whole city.

A few days pass, then a week. Then two weeks. Maybe this whole deli thing was just talk, I think. But Gab's family isn't like that. There's no "blah blah blah," as Kay would put it—"just do." (Like her syntax in English, Kay's life doesn't have a conditional or subjunctive tense—only action.) And what about all the loans we've lined up, the credit cards we've taken out, the money that's just sitting in our bank account?

Soon Gab and Kay have to start thinking about going back to the lives they left behind before we started the deli search. Gab, when she left her job as a corporate lawyer, was regularly putting in seventeen-hour days, and would sometimes sleep in a hotel next to her office rather than take a fifteen-minute cab ride home to Brooklyn. Kay had been halfheartedly taking classes at a community college so close to the barely cooled-off wreckage at Ground Zero that students wore face masks in class. Neither of them wants to go back.

Two weeks later Gab announces that she thinks we can make Salim's deli work.

"But you said it was too small."

"I didn't say it was too small. I said it was small. What's wrong with small? Are we such big people? When did we decide to open a Costco?" Small, she goes on, means that Salim's deli is just right for our family, since we're only aiming to run a modest business that will fulfill Kay and pay for her house, not make anyone rich. Small is perfect. Small means we won't have to hire a big staff after the store gets on its feet and Gab and I aren't working there anymore. Small means we won't be taking an enormous risk with our savings. ("Maybe we can even cancel one of those credit cards I took out," Gab says.) Small also means that Salim's deli, though it is in a sexy, gentrifying neighborhood, is relatively cheap: one hundred and seventy thousand dollars with equipment and inventory included. The rent is a little high (thirty-five hundred a month), but for that little money overall we won't find any other stores in Boerum Hill unless they have a hole in the ceiling.

Small is beautiful, Gab says. Small makes sense.

We decide to go back to the store on a weekday night. Part of me is intrigued, and part of me wants to make sure that Gab isn't succumbing to desperation. She isn't acting desperate—she's thought about it for two weeks—but still, when you're property-hunting and you're running out of patience it's easy to make bad decisions. New York in particular has a way of making people twist reality in their heads. *Who cares if the apartment is beneath a flamenco studio? I'll get used to the noise! Yeah, I know the whole apartment has only one window facing a brick wall, but I'm never at home during the day.*

We arrive at eight o'clock in the evening on a bitterly windy night. Salim's store is on Atlantic Avenue, the Broadway of Brooklyn, a high-speed thoroughfare that goes from one side of the borough to the other, nearly eight miles in distance. On Salim's block it is jammed with stores and low-rise apartment buildings, though many of the stores seem empty. About a block away the landscape features a large void centered around the Brooklyn House of Detention, where male prisoners wait to be sent upstate. Parking lots with rattling chain-link fences take up much of the area, giving it a windswept feel, especially on nights like tonight. Salim's deli, which has a teal-and-yellow awning dripping with pigeon poop, is the only convenience store around for several blocks.

"Teal and yellow—what does that mean?" I ask Gab. The color of a deli's awning often tells you what kind of store lies within. In Manhattan, an evergreen awning tends to signify a Korean deli offering fresh produce, cut flowers and upscale products—the Starbucks of the deli world. Red and yellow, on the other hand, usually means a bodega run by Dominicans, where the groceries tend to come in cans and jars and the prices tend to be more affordable—the Dunkin' Donuts of New York's convenience stores. In poorer neighborhoods, where supermarket chains usually decline to set up stores, bodegas are the traditional place where families shop for groceries. Bodegas also often tend to be neighborhood hangouts; in front of Salim's store I notice that there are milk crates and a wooden bench, where undoubtedly in the summertime old men sit around and do stuff that old men do on city corners.

"Salim is Arab, if that's what you mean, but I think he bought it from the building's owner, who's Puerto Rican or Dominican and ran it as a bodega. It's kind of a mixed-up place—a little of this, a little of that. Why don't you go inside and get me something to drink. I'll wait in the car."

I exit Kay's Honda and wait for the light. While crossing I take stock of the apartment building housing Salim's deli, a brick walkup that appears to be in dire condition, slumping sideways and spalling bits of facade. Like all of the attached row houses, it is a couple times as tall as it is wide, the shape of a cigarette pack. Its level roof sits four stories off the ground, exactly the same height as most of the buildings in this historically landmarked neighborhood. There are similar buildings in every direction, most of which appear to be in flawless physical condition, but Salim's seems to have been left over from a different era. On the exposed side of the building facing leafy, pleasant Hoyt Street, everything sags, everything is crooked—the black fire escape entangled in cable TV wires, the graffiti-covered garage, the peeling windowsills framing bedsheet curtains and flags from countries I can't identify. The whole building seems to be leaning in a separate direction, as if it no longer wishes to be part of the block.

Opening the front door, which features one of those annoying brass knobs that require a special sequence of jiggles only the regular customers know how to perform, I find the interior worse than I had imagined. The space is as claustrophobic as the inside of a damp shoe box. The ceilings are too low, the aisles too narrow. If the North Korean deli was dismal, at least it had the potential to be fixed up; the space was reasonably large, and the building itself didn't seem structurally unsound. Salim's deli isn't just hopelessly tiny—I count seventeen paces from front to back and less than seven across—but it appears to be rapidly falling apart, as if a passing truck could make the whole thing crumble. There's even—and now of course I know why the lease is so cheap—a hole in the ceiling the size of a volleyball, as if an elephant's leg had come through, and that hole is currently dripping little bits of plaster. Other parts of the ceiling appear to have caved as well—over by the checkout counter, back by the stockroom—but unlike the one over the deli counter, these have been covered with sheets of aluminum, then painted, and now support little stalactites of dust that wave back and forth in unison every time someone opens the door and the wind comes in. Not one angle in the store stands square—the space is like some crazy nonrectilinear world invented by Dr. Seuss—and the coating of fuzz isn't limited to the ceiling: it's as if the ancient bottles of Log Cabin maple syrup on Salim's shelves had all spontaneously exploded before a great gust of ash blew through. As for the floor, I notice that in certain places it makes an alarming squish, raising the terrifying question of how it manages to support the weight of Salim's enormous, chrome-plated KustomKool refrigerators, which are the one impressive thing about the store, shining brilliantly like waxed Ferraris. And the smell, oh, the smell—a mélange of kitty litter, leaky air fresheners, pastrami, wood rot and Freon.

This isn't going to work. Not even Gab's family could make this into a successful business. There's too much to be done and too little to work with. How would Gab be helping out her mother by giving her a store like this? The part of me that worries about desperate, wishful thinking was right, and the only question now is, How will I break it to her?

I'm about to walk out when I remember that Gab had asked me to buy her a drink. Opening one of Salim's KustomKools, those shiny, chrome-plated refrigerators, I reach for an iced tea, but in order to find one that isn't "infused" with sea algae or something unnecessary, I have to poke my head way in back. Inside, I don't know what happens—maybe I get a chestful of Freon, or maybe I just get second thoughts about telling Gab what I really think—but when I come out it's like, *Hey, this place isn't so bad. Don't be so critical.* Things even look a little different, as if I fainted and woke up in a different store. The dust-coated bananas look perfectly edible, and the dimensions that a moment ago I'd judged impossibly tiny now seem more than adequate. Above all, I suddenly I remember that location is everything, and we're in Brooklyn.

So I go outside, skirt the traffic on Atlantic Avenue and jump into the car.

"Here you go," I say.

"What is this?" Gab says, holding the drink I've gotten for her. "Strawberry Yoo-hoo?"

"They didn't have any nondisgusting flavors of iced tea, and so your choices were pretty much King Kobra Malt Liquor or Nutrament. Sorry."

Gab looks disappointed, but when I tell her what I thought of the store, it doesn't matter. "Really?" she keeps saying. "Really?" Her eyes swell with tears, and we embrace over the emergency brake and the strawberry Yoo-hoo. As we hold each other, I glance over Gab's shoulder and see the deli's weird yellow-and-teal awning glowing at the end of the dark block. A truck passes by, and it looks as if the deli is winking at us.

THE NEXT DAY I call my parents in Boston to tell them about our plans. They are, bizarrely, thrilled.

When I first informed my parents about the deli a few months ago, I expected them to be mortified. "No, Ben!" I anticipated hearing. "Don't squander your education and upbringing. We beg you!" But the truth is, they were downright enthusiastic.

"How exciting!" my mother cried, as if it were an art gallery we were opening. She even offered to come down and help decorate. Her main concern seemed to be that we sell the right kind of mustard and "stay away from that vile diet tonic water."

My father's attitude was disturbingly upbeat as well. "Could be an interesting experience," he said, "sort of an ethnography, a participatory study into the lives of the urban underclass. Orwell worked as a dishwasher, you know. Conrad spent his early life aboard ships." Which sort of made me want to remind him that the deli was *not* a semester abroad.

My father is a cultural anthropologist, which means that in his eyes everything is potentially "an interesting experience." Some professors see the world in terms of colliding atoms or fizzing amino acids; my father is a junkie for the mechanics of human interaction. He's a man who truly lives his profession—joyfully, too.

For the most part, being the son of an anthropologist is a wonderful thing, especially when you're growing up. For starters, there tend to be a lot of blowguns and spears lying around the house, and among your friends you're usually the only one whose parents own an extensive collection of books on devil worship. Also, cultural anthropologists are supposed to be relativists, which tends to undermine their authority as parents. For instance, if at ten o'clock, an anthropologist tells you it's time to go to bed, you can remind him that a ten o'clock bedtime for fourteen-year-olds is a Western cultural construct and that if our family were Masai cow herders he'd probably want me to stay up all night watching out for lions.

But while my father is definitely a classical Boasian cultural relativist, he's also a strict, thoroughgoing New Englander, from a family deeply set in its Puritan ways (so set that after coming over on the *Mayflower* it spent the next ten generations stubbornly rooted in Plymouth, presumably so that it could get on the first boats back if people started returning). These people make a strong case for the anthropologist's argument that culture, rather than just our material conditions or traits hardwired into our brains, determines our behavior. They're modern-day Puritans, some of them living so far in the past they're still trying to decide whether it was a good idea to leave England, and have a technophobic aversion to things like dental floss. Someone once said there are two kinds of Wasps in the world: the fearless, fun-loving George Plimpton variety and the dour, fun-fearing variety, like my family. And whereas my father's professional instinct is to be against rules, or at least question them as tools of social control, his Puritan side is rather in favor of them.

Not that his rules are so onerous. My father's rule book when I was growing up was *The Elements of Style* by William Strunk and

E. B. White, which he gave me a copy of in ninth grade. Most people think of *The Elements of Style* as a book about writing, but it's actually about character—specifically, how to be a crusty old man. As a teenager, I hated it, of course. Instead of teaching you to unlock your inner Salinger or Hemingway, it encouraged you to think of writing as a discipline. Strunk and White saw style as dangerous ("Approach style warily," they advised, as if it were a recipe for a homemade bomb) and creative writing in general as "the Self escaping into the open." Good writing, they argued, must be constrained by values such as modesty ("Place yourself in the background"), consistency ("Hold a steady course") and respect for tradition ("Prefer the standard to the offbeat"). To achieve style you first had to achieve control, which specifically meant not unleashing that unruly, appetitive Self. A good writer did not show off so much as vanish into thin air.

Of course as a teenager I failed to follow Strunk and White's rules, in writing or in general. Nor did it occur to me that growing up with a plethora of rules was in any way connected with a hyper-controlled Puritan background. I didn't think of us as having a "background"—we were just people who happened to live in the same place, Greater Boston, where nearly all of my father's relatives had lived for nearly four hundred years. It didn't change the way we thought or acted. Oh, sure, practically everyone in my family was named after a fanatically devout bootmaker or indentured servant from the seventeenth century, but history didn't determine our actions. Those ritual-laden family reunions every summer in Plymouth? Inconsequential. This was silly, of course. In the sixties and seventies, my father's generation did everything possible to escape their own Waspiness, cutting themselves off from that embarrassing culture of pink pants, country clubs and names like Flick and Bunny. Instead, they gave their children names like Vishnu and Cuauhtémoc and married people from non-Brahmin backgrounds. However, the old values must have run deeper than they realized, because many were passed on to my generation more or less intact (if less and less embedded inside a meaningful context). It could be confusing—in fact, it was meant to be confusing. As my grandmother once said, "You're not supposed to talk about Wasp values. You're just supposed to have them." Which is what made a source like *The Elements of Style* invaluable, insofar as it helped articulate the values that, whether wholly admirable, like Strunk and White's emphasis on modesty, or questionable, in the case of their obsession with control, simply happened to be the ones I grew up with.

But the big question wasn't what Wasp values were; it was how to reconcile them with the wide-open embrace of the world my father seemed to encourage as an anthropologist. How did you get the two worldviews to mesh? Most of the time the conflict consisted in harmless skirmishes over politics or the culture wars, or I'd feel the tension internally, as in the realization that no matter how much you wanted to be a Rastafarian or a lobsterman, you'd never escape your inherited identity. Out-and-out conflict was a rarity, though, in part because while my parents had plenty of rules, they were against telling anyone what to do, especially their own children—even more so now that we were grown. And besides, the Wasp-Puritan morality is so good at getting inside people's heads and turning them into mild-mannered, stability-oriented replicas of their parents, they didn't really have to.

After I tell her about the deli, my mother sends me a gift: something from L.L. Bean called a "mountain town jacket" ("an updated, casual take on the classic chore coat") and matching khaki pants. As mothers tend to, she is worried that I'll be cold, and the outfit she sends actually turned out to be quite comfortable and warm, though instead of looking like a future deli clerk, I look like I'm off for a little trout fishing on the Beaverkill.

However, she then makes it clear—well, clear for people who, whenever possible, avoid saying anything directly—that there is one aspect of our new life she'd rather see end as soon as possible:

"So does finding a deli you'd like mean that you can start thinking about moving out?"

This is the real reason she's excited about Salim's deli. My parents have always been uneasy about us living with the Paks. "A young couple needs privacy," my mother said to me recently, briefly terrifying me with the thought that she was going to start talking about our sex lives. "You need to be able to create your own identity as a couple and develop it inside your own space." I could not agree more. Maintaining your own identity, let alone developing it, can definitely become a problem when you find yourself sharing underwear with your father-in-law. Maybe if I could get the Paks to not be so damn communal and occasionally knock on a closed door (there's no point in even having doors in the Paks' house; it's like they're not there), we could develop a modicum of personal identity, but I fear it will take longer to train them than I hope to be here.

In my family, cohabiting with elders after a certain age violates one of the basic laws of the universe. My parents sent me to boarding school when I was fifteen, and in case I didn't get the message as to what that meant for our relationship, the school was eight hundred miles away, in Colorado. My parents had strong feelings about independence—they themselves, as children, had been sent on summer-long ordeals out West for toughening. It was simply part of childhood: the parents found the most oppressive summer experience imaginable (usually some nightmarish camp in the wilderness staffed by the recently deinstitutionalized), then waved good-bye. And when the time came to really move out, whether it was to boarding school or college, you knew you were never coming home—for instance, my parents let my room to a tenant practically the day after I was gone.

Don't get me wrong: I'm not complaining about the fact that my parents didn't want me to live with them. And I would hate to create the image of them as stereotypically frigid Wasps, more interested in polishing the china than attending to the messy emotional needs of their children. While they shipped me off to boarding school during a phase when I wasn't the most pleasant teenager to have around (at the time I had decorated every inch of my room's walls with Richard Avedon's pictures of severed cow heads), I think they thought holding on to their children was selfish, because it would prevent us from growing up and moving past adolescence. Being a kid in the suburbs was too easy in some sense; moving out was the necessary challenge to spur growth. It was their duty to let go, whether they liked it or not.

For a family like Gab's, however, nothing could be more normal than parents living with their adult children. Koreans, like many Asians, have a strong tradition of filial piety—that is, of dutifulness to one's parents. In America, kids are supposed to antagonize their parents: they're supposed to torture them as teenagers, abandon them in college, then write a memoir in which they blame them for all their unhappiness as adults. But in Korea they serve them forever, without a second thought. They take care of them, support them, and frequently orient their entire existences around them. For instance, almost all of Korea's elderly cohabit with one of their children, usually the first son, whose wife is expected to essentially become a live-in servant to her in-laws. These obligations aren't etched on a tablet. It's not like Gab ever said to me, "I am a dutiful daughter from a Confucian-based society and must honor my parents," the way she would in a Hollywood movie. She just did things that to me seemed above and beyond the call of duty, even for a devoted daughter, like bringing Kay and Edward on vacation with us, or sharing our income with them even when they didn't need it.

Of all people, I assumed my father, the authority on culture, would understand this, but he seemed as baffled as me. "You mean, Gab *wants* to do all those things for her parents? She's not being forced? What a system." At the same time, it's not as if the Paks don't value independence. When Gab was growing up, her mother pushed her to become as financially independent as she had been forced to become at her age. "Never depend on a man," she would say. "Always be able to take care of yourself." And the Paks *are* independent—they're the ones living in a foreign country, after all, while my family stays as immobile as Plymouth Rock.

"DON'T LET IT KILL YOU"

THE NEXT NIGHT I COME BACK TO BOERUM HILL SO I CAN inspect the neighborhood and make sure the store isn't near any slaughterhouses or toxic waste sites. It appears as if dealing with the challenges inside Salim's building will be more than enough.

Before I do that, though, I stop by the store so I can meet Salim.

The first time I see him he's standing at the checkout counter, a tired-looking Arab-featured man not that much older than me watching a TV show and eating his own inventory.

"Salim?" I say, sidling up the counter.

"Yes?" He guiltily puts away the BBQ-flavor chips. "How can I help you?" His voice has a Middle Eastern accent, but not very strong.

I introduce myself as Gab's husband, and behind his heavy-lidded eyes I can him trying to retrieve information from his memory about Gab, like *Wasn't she Korean? What are you?*, before he cautiously extends a BBQ-chip-stained hand.

"Yes, she called and said you'd be coming by." There's a hint of relaxation, but the suspicion lingers. *Who calls the shots—you or your wife? Or that mother-in-law of yours?*

"So have you owned the store a long time?" I ask, trying to make conversation.

"Ten years," Salim says, seemingly wincing at the thought. *And you? What were you doing the last ten years? Brushing your pony?*

"Are you familiar with the neighborhood?" he asks.

I explain that Gab and I used to live in Fort Greene, just a mile or so away.

"FORT GREENE?" he virtually explodes.

"Yes . . . I . . . but it wasn't for a long time . . . and I really didn't like it." *What could Salim possibly have against Fort Greene?*

"YOU MEAN FORT GREENE, *BROOKLYN*?" he repeats, leaning across the counter.

I nod fearfully.

"Tell me, if you lived in Fort Greene," he demands, "then you must know the store over by the park—the one on the corner. Yes?"

"Oh, sure, I know that place."

"That's my cousin's store—Ibrahim's!" Salim cries joyfully. "Do you know Ibrahim?"

"I, uh, sure. Doesn't everyone?"

Salim starts looking for the phone and threatening to call Ibrahim right away. "Where's that damn phone?" he mutters, while tearing through piles of newspapers, receipts and other garbage around the register.

"Salim, you don't have to do that, really. I don't think Ibrahim will remember me . . ."

Salim has now located the cordless phone, but no matter how hard he jabs it, he can't get it to dial, perhaps because it's encrusted with enough mustard to dress a hot dog. "I swear, this place is becoming a pigsty," he says, as if it weren't his own store. But then he forgets the whole business and turns his attention to the lottery machine, where a customer is waving a piece of paper at him, which Salim absentmindedly scans.

"No money this time, my friend. Better luck tomorrow." The customer walks out without a trace of a reaction. Salim turns back to the checkout counter.

"Now, where were we? Oh yes, you were thinking about buying my store. You want to see the books? Meet the landlord? Have a look at the basement? How soon can you buy?"

"We're not there yet," I say. "I just wanted to come by and introduce myself. We like the store a lot."

Salim looks unimpressed.

"That's good," he says, "but if you make me an offer, don't insult me. This store may not look like much, but I promise you it is worth more than you think. I am not the first owner. There are people in this neighborhood older than both of us who have been coming here their whole lives. They have spent more money in this place than they have on their own apartments, their own savings. I will not sell to just anyone." He folds his arms across his chest.

"Well, that's good to know." *Is this some kind of bargaining strategy?*

"Make me a good offer," Salim continues, "and on your way out of the store, take anything you like."

"Anything?"

"Anything."

So I ask for a pack of Parliament Lights, Gab's brand of cigarettes.

"That's too much money," Salim says. "Pick something else."

Why do I have the feeling that doing business with Salim won't be easy?

BACK OUTSIDE IT is a warm December night, so I start walking toward Smith Street. Boerum Hill still has blocks that are visibly poor, and it is more industrial, with housing projects that seem a lot bigger and more intimidating than those in Fort Greene, where Gab and I used to live. At the same time, Boerum Hill has Smith Street, maybe the trendiest place to open a restaurant or boutique in the whole city. Smith Street is a good place to live even if your idea of paradise isn't a neighborhood packed with stores selling hand-printed baby kimonos and touchless cat massages. You can almost forget that the housing projects, the Wyckoff Gardens and Gowanus Houses, which have so many buildings they essentially form a neighborhood unto themselves, are only a block away. Ditto the Brooklyn House of Detention and the general seediness around State Street, with its hot-sheet motels, job centers and stores like 99¢ City. They are there if you want them to be.

Like all the surrounding neighborhoods of brownstone Brooklyn, Boerum Hill started out as a middle-class community, and despite its disrepair, you can see that background in a building like Salim's. Probably just a single family had lived in that entire four-story building once. The second floor held a dining room with a parquet floor, a chandelier and special side rooms for entertaining. The backyard contained a patio or a garden, and the garage was where a horse-drawn carriage was once parked. Or so I imagined.

At some point, though, Boerum Hill fell on its luck. Maybe it was the Gowanus Canal, a festering, reportedly body-filled outlet for factories and junkyards, that set off the decline. Or maybe it was after the city decided to plant a pile of public housing and social services in the neighborhood. In any case, at some point those gorgeous brownstones such as Salim's went through a long and dark period of decay, which some of them still hadn't come out of.

The first time artists, writers and activists started coming back to Boerum Hill was in the 1960s, as part of the so-called brownstoner movement. Not all of these people were trying to make a political point by moving to a "slum"; some were just looking for old, affordable apartment buildings with character where they could raise families. Nonetheless, the movement helped foster an image of the borough as a kind of ideal community where classes and races mixed. It was the dawn of a new era in urban living, exemplified by the appearance of *Sesame Street,* featuring a neighborhood that looked a lot like brownstone Brooklyn. This image depended on the brownstoner movement not being *too* successful, however. That is, it couldn't attract so many middle-class newcomers that the old-timers, the working-class Puerto Ricans and blacks, were totally pushed out. And in fact it wasn't too successful, thanks to the race riots, the crack epidemic and the sky-high homicide rate that characterized the County of Kings in the late seventies and eighties. The area around the Wyckoff Gardens and Gowanus housing projects became one of the most violent parts of the city. Much of Boerum Hill remained bombed out, and property values stayed relatively low.

But then The Big Change happened. New York as a whole saw crime plummet in the nineties, making neighborhoods like Boerum Hill ripe for another "discovery." That's when Gab and I moved to Fort Greene. As the second generation of brownstoners, we were attracted by the trees, the beautiful old buildings and the open skies—but also by that vision of Brooklyn as a place where people from different classes and backgrounds mixed. It was strange: even though I was a year or two out of college the first time I stepped foot in Kings County, I felt like I had been there many times before, and my experiences had always been pleasant, and I had friends waiting to see me. In fact, one weekend I was walking to the subway when I passed a group of children playing in Fort Greene Park. They were wearing cardboard hats and beating a piñata—it was a birthday party—and among them stood a special visitor whose presence made my heart surge, because everything then made sense. It was Big Bird, as comforting a sight as a doting uncle or beloved pet. I was in the land of Mr. Hooper, Guy Smiley and Snuffleupagus. And tonight as I walk through Boerum Hill's streets I think, What bad could happen in a place where the solution to every problem is to sing a song, plant a vegetable garden or put on a puppet show?

OVER THE NEXT few days things gradually become more tense. Kay announces that she wants the store before Christmas so we can capitalize on holiday sales of beer and lottery tickets. This is impossible. Christmas week is less than a month away. Not only do we still have to convince Salim to sell us the store—to prove to him that we're worthy—but then we have to agree on a price and a contract, get landlord approval, hammer out a payment schedule and so on, then get our licenses and insurance policies in order, and then, only then, after what I would imagine to be a lengthy period of renovations, move in.

Only I forgot one thing: this is a convenience store, and making money comes before anything as trivial as fixing a hole in the ceiling. Also, this is my mother-in-law talking, the most impatient person on the planet.

"If Salim not say yes before Christmas, then *no deal*," she insists.

Kay also announces that she wants to underbid Salim by fifty thousand dollars, which, given how sensitive he appears, strikes me as unwise. But Kay has her own ideas about strategy. "I never pay full price," she says, and it's true: I've seen my mother-in-law try to bargain with everybody from car mechanics to waiters. She's incorrigible—to her, price tags are mere starting points in a negotiation—and I suspect that more than half the time she does it just for fun. But this time she says it's important.

"If we offer Salim full price," she says, "he not respect us," which will have repercussions later.

So Gab offers Salim one hundred and twenty thousand dollars, and rather disturbingly, he accepts.

"He what?" I stammer. "Should we have gone even lower? What if the store isn't even worth one hundred and twenty thousand?" This is not a pleasant feeling at all, but after resisting Kay's low-ball offer, I can hardly take a position against it now that it's been accepted.

Salim seems rather pleased. "I like your mother-in-law," he says. He promises to vacate the store by December 23.

Now the process begins to gather speed, another worrisome development. Gab's family seems comfortable banging from decision to decision, but I'm more circumspect. I come from an academic family, and we like to think things through—then think about whether the process of thinking them through was as thorough as it could be, then write a book about it. (A book that takes twenty years.)

But maybe it's better not to reflect. I have a feeling that if I think too long about Salim's deli, or perhaps much at all, I'll have second thoughts.

DESPITE THE RUSH, we manage to set up a deal in a more or less orderly fashion. We skimp on things like the observation period, wherein the new owner traditionally sits behind the register with the old one making sure that the business stands up to the owner's claims. Usually the observation period lasts a week. Kay pronounces herself satisfied after one shift. Half a shift, actually.

It looks, nevertheless, like it's going to be a smooth transition. Then one day Salim calls and says he wants to modify the deal. He says he wants us to send part of the money we owe him to an associate in Lebanon.

"Ha ha, that's funny," I laugh. "You mean like in the Middle East?"

"I'm not kidding," Salim says. "What do you think I mean, New Lebanon, Pennsylvania?"

Swallowing my amazement—things were going much too well, I realize—I try to picture how I would send thousands of dollars to a country I've never visited halfway around the world. Does he mean to a bank? Do they have banks in Lebanon? Would it be to some kind of money changer at a bazaar?

"Western Union will be fine," says Salim, while assuring us that this is just a normal way of doing business. Part of me knows that it is, but you know what I'm thinking: *This couple thought they were buying a convenience store in Brooklyn and ended up laundering money for an international crime ring that sold kidnapped American children into slavery and invested the profits in pornography and heroin. Tonight, Steve Kroft will take you to Auburn state prison in upstate New York and interview the husband, a former literary magazine editor who says he was framed . . .*

And then I feel guilty. Guilty because during all thirty seconds that I have such paranoid thoughts, I am prejudging Salim, am I not? Would I be suspicious if Salim were Swiss and asked me to send money to Switzerland, which is also a country I've never been to halfway around the world? *Yes, and if he were Swiss and asked me to send all that money there I'd say, You're out of your mind!* But somehow in Salim's case, because Gab and I don't want to entertain even the possibility of prejudging him, we say okay, despite the alarm bells going off in our heads.

"Listen, it's pretty hard for me to imagine Salim involved with anything nefarious," Gab rationalizes. "Would you spend seventeen hours a day selling Yummykakes if you had the power to be an international crime lord? Besides, he's too nice a guy. I can't see it."

Neither can I. It just doesn't add up.

Then Salim calls again. He's changed his mind: instead of sending the money by Western Union, he wants us to send it to the Middle East with his cousin Farouk, who's going there on business in a few days. Which of course we say yes to, plus a series of other last-minute requests. Things keep changing, taking us out of our comfort zone. *Now the money is going with Farouk as a cashier's check. Now it's going to Salim's accountant, a Hasidic Jew in Crown Heights. Now some of it is going to the hopelessly fickle-minded Salim at the closing.* But it's not as if Salim isn't helping us too.

First of all, he's letting us pay him some of the money we owe him over the course of twenty-four months, with money we earn at the store. And he's not charging us interest. "Muslims don't believe in interest," he says. "It's un-Islamic." Though I wouldn't have guessed that Salim was religious, I could not be more grateful.

On the day of the closing, Gab goes to meet Salim at his lawyer's office in downtown Manhattan, while Kay and I prepare to open the store.

The countdown has begun. In three hours we will become deli owners. When Gab arrives at the lawyer's office, Salim seems to have suddenly gotten jittery. He keeps jumping up from the conference table where papers are being signed to look nervously out the window at the traffic on Broadway while yelling into his cell phone in Arabic.

"Everything okay?" Gab asks.

"My wife is outside in the car, but there's nowhere to park, and the police keep telling her to move. They're harassing her."

Gab is horrified. "Tell her to park in a lot. You know what the police here are like." Ground Zero, barely a year old, sits only two blocks away.

But it turns out Salim's wife doesn't drive. *Oh no,* Gab thinks. *Something's going wrong again.*

But then, for whatever reason, the police leave Salim's wife alone, and Salim stops fretting. Meanwhile, it gets dark outside. Salim's lawyer taps his foot and makes small talk while Gab signs paperwork. *Something else will come up,* Gab thinks. *It always does. There always has to be something.*

"We're done!" Salim finally says, handing over the store's primary set of keys. (Kay and I have the backup over in Brooklyn.) "Congratulations. Welcome to the wonderful world of small business."

Gab isn't sure if this is a joke.

"Where are you off to?" she asks as they exit the building.

"Arizona," Salim says. "I have a cousin out there who owns a gas station."

He gets in his car—a brand-new SUV plastered with Day-Glo orange parking tickets—and waves. "Don't let it kill you," he says, and he and his wife ride off through the maze of security checkpoints, into the night.

AMATEURS

TODAY IS MY FIRST FULL DAY AS A DELI OWNER, AND I'M
standing next to the cash register, trying to figure out what is missing. A few minutes ago, at four o'clock, the day shift quietly ended,
and now there's a lull. After walking in I slipped behind the cold-
cut display and felt a surprising shiver of excitement as I entered
the narrow space where the cashiers stand. Where I am now is like
a stage (it even has a little platform), but so constricted is the space
that it feels like the gap between two cars in a parking lot, without
the headroom, thanks to the overhanging illuminated Marlboro
display. Behind me is a sink filled with wet coffee grounds; to my
right is a vinegary-smelling deli slicer covered with bits of lettuce

and ham; to my left is a lottery machine spitting out scraps of paper and sputtering like an angry robot. Yet my first thought upon entering this space was not that it was filthy, cramped or unpleasant, but that *something* that I can't quite put my finger on isn't here. Finally, after a few minutes, I figure out what it is: I'm looking for a chair.

After so many months of searching for a store, this is how the next phase begins. It seems unreal to be on the other side of the checkout counter. Is the store really ours? Could Salim somehow change his mind and take it back? Now that we're here, all I want to do is to put our stamp on this place and make it our own. There's no time, though, for even now, during a brief moment of calm between shifts, as the wave of evening commuters prepares to crash over us, there's an endless list of things to do, and it's all I can manage to stay out of Kay's way.

"Excuse," my mother-in-law says after hip-checking me into the sink. She and Gab have been here since six A.M.; now Gab is going home to collapse, leaving me till one A.M. with her mother, who has yet to stop moving for a single second.

"The checks for the deliverymen are in the cash register, under the drawer, and there are three of them, just in case the beer guy shows up," Gab says before leaving. "Not the beer guy who delivers Heineken, but the beer guy who delivers Brooklyn Lager. Next to the register is the price list, and I've attached instructions for making a void, in case you have to. Don't forget to refresh the cash supply every few hours, and don't try to do the lottery machine yourself, or put too much meat on people's sandwiches, or too much sugar in their coffee. Don't forget to ID anyone who looks underage and, oh God, am I forgetting anything? Yes! Turn on the awning lights when it gets dark or people will think we're closed, and if anyone from upstairs comes in, ask if they can turn up the heat—it's freezing. And your parking meter! Did you park on the street? The fine is one hundred and five dollars as of this week. Can you keep all that in your head?"

I nod and make a cocky face like *Who, me?* But the truth is, I have never felt so ill-prepared in my life. Yesterday, while Gab was at the closing, I got a small taste of the action in the store, but Kay made me spend the whole time stocking (Kay is now the boss, and we're not supposed to disobey her—not that I would be inclined to), and when we got home Gab advised me that today would be much, much harder. I had no doubt that she would be right. Still, at that point I wasn't nervous. When you live in New York you shop at delis every day, and you become accustomed to seeing what clerks do. It's easy to think, *I can pour a cup of coffee. I can butter a bagel. I can punch a lottery ticket. So can anyone.*

It is only after stepping up to the register that I realize how wrong I am. A deli worker is lucky if he gets to focus his attention on *just* buttering a bagel, pouring coffee or punching a lottery ticket. Much of the time he has to do at least two of those tasks at once, while in his mind he has to be doing at least seven, no matter what's going on with his hands.

And then there's the cash register, the bane of every clerk-in-training's existence. Ours, a Royal Alpha 9150 cash-management system with fifty daunting, multicolored keys, conspicuously lacks one of those nifty handheld price scanners I was looking forward to beaming against customers' behinds. The cash register has an effect on me similar to quadratic equations and French movies—that is, it makes me yawn uncontrollably and feel instantly and hopelessly defeated. Kay says I only need to learn how to use about five out of those fifty keys, but every time I look for them I get lost in a sea of "CONF-L", "$\lim_{n \to \infty} \left(1 + \dfrac{1}{n}\right)^n$" and MULTI-TAX LEVEL T.

Embarrassingly, though, my biggest struggle is with the money itself. I have always had a hard time handling cash: my hands go meaty and numb when I touch it. It started at a young age, when my parents caught me strutting around our house triumphantly showing off a couple of dollars I'd saved. "Put those away!" they barked at me. After that I noticed that my parents were always washing money in the laundry, leaving it in places where they would never find it, or storing it in undignified locations like sock drawers. They weren't intentionally careless, but they seemed careful not to be *too* careful with it either.

"Here," Kay says, handing me a stack of twenties. "Count this."

As soon as I start counting, the bills squirt from my fingers and land on the floor. Kay gasps. Both of us bend down, taking our eye off the open till of the Royal Alpha for a dangerous second.

"Try something else," she says, handing me a Snickers bar. "I want to buy this. Pretend I am customer."

Taking the bar, I turn unsteadily toward the register, where the first symbol I see looks like a Mayan hieroglyph.

"Some kind of problem?" Kay says, watching me stand there with my mouth hanging open, a single digit frozen in midair.

I turn to her and wince. "How much is it?" I ask. "The candy bar, I mean."

"You don't know? I thought Gaby gave you price list."

Our store has over a thousand different products, only a third of which have price tags. For someone like me who struggles every day to remember his own debit card PIN, this is going to be a serious challenge.

"She did," I admit. "I just haven't had a chance to memorize the candy bars yet."

"Sixty-five cents," Kay says, trying not to sound impatient. Then she shows me which buttons to press, a sequence scarcely less complicated than the one presidents use to unlock the nation's nuclear arsenal, and at the end of it all the cash drawer pops open.

"Well, there, we did it," I say, trying to summon a jocular air. "I guess we can go home now."

Kay frowns. If this was an audition, I just failed.

SHORTLY AFTERWARD, MY first customer arrives, a man with a sour expression and a wispy comb-over. I can't help thinking how tired he looks, how sad and beaten down, the way his gray suit bunches at the elbows and magnifies the smallness of his shoulders. His tie is twisted. *I wonder if he has a family to go home to. God—to be drab and middle-aged and not have a family? Is this all he's having for dinner—corned beef hash and a loaf of Wonder bread? I can't bear it, just the thought of him in some dismal little studio smelling of grease, sitting on the edge of a cot and eating off a Styrofoam plate.*

"You new or something?" the man asks.

"Huh?" I've been turning the loaf of Wonder bread over and over in my hands, absently looking for a price tag. Now I discover, with some help from Kay, that it's printed right on the plastic wrapper.

"Sorry," I say.

The man smiles benevolently. "Don't worry about it. Everybody here is new at some point. That's what makes New York so great. What country are you from?"

If only, I think. *Then I'd have a decent excuse.* I glance at Kay, who is appraising me skeptically over folded arms. I've never been a great worker, but not because I don't work hard. I just tend to focus on the wrong things, like how people look, what they're wearing and whether they use words like "fortuitous" properly. Gab once called me a "big-picture person," which can be read two ways: either as a straightforward compliment or as a euphemism for having one's head up one's ass. I think she might have meant both.

The thing of it is, I'd like to be a good cashier. To be inept with cash, such an elemental part of everyday life, would seem to bespeak a shameful and fundamental deficiency, like not being able to drive because you've always had a chauffeur, or not being able to cook because you've always had your meals prepared. Kay says there are workers who "you teach right hand what to do, but left hand not learn," and I don't want to be one of them.

There's even something sort of appealing about cashier work— the enviable hand-eye coordination, the mental stamina, the unflappable cool during a rush. So for the next half hour I attempt to prove to Kay that I can work the register as fast as anyone, resulting in a succession of over-rings, nineteen dollars in extra change for a grateful customer buying cigarettes, a decaf coffee served light and sweet instead of regular and black, as requested, and a turkey sandwich that never even gets made (the customer eventually walks out, cursing).

Finally, Kay nudges me aside.

"You go stock," she says.

"Again?"

She nods.

Disappointed, I trudge to the back of the store. I can't blame her for banishing me. If you can't be useful behind the register, it's best to stay clear of those who can. In a space this small, you're either a help or a hindrance, and besides, the way my mother-in-law works, you're in danger of losing an eyebrow in the slicer or getting accidentally doused in fresh coffee.

Sometimes I wonder what Kay thinks of me. I think she respects what I do as an editor, though when she worked at a 7-Eleven she always used to ask why the *Paris Review* wasn't on the magazine rack next to *Pro Wrestling Illustrated* and *People*. I think she thinks that like a lot of men, I'm sort of hopeless when it comes to such chores as taking out the garbage or keeping the car filled with gas.

Her biggest concern, though, I think, is that like many Americans, I've forgotten what it's like to suffer. ("American people, you cut off they finger, they gonna cry," Kay once said to me. "Me, you can cut off my whole hand and I not even care.") Forgetting what it's like to suffer can be a good thing, since suffering can make people too cutthroat for society's good. But suffering also breeds certain capacities that are easily lost, such as the ability to focus and a willingness to engage with conflict. These are things that I believe Kay thinks I'm incapable of.

Which doesn't make me completely useless. With my repertoire of professional communication skills honed as a member of the media, I can serve as a cultural interlocutor of sorts, educating my mother-in-law about the subtler aspects of American culture. For instance, recently I taught her the meaning of the words *skanky* and *Eurotrash,* and explained to her what a platypus is. I also had the occasion, on a recent foray to an International House of Pancakes, to explain to her the maple syrup–making process. ("You see, it's just sap.")

The sad part is, Gab actually expects my being a "big-picture person" to be an asset at the store. "You know what people want," she says. Gab says that her mother's business philosophy is similar to the way she drives, which is that when she gets on the highway she prefers to stay in one lane and never get out. "It has the virtue of being consistent," Gab says, "but everything she learned about American tastes is fixed in her mind from twenty years ago," from convenience stores in Texas and Ohio, where the Paks first came when they got to the United States.

As I'm lost in these thoughts, I hear Kay's voice summoning me back to the checkout counter.

"You bag," she says. "I do register."

The evening rush is here. You'd think a subway car had stopped outside our door. Customers arrive in waves—the door will not

stay closed—and stand at the register, heaving armfuls of groceries. They're tired and grumpy and want to get home. Fortunately,
you can be a terrible bagger and not slow down the line, because
people rarely discover that you've placed a gallon of milk atop
their eggs until after they leave the store.

Kay's register technique is dazzling. Even when she's punching
the keys four or five times a second, every stroke is perfect, and the
sound it makes is like a galloping herd of horses. When she stops
you can hear a penny roll, and you almost expect the Royal Alpha
to let out an exhausted sigh. Kay's steady presence makes people
feel that the universe is a just and orderly place, and someday they
will see their families again. It is impossible to look at her and not
feel some faint yearning to be a cashier.

THE GHOST

IT TAKES ONLY A FEW DAYS TO NOTICE THAT THE STORE HAS certain patterns. During the night shift, for example, the early hours are often too busy, but the later hours usually aren't busy enough, and yet it's hard to devote the slow times to something useful, like reading a book, because you never know if you're going to have two minutes or a whole hour until a customer breaks your concentration. If we had a computer in the store, the Internet would be perfect, with its bite-sized doses of mindless information. When a customer walks in I try not to make it too painfully obvious what I'm thinking, which is *Stay! Please! Tell me anything! I want to know all the mundane details of your boring life—just give me some companionship!*

Such is the boredom, in fact, that I end up rationing inane little chores over the course of the evening so that I have something to look forward to, like *Eight o'clock, clean lint out of pockets. Nine o'clock, clip fingernails (left hand only—save right for later). Ten o'clock, recheck pockets for sudden lint regrowth. Eleven o'clock, count tiles in floor.*

On nights like these the pleasure that comes from stocking shelves can be positively kundaliniesque. Stocking is a repetitive task that's either meditative or inane, and it can yield deep thoughts about, say, the nature of time, or more useless ruminations, such as, *Do toilets on Amtrak trains open up straight onto the tracks? Why do some people tattoo their own names on their bodies? Was Fred Rogers, the actor who played Mr. Rogers, really a Marine sniper with over one hundred "kills" in Vietnam?* Yesterday while stocking I thought about an ad I saw on the subway for public school teachers that said, "Get a job that matters! Nothing is more important than the next generation!" And I thought, Well, not to be cynical, but what makes "the next generation" so important? I mean, wasn't the current generation once "the next generation"? What happened to them? Were we only important while we were in the process of becoming something?

People want to believe the future is important, because that gives the present meaning. But if you do something like stocking shelves every day, you can find that faith in question. It's like the moment in the movie *Groundhog Day* when Bill Murray realizes that nothing surprising or momentous will ever happen to him again, which forces him to ask, If you decide that the future *isn't* important, how do you find the capacity to care?

What's interesting to me about this is that the Paks, who from moment to moment have rarely been assured of anything since they came to America (it was only a few years ago that they had the means to buy a house, for instance), are not in the least prone to agonized reflection about the potential significance of every decision. When I think of the word *existentialist,* I think of beret-wearing, Gauloise-smoking philosophers, which the Paks most definitely aren't, but existentialists they are. They don't think about what the moment means, and they tend to live in it fully. (Then again, given the hectic pace of their lives, they don't have time to do otherwise.)

I, on the other hand, cannot but see cosmic significance in every single decision. Every purchase is a test of moral fiber. Every thread on my body is a statement of character. Nothing can pass my lips—not food going in, not words coming out—without being subject to the strictest scrutiny. There is no such thing as being passive or neutral: we are always revealing ourselves and asking to be judged.

This is undeniably the result of neurotic bourgeois narcissism and overeducation, but it's also specifically tied to the Brahmin upbringing, which insists that in everyday life there are no unimportant details; in fact, the smallest details are the most important, because they're the most revealing. "Manners maketh man," wrote William of Wykeham, but for a Wasp this statement probably does not go far enough. *Manners maketh all*—from how we judge ourselves to how we judge other people. Everything from the volume of your voice to the size of the logo on your shirt tells a story. And with the sort of constant coding and decoding that goes into, say, walking across a room, it's a wonder most Wasps aren't too clogged with instructions to get out of their chairs.

Incidentally, the anti-Wasp revolt led by boomers like my parents didn't help unclog the program either, because not only did it fail to erase its prime directive (Every decision matters), it added more layers (Have you considered the impact of your toilet paper preference on the the coral reefs?) of introspection.

When my ancestors on the *Mayflower* came over (there were thirteen of them who survived), they were, in physically separating themselves from the Church of England, doing rather than thinking. However, it's astonishing how quickly after that one bold act they reverted to being inward-looking. Here was a gigantic, fertile, undeveloped continent teeming all around them, and they decided to stay in Plymouth, banning maypoles, marrying each other and farming the area's hopelessly scrubby soil (poor even by New England standards). They didn't want to continue going west. They didn't want to check out the Great Plains, the Adirondacks or the Okefenokee Swamp. They didn't even want to go to Boston, which had a better harbor and all the latest styles in buckle shoes. They were so-so at making money, and they weren't very adept at politics. What they were good at was observing, explaining and rendering opinion; they became historians, lawyers, writers and clergy. They were good at being fussy, particularly about the past; like their forefathers, they tended to see the world as degenerating the further it got from the plain and simple. They were America's anchors, its grown-ups, its chaperones on the great global field trip into the future. You could almost feel bad for them, trying to be the voice of restraint in "the country of the future," as Ralph Waldo Emerson put it. Here they were in the most relentlessly forward-lurching nation the world has ever seen, trying to remind people that it doesn't always get better—sometimes it gets worse. By the same token, it's hard not to see them as the people in the movie theater shushing everyone else, even though the movie is *Cannonball Run II.*

You can get lost in thoughts like these while stocking cat food, but the good thing is that you're accomplishing something at the same time, and if it's a good night, when you're done the hours have flown by and it's time to go home.

SOMEONE SLIPS INTO the store today while I'm back in the grocery shelves eating a bag of chips. Hearing street noise come through the door, I turn, but whoever it was seems to have poked their head in and left, as customers sometimes do. (What are they looking for that they don't see in one split second?) It's been a slow afternoon. I go back to the chips—sampling the inventory is one of my other ways of passing time—until I realize, some ten minutes later, that whoever came in is still here and has been in the store the whole time.

It's my father-in-law, Edward, a ghost if ever there was one. He's an air-conditioner and refrigerator repairman.

"I didn't know you were here," I exclaim upon locating him in the stockroom. He's lying flat on his back with his entire left arm up inside one of the KustomKools, as if he's delivering its baby. He smiles wanly and declines to shake my hand, apparently because while my hands are covered with junk food crumbs, his are covered with engine grease.

"You want me to turn off the refrigerator?" I ask. There are spinning fans in there and red-hot coils, but he wants me to leave it on, because he would rather risk losing a fingertip than raise the temperature of the bottled water a couple of degrees.

When he's finished Edward comes up to the counter with his dinner, a box of powdered doughnuts and a foot-long barbecue-flavor Slim Jim, which, like me, he has taken from the shelves. Unlike me, he insists on paying, with a twenty that he refuses to accept the change from.

"So where are you coming from?" I ask him.

But Edward is already gone, apologizing profusely as he backs through the door. "In a hurry" he says, giving me the both-hands-on-the-steering-wheel signal and an enthusiastic grease-covered thumbs-up. Then he gets in his brick-colored Econovan, which always looks as if it's got barbells or rocks inside, and drives off squeakily toward Manhattan.

And thus concludes one of the most extensive verbal interactions I have had with my father-in-law in months. And I live with the man.

Before we got married Gab told me her father was an enigma.

"No one in this family knows what he does all day, where he goes, who he sees, how he makes money. All they know is that he works," she said. However, within a few years I felt like I had a handle on my father-in-law. Edward is an artist trapped in an air-conditioner repairman's body. His medium is music, specifically sentimental old Korean war ballads, which sound like Bing Crosby crossed with a samurai movie sound track. He loves to sing. He will sing at night after he comes home and has eaten a bowl of ramen while sitting on the floor. He will sing on Sundays, after he deliberately locks his cell phone in the Econovan so he can't hear his clients' calls, while lounging around the house in a pair of over-sized flannel pajamas. He will sing in the car, since that's where he spends most of his time, and hone his technique by listening to tape recordings of himself that he makes with his home karaoke machine, a bar-quality VocoPro Wanderer.

The rest of the time he is pretty much silent.

When I moved into Kay's basement, I thought I might get to know my father-in-law on an even deeper level. However, Edward is probably the one person in the world you could share a tiny little house with for an entire year and learn next to nothing about. He's always out, and when he's home he's always asleep or singing by himself, and if I do happen to see him, it's like it was in the store: he materializes out of nowhere right next to me, stealthy, all-knowing and intermittently social like a cat.

I have discovered one thing about Edward in the last year, though. Before we moved into Kay's house I used to think that the job of a self-employed commercial refrigerator repairman belonged in the hierarchy of hellish occupations somewhere near coal min-ing, which it shares quite a few traits with, actually, starting with the fact that HVAC men spend a lot of time wedged inside dark, narrow spaces filled with hazardous gases and sharp objects. But it's actually worse. Refrigerator repairmen are the only people in this world standing between civilization and the Dark Ages— they're the ones keeping the food fresh. Like gods, they have the power to turn us back into cavemen eating berries and insects, and thus their work never ceases: they remain on duty so long as their clients, the shopkeepers of the world, have things like sushi and potato salad that need to be refrigerated. In Edward's case, it's less the sheer amount of work that makes the job brutal than the frantic telephone calls at ungodly hours from hysterical deli owners, and being the only car on the Brooklyn-Queens Expressway on Christmas morning. Sometimes he doesn't get any service calls for a few hours, but it's never long enough that he can take a real vacation or venture far from the Tri-State Area. In fact, I've only seen him outside a forty-mile radius of Times Square once, and that was for our wedding in New England.

The odd thing is, I don't think Edward minds his job. In fact, I don't think he'd trade it for the world. Why would he? As a refrigerator repairman, you get to indulge in three of life's greatest pleasures: driving, smoking and tooling around with machines. Add to that virtually unlimited time for listening to music while becoming familiar with every inch of New York City's roadways, as well as membership in the great urban fleet of repairmen, town car drivers, deliverymen and tow truck drivers, and you have what for some people amounts to something very close to The Good Life.

Nevertheless, this year Edward will turn sixty, and the Paks have begun trying to coax him into a line of work with less lifting of heavy objects and less time spent around poisonous gases. Edward may be quiet, but he can also be impossibly stubborn, and like most independent operators, he's less than the ideal judge of when to let go. (There's also a bit of a martyr's streak: for instance, Edward refuses to wear a gas mask when he's around toxic fumes, out of fear that he might unnerve his clients' customers.) Yet honestly, I don't know what we'd do if he decided to retire right now. Kay's household needs funds. Not only is the house itself heavily mortgaged, but inside it are four adult mouths needing sustenance— and often many more, given the steady stream of house guests. At the moment the store isn't bringing in any money, and it won't until we pay off our debts. Sure, I make a contribution, but my already paltry earnings are down sharply this year because there's no time to pursue the freelance magazine work I usually supplement my meager editor's salary with. Gab, of course, made quite decent money when she was a lawyer, most of which got eaten up by student loans we're currently scheduled to continue paying off till the year 2037, and the rest of which we successfully garnished into the nest egg that became the store. That leaves Edward carrying most of the load. Lately he's been seeking out additional jobs, adding to his client base and not coming home for days, worrying everyone with the impact this will have on his health. He sleeps in his van and eats at his clients' stores. The only way anyone can see him is to call him and tell him that one of our refrigerators is broken, and even then, if you're not paying attention, he might come and go without your realizing it.

"THE SQUARE ROOT OF A DOUGHNUT"

THE HOLIDAY SEASON COMES AND GOES, WITHOUT QUITE THE oomph in beer and lottery sales Kay had been expecting. Part of this, I hypothesize, is that Boerum Hill, being popular with young, single New Yorkers who tend to come from other parts of the country, sees its population drop over the holidays, as people go home to visit their parents. Kay has a different explanation: it's freezing outside, and after Christmas we had a blizzard. "People not want to go out even for beer," she rationalizes. Although it's frigid in the store as well (there's only one radiator, whose functionality I have yet to determine; I have a feeling we're being kept warm by the carafes of stale coffee on Salim's coffeemaker), I notice that Kay is wearing only an orange T-shirt with cut-off sleeves. Maybe she keeps warm thinking of what the shirt says: COSTA RICA! (A place she's never been to, incidentally.)

After a week at the register, I'm making fewer mistakes but hardly at ease. The store has a regular crowd of customers, people who come in and hang out and sometimes watch an old color TV propped above the cold-cut display. It's never the same crowd, or at least it hasn't been since I started trying to remember faces. Some people have gone out of their way to be welcoming, which is weird, I guess, because they're welcoming us to our own store; others, more disconcertingly, act as if we're not even here. Tonight, after a long day at the *Review*, I come in and find one of the largest crowds I've seen yet, watching a movie. I'm not in a very crowd-friendly mood. I had a pile of unread mail and manuscripts on my desk at the *Review*, only a fraction of which I was able to dispose of, and some of which I've brought with me to the deli.

"What's on TV?" I ask, trying to be upbeat. A cheerful deli owner.

No one answers, so I take off my backpack and drop it heavily next to the coffee machine. The people watching TV are blocking the aisles and creating a gauntlet of cigarette smoke and malt liquor breath for the enjoyment of customers who come in to actually buy things. Meanwhile, on the TV voices are screaming, blood is splattering and some sort of electric knife or chain saw is droning painfully. It's not exactly a scene that puts you in the mood for a sandwich.

"*Scarface* again?" I sigh, not really to anyone in particular.

"*Chucky Two*," a voice from the crowd shoots back.

"Oh. Thanks." I look around the store. In the beer aisle a man in a wheelchair has fallen asleep with a smile on his face and is snoring blissfully, emitting soft liquid sounds. Next to him is a woman in a subway booth operator's uniform, who had evidently grown tired of watching the movie on her feet and made herself a pillow out of hot dog rolls, is laughing hysterically.

"Man, I'm glad I don't have to live with Chucky," she says. "He's so bad."

Maybe I can hide in the stockroom and read, I think wishfully. But as I venture back I hear voices there too and smell something pungent and sickly sweet, like an air freshener—except it smells as if it's on fire.

"What's going on back here?" I demand, sweeping aside the stockroom curtain.

The stockroom is not a real room but an alcove walled off from the main part of the store by the refrigerator. It is inadequately lit and filled with stacks of cardboard boxes and bags of leaking garbage. I try to spend as little time in there as possible, because the floor feels about as sturdy as wet tissue paper and the shelves are lined with thousands of pounds of beer and other liquids.

No one answers, so I squint, and in the smoky haze I begin to discern bodies: three, maybe four, seated on milk crates.

"Can I help you guys?" my mouth says, not because I want it to but because sometimes my mouth says things without asking me first, to fill up awkward silences.

"I don't know," someone finally says. "That's not the question."

"What's the question?" I ask the figure, who appears to be made out of smoke.

"The question is, Can we help *you*?"

The voice has an undeniable element of nastiness, and now one of the other bodies is standing up. Clearly, I interrupted something—a card game? some sort of business transaction?—and my entrance wasn't very diplomatic. Who am I anyway? To someone who's never seen me before, I probably look like just another customer—only demanding information I'm not entitled to.

Suddenly a door in the back of the stockroom creaks loudly and opens halfway. The bathroom. A vigorous rush of liquid. Then a voice, unmistakably African-American and young.

"Ben, that you?"

"Yes, hello, Dwayne?" I cry. Dwayne is one of Salim's old employees, the only one we have kept on. It must be him back there in the bathroom, I reason, but whoever it is doesn't reply. Or, rather, he lets his vigorous dialogue with the toilet bowl reply for him, while the rest of us wait. And wait. And wait. Finally, a human Brinks truck waddles out into the stockroom. He is dressed like a farmer-gangster (Oshkosh B'gosh overalls, oversized New York Rangers shirt, red bandanna) and walks a bit stiffly, like a rusty robot samurai, but with instantly recognizable authority.

"Yo, Marvin, sit the fuck down," Dwayne says. "That's Ben, the new owner."

Marvin sits down, fast and hard. But another man even bigger than Dwayne stands up.

"You mean the new owner *of this store*?" he grunts.

Everyone looks at me as I nod dumbly, feeling as if I've just been identified as the perpetrator of an unspeakable crime. My center of gravity has suddenly dissolved. The floors are tipping from side to side. I want to spread my feet wider or put my arm against the wall, but there is nothing for me to hold on to except smoke.

The man takes a menacing step forward, halving the distance between us, and not even Dwayne moves to stop him. Then he lunges, wrapping me in his arms like a terrible bird, and as I surrender the battle to maintain my balance, my face collapses into the base of the giant's neck, where at last I identify that odd scent I had first detected outside the stockroom: a French Vanilla–flavored cigar, undoubtedly one of the Dutch Masters we sell ourselves.

I met Dwayne once before. He is thirty-four and has worked at the store since he was eighteen. Half of what he says I can't understand, either because he says it too fast or because what he says turns my brain inside out. Two hours after I met him, though, I knew his life story: where he grew up (three blocks from the deli, in the Gowanus Houses), where he was shot (around the corner) and what he'd ordered in the mail the previous week from the ninja supply company (eight throwing stars, five knives, a pair of nunchakus, some kind of truncheon and a pair of slingshots with ball-bearing ammo—one for him and one for his sixteen-year-old daughter, Keisha).

The first thing Dwayne said to invert my cerebral cortex was that he has a cousin with some gifted children.

"They're so smart they can tell you the square root of a doughnut."

"What?" A second earlier we seemed to be having a discussion about hubcaps. The segue to the cousin's kids eluded me.

"They're so smart they can tell you how fast it takes spit to fall off a roof."

Huh? I looked around—was the cousin or one of his kids nearby? Is he a hubcap designer? I would soon learn that this is quintessential Dwayne, though. As he would say, my brain moves "slower than water going uphill," while his brain moves like Renee, the drunk down the block who drinks Colt 45 "like a snowball going down a snowhill." After touching on the cousin's kids and hubcaps it was on to why you can't eat Chinese food after drinking beer ("You'll mess up the alignment of your stomach") and how to escape from a police choke hold. Only a genius (like Dwayne) can see the connections.

As for the interaction in the stockroom, it's easy to see why Marvin sat down so obediently. Though built like a steroid-enhanced turtle, Dwayne is hardly the biggest person to walk through the front door. (That would be the rapper Biggie Smalls, who, according to store legend, was so big that Dwayne had to come out from behind the register and rearrange several racks of snack food so he could move around.) What makes Dwayne menacing is his aura, a radiant hum of pure aggression. Dwayne's body also bears evidence to back up the threatening air—scars, contusions, welts, burn marks, swelling, some of which looks recent. As with a fighting dog, everything you could grab on him in a struggle seems to have been shorn off. And yet at the center of it all is this dapper little mustache, almost military in its trimness, perfectly balancing the rest of his plumlike face, plus a bookish little pair of spectacles that has to stretch so wide to get around his head that looking at him makes me wonder when they're going to *snap!*, sort of like Dwayne himself.

Salim made us promise to keep Dwayne on, and said we'd be sorry if we didn't, but left us to guess why. There are several possible reasons. One, as anyone who has lived in New York knows, African-Americans almost never operate or work at delis. The reasons aren't clear, but the deep-rooted enmity between Korean-Americans and blacks is certainly part of it. (Many Korean deli owners simply refuse to hire African-Americans.) For that reason alone, it would certainly not endear us to the store's many African-American customers if we came in and immediately let go of Dwayne. We also wonder if Salim's insistence could have to do with the deterrent power of Dwayne's physical presence or his ties to the community after so many years in the store.

Almost immediately, though, we realized that if these are reasons at all, they are deeply secondary. After one shift with Dwayne, Kay called him the best worker she has ever seen. He is energetic, takes initiative and seldom makes mistakes. As Dwayne himself would say, some workers tend to "sleepwalk," but Dwayne is as perky—and still talking a mile a minute—when he gets off work as when he gets on. Most striking of all, though, he seems to be omniscient, to have almost complete awareness of things happening in and around the store, whether it is the presence of shoplifters, undercover inspectors from Consumer Affairs or someone silently struggling to find canned olives on the shelves.

To Kay and Gab's delight, Dwayne's powers of observation also extend to other workers, including, of course, me. He can spot my mistakes while simultaneously engaged in three other tasks, then remember to point them out several hours later or even the next day, when customers aren't around. "You know, Ben, you charged that lady from the real estate agency tax on her milk, but dairy products are tax-free. Just FYI for the future. You can chew on it now and taste it later. Swallow it now and digest it tomorrow."

The problem is that Dwayne has groupies, devotees and disciples, people from all over Brooklyn and every demographic in the neighborhood who come to see him.

"So, Preach," as his fans call him, "you goin to the Founders Day party this year?" Or "Preach, what *really* happened to Jam Master Jay? You suspicious?" Or "Is Lil' Kim trying to make herself a female Michael Jackson? What's up with that nose?" Or "Dwayne, I've been offered a job at a West Coast law firm doing the kind of structured finance work I love, but I'm also on the verge of making partner here, and I don't want to leave New York. What should I do?" Preach has been performing in this pulpit for years, his métier being the bombs-away freestyle jeremiad, a brilliant, crude and Yogi Berra–ish soliloquy that attracts customers as much as his famously well-fortified sandwiches. As long as his fans show, he's never going to be shy about responding, and he's certainly not going to censor himself. He'll be loud and profane, and not all customers will be charmed. "Did he say what I think he said?" "Who owns this store, letting people talk like that?" And his friends can be even worse. It doesn't take someone who can calculate the speed of spit to see troubles ahead with Dwayne.

THEY SAY THE hardest part of running a business is finding good personnel, but with a convenience store it should be easy, right? We're not necessarily looking for register gods like Dwayne or Kay. We're looking for people whose technical competence maxes out at Velcro shoes. The employee we hire could even be the sort of person who, like me, forgets the price of a forty-ounce bottle of Miller Genuine Draft milliseconds after typing it into the cash register, as if the number never even existed in their brain. The only necessary qualification is that they must show up for work every day and not steal our money.

Kay puts an ad in the Korean newspaper, and applications soon start to flow in. Our first interviewee is a cheerful but somewhat down-on-his-luck-seeming middle-aged man whose bald pate and perpetual five o'clock shadow make him look like a Korean Homer Simpson. Because Koreans think it rude to ask someone their name until you know them well, he is simply known as The Man (*ajashi*). The Man has zero retail experience, but he used to be a computer programmer, which perhaps will translate into register skills. Also, he has a Social Security number and a pulse, so Kay hires him on the spot.

Things go well the first few days; The Man seems eager to please and won't let anyone else do a speck of work while he's on the job. But then he starts missing shifts, as if he's suddenly decided that coming to work is, well, optional. "Oh, my stomach was hurting," he tells Kay after not showing up one day. "I think I ate too much for breakfast." Being the bighearted person she is, Kay gives him a second and a third chance; then, being a temperamental, nononsense businesswoman, she turns on him ferociously. She gives him the money he's earned and kicks him out of the store in front of some disquieted-looking customers. The Man actually has the gall to look wounded as he walks out, but something tells me he's experienced this before.

Our next hire is also a middle-aged Korean ("The Man II"), but temperamentally he could not be more different from The Man I. The Man II comes from a military background—he served both in the Korean and the U.S. armies—and has his shit wired alarmingly tight. Unfortunately, he's also a bit opinionated.

"Who did you vote for in the last presidential election?" he demands of a shaggy young woman who came into the store to buy cat food.

"Um, Gore?" the surprised woman says.

"Ronald Reagan is the greatest president ever!" The Man II shouts at her, slamming her 9 Lives Liver and Bacon Dinner on the counter. Later he questions the patriotism of a customer who tries to buy European beer and accuses Dwayne of stealing, and before he can inflict any more damage Kay jettisons him as well.

Our third hire, The Woman (*ajuma*), has no problem showing up for work and does not have a personality like weed killer. Her only drawback is that she seems to have misled the employment agency about her age, which listed her as a mere fifty-five, the same age as Kay. Now, some Asians do tend to age well (studies show that Korean-American women live longer than any ethnic group in the country), but there's simply no way this woman was born after the fall of the Chosun dynasty (1392–1910).

"Oh my God," gasps Gab after watching The Woman totter around the checkout area. "She's too frail to work in a convenience store." The Woman looks like one of those sweet little grannies driving a Buick through a crowd of pedestrians in the parking lot at the mall.

"Ready for work, boss!" she announces with crushing enthusiasm every time she sees me. (This might be the only English she knows.) We position her next to the register and forbid her to go anywhere else, lest a roll of toilet paper fall off the shelf and break one of her collarbones. For a few days we watch as revenue inexplicably plummets during her shifts, until we realize that she's handing out change like a broken slot machine. So we try giving her a box of drinks and ask her to stock the refrigerator—not too taxing a job, but maybe hard enough that she'll reconsider working for us (Kay can't quite bring herself to fire someone older than her)—then watch as she fills all eleven shelves of the KustomKool with the dreaded Diet Kiwi Lemonade, a nonseller. So as a last resort we transfer her to the morning shift, to be a kind of auxiliary coffee server, which seems to go fine at first. Then the morning shift's revenue starts plummeting as well, and the commuters, our most reliable source of revenue, the bedrock of our business, inexplicably start disappearing, and as panic sets in, one morning an oxlike secondhand furniture dealer from down the block barges in and bellows in an outerborough accent:

"Don't you people know how to run a store?"

Startled, we ask him what the problem is, and he tells us that every day this week his morning coffee has been either room temperature or flat-out cold.

"I've been living in Brooklyn my whole life, and I've never seen such an incompetently run convenience store!" he goes on, rattling off a half-dozen other complaints. "You're unbelievable. How do you screw up deli coffee? It's not even supposed to taste good. I want the old store back, with the people who used to work here. Your family stinks!"

After the furniture dealer leaves, I touch the hot plate on the coffeemaker, which I shouldn't be able to do. Cold as a nicely chilled bottle of Diet Kiwi Lemonade. Did anyone tell The Woman that she had to turn on the switch on the hot plate every morning?

No, of course not, because no one would have thought it necessary? Then I go outside and notice that the trash can on the corner is overflowing with our coffee cups and the sidewalk is covered with frozen coffee. Oh, well. *Good-bye, morning commuters! I hope you find service as shitty as ours at whichever convenience store you abandon us for, and come back to our deli someday!* But I know that's unlikely.

THE ACCIDENT

STAFF MEETING AT GEORGE'S TODAY. SINCE BUYING THE STORE
I have quietly gone back to neglecting my duties at the *Review,*
which I'm hoping won't be revealed in front of my fellow editors.
Maybe I should skip this meeting and blame it on the deli. It wouldn't
be untrue in the slightest to say that I am worn thin by working so
many night shifts (four a week since we started, plus endless running around during the day trying to get equipment, dealing with
distributors, and so on). But again, is it really something I want
George to focus on—that my attention is elsewhere, rather than on
the *Review*? For all I know he's forgotten our conversation about
the deli already, and will be far less understanding the second time.

Then again, it's not like staff meetings at the *Review* are all that businesslike. The editors who aren't off at writers' colonies or in Paris stalking Kundera file up to George's living room, plop down on the couches with their yellow notepads, and endure around ninety minutes of gossip from Elaine's, the famed writers' hangout on the Upper East Side, with only the occasional feeble effort at following an agenda. Whenever a genuinely pressing issue pops up, such as the *Review*'s chronic lack of funds, there is invariably the same solution: party. (This always reminds me of the scene in *Animal House* when Delta Tau Chi learns that Dean Wormer has put the fraternity on double secret probation: "He's serious this time." "You're right. We gotta do something." "Know what we gotta do?" "*Toga party.*")

"But who will help us?" George will then cry. "Who will perform the readings? Who will provide the publicity? Who will find us a venue?"

"Yankee Stadium!" someone on the staff will shout. "Someone call Steinbrenner."

"No, we'll have a party inside the Brooklyn Bridge!"

"No, we'll do it at LaGuardia, and have readings on the tarmac and shoot fireworks at the planes!"

"Call the Port Authority!"

"Call Norman Mailer!"

"Call Swifty Lazar!"

"No, call Bobby Zarem! Swifty's dead!"

George loves this. No matter how incoherent it is, seeing the staff brainstorming makes him feel like we're getting things done *and* having fun at the same time. So thoroughly unproductive are most *Paris Review* meetings, so exhaustingly frivolous, that people tend to wander back to their desks afterward in a daze of guilt and have deeply *productive* afternoons—unless, of course, they've had too many of George's beers, in which case they pass out in one of the slush-reading chairs.

Today's meeting is different, however. As I'm waiting for it to start, someone asks me if I've noticed how changed George seems since his accident. "Accident?" I say. It turns out that the other night George fell at one of his private clubs and smashed his head. He spent the night in the hospital, and since then he's been, well, with head injuries it's hard to tell. He's up and about, but definitely not himself.

When he walks into the meeting, he seems considerably frailer than the last time I saw him.

"As you may or may not have heard," he begins by saying, while staring at the floor with uncharacteristic vagueness, "I've had a bit of a mishap. That blasted floor at the Colony Club is harder than it looks. I mean the Century Club—or was it the Brook? Anyway, that floor was marble, pure marble, I can tell you, and now I'm a bit of a mess, as you may or may not be able to tell."

George is too modest to realize that right now he looks like a man who got yanked out of bed in the middle of the night, thrown in a van and dropped by the side of the road out in the country, but we won't point it out for him.

"Are you feeling any better?" one of the editors asks.

Rotating his eyes but not his head (too painful, apparently), he says to her, "I can't read or write. I can barely talk on the phone. I can't even make sense of what I'm watching on TV. All I want to do is sleep and drink ginger ale." He holds up one of those little green bottles of Schweppes.

The staff looks stricken, and George obviously notices. None of us have ever seen him in such awful condition.

"I'm sorry for being like this. It's damn embarrassing." At that point I wonder if the meeting will end right there. But George roused himself from bed for a reason—he wants to say something—and seems to find a reserve of strength.

"Listen all," he says, perking up. "Being like this has gotten me to do a bit of thinking I wanted to share with you."

The living room is silent.

"I will recover from this mishap," he continues, "eventually. But who knows what could happen after that? I could have a stroke while playing tennis, or I could be run over by a bus while crossing York Avenue. Do you hear what I'm saying?"

The staff nods. We've heard this speech before. After the bus-on–York Avenue scenario—in case that wasn't vivid enough—he'd come up with a half-dozen more. ("I could be crushed by a falling bridge. I could fall into the polar bear den at the Central Park Zoo. I could be mortally wounded in a freak trampoline accident.") Talking this way revealed that even George worried about death and, in particular, the future, which is only natural in a seventy-five-year-old. It wasn't quite as morbid as it sounds, however: part of him, the bon vivant, the seeker of fun, clearly looked forward to adding death to his repertoire of experiences and the stories he would be able to tell about it afterward.

"I think we get the picture," one of the editors says after George starts going down his usual path.

"Good, good," says George. "Excellent. Because what I'm trying to say is that you mustn't take anything for granted. The corner-stones of reality shift overnight, and things are forever different. Life makes sudden turns without warning, do you hear?"

He looks around the room, to see if we're all listening.

"Very well, that's all I'm going to say. Now, has anyone seen Page Six today? I hear there's an item . . ."

At this moment I realize that in a funny way, the *Paris Review* is like a deli: it's a throwback, an institution that doesn't quite fit in the modern world. It's not big or corporate. It doesn't have a lot of swagger or muscle. There's no marketing director, IT manager or human resources department. George likes to pretend we're some kind of global institution—he's always adding people he meets to the masthead with grand titles like "Moscow editor" or "Special ambassador to the Southern Hemisphere"—but the magazine is tiny and parochial, even a bit homely. (For decades its business manager was a lovable old grandmother named Nicky who worked out of her attic in Flushing and never came into the office. Although she was only a few miles away, many people who worked for George had never met Nicky in person and only knew her by her Queens-inflected warble.) Nestled in the shadows of Manhattan's media titans—the Condé Nasts, the Times Companys—it's an amateur among professionals.

But being small can be a virtue: in the case of a deli, smallness means that the person who's poured your coffee for the last twenty years and whose children you've put through college is likely the owner, not some faceless corporation in an office park with square bushes in Odessa, Texas. In the case of the *Review,* smallness means that George has the freedom to make unconventional, ad hoc, *interesting* business and editorial decisions, things that a larger and stiffer, more bottom-line-oriented institution wouldn't allow.

Such as the slush, for instance, that morass of unsolicited manuscripts sent in by the masses trying out to be the next Jeffrey Eugenides or Ann Patchett (both slush discoveries). Like a lot of the magazines considered its peers, the *Review* can afford to rely on literary agents and published writers to provide its material. Unlike larger places, however, it chooses to concentrate a major part of its office resources on the slush. This comes at considerable inconvenience. We receive something like thirty thousand manuscripts a year, an amount so massive one of the biggest challenges is simply finding space for it. One of the quintessential *Paris Review* experiences is opening a cupboard to look for a coffee mug and having an avalanche of short fiction land on top of you. You open a closet meant for coats and there's a stack of cardboard boxes containing unsolicited manuscripts. You sit down at your desk and stretch out your legs, and *bump*—there's a whole milk crate of human creativity. There's slush on the shelves in piles reaching up to the ceiling, slush in the basement in ice coolers and picnic baskets, slush under the toilet, slush over the sink, slush spilling into a rat-filled tunnel that extends from the basement of George's building all the way up to East Ninety-sixth Street. There's so much slush it makes you wonder if everyone in the country, instead of watching reality TV and playing video games, is writing short stories. But George insists that we read every submission, because nothing in the world gives him greater pleasure than the Discovery, that once- or twice-per-year moment when you unearth a new talent laboring in the shadows. When it happens, our office is literally filled with joy.

Being small also creates problems, however: just because you don't have a marketing director doesn't mean you don't need one; ditto subscription fulfillment, fund-raising, a permissions department, etc., all of which George doles out to the staff (who are generally as unqualified for such jobs as you would think) on top of their editorial duties. It's do-it-yourself publishing, and a lot of the time, given the late-boarding-school atmosphere of the magazine, it doesn't get done.

Lately, some worrying signs have begun to appear. The *Review* has always had an untidy, overcrowded office that more resembled the headquarters of a high school yearbook than a real-world magazine. Six editors share a converted studio apartment so tiny that as they sit there reading manuscripts all day, they can practically communicate without talking. ("Is that your stomach growling or mine?") In recent months, however, the slush has begun to reach unprecedented heights, overwhelming all efforts at control. It's like a mutant lab creature run amok, or an invasive weed colonizing a hapless little pond. Poetry alone—my God, the world produces a lot of poems—is so backlogged that we don't even read what comes in for an entire year, and the piles just keep rising and rising. Among staffers, the inability to make headway is breeding despair.

Meanwhile, this dysfunction is being broadcast to the world via bloated, error-ridden issues that the editors themselves are reluctant to read in their entirety. Even the *Review*'s famously well-attended cocktail parties in George's apartment have gone slack.

So George is absolutely right to worry: the situation at the *Review* feels ripe for a crisis. The issue is whether he worries enough.

LUCY

MY HANDS CAME BACK.

After a few weeks behind the register, my hands have returned to being the reasonably obedient appendages they used to be. Money no longer causes them to spaz out and seize up, and one reason is that I've accepted that I'm never going to be able to keep them clean, and when someone fishes deep inside their pocket for some cash, as if they were rearranging furniture inside their groin, then hands me a bill so damp it might as well have been underwater, I no longer flinch. Money is money.

Tonight while on duty I meet Chucho, our wheezy, purple-faced landlord.

"I live in this building thirty years," he says. "Bought it with a lottery ticket back in"—he inhales deeply—"seventy-three."

"For how much?"

"Forty thousand."

"Forty thousand dollars? Wow! That's a lot of money. For a lottery ticket, I mean."

"Guess how much the building's worth now."

"I dunno. A million?" Chucho has already established himself as a landlord who plays hardball—we're freezing right now partly because he refuses to spend money on heat—so I try to pick a low number. I don't want him to think that I think the building is nice.

"Seven."

"Seven *million*?"

"Yeah. Easy. No problem. Someone offered me that last week."

"Wow. Seven million is a heck of a lot of money." *For a building falling sideways.* I'm not sure I believe Chucho. I could see the location alone justifying one or two million, but with floors as soft as boiled lettuce? It's a delusion. Even more disturbing, however, is the question, Is he shopping his building?

"You know, my wife got shot where you're standing."

"What?!"

"Blam!" he says, pointing a finger at my stomach. "Blam! Blam! I used to own this store."

"Yes, I heard that."

He nods and breathes in noisily, evidently lost in memory.

"I'm so sorry," I say. "That's terrible."

"Sorry for what? My wife? She lives in Virginia now."

"Oh."

"My brother got shot here too, except he was outside." Another deep breath. "And he didn't make it."

Silence.

"So are you gonna gimme a lottery ticket or what?"

I give him a Lotto ticket for free and he goes upstairs.

The lottery machine, a clunky blue cash register–like contraption that as it spits out scraps of paper makes noise like a screwdriver inserted into an electric pencil sharpener, sits next to the actual cash register in the checkout area, forming a bulwark against the reaching arms of shoplifters. A few days after we bought the store I asked our liaison from the state lottery commission, a hennish Indian-American woman named Glenda, how to go about getting rid of it.

"Get rid of it?" fluttered Glenda. "No one ever gets rid of their lottery machine!"

"Why not?" I asked. For a moment I had a vision of the machine trailing me around to the end of my life, like an unkillable parasite. I would never be able to escape the horrible grinding noise, and there would always be an old woman in a nightgown and army boots standing next to me and shouting, "Three! Seven! Two! Four!"

But it turned out that what Glenda meant was that nobody who had a lottery machine in their store would even consider letting it go, because getting one in the first place could be such a struggle. In seeming recognition of the vast power that lottery machines possess, the state lottery commission allows only a certain number of stores in each neighborhood to have them. If you didn't have one already, you could spend years waiting in frustration for your chance to become an approved vendor of state-sanctioned con games primarily afflicting the poor and needy.

Glenda said she'd start the process of disenfranchising us as lottery vendors in a week or so, but first she wanted us to think about it long and carefully.

"You're new to the business," she said. "I don't want you to make an impulsive decision and lose all your money."

Yes, I thought. *That would be like playing the lottery.*

So I study the lottery machine's impact on the store, how much money it makes for us and what sort of people it attracts. Economically, it's a no-brainer: for every dollar of tickets we sell, our take is a pathetic six cents, and that's before you factor in the cost of paying someone to sit there and operate the machine. (Kay once spent an entire hour punching in numbers, and at the end she calculated that as store owners we had barely earned three dollars—the same profit we'd make on a six-pack of beer. And please don't even ask whether we get a portion of winning lottery tickets; unless you sell the one and only jackpot winner, you get nothing.)

As for the customers, what can you say? The typical lottery customer is apparently someone who woke up and almost got run over by a bus outside their apartment building, then memorized the bus's license plate number and realized that it had four digits in common with their mother's birthday, which prompted them to visit their mother's old neighborhood and play the lottery at the local store using a combination of (1) the number 9, representing the floor of the apartment building where she used to live, (2) the numbers 6 and 3, 63 being the year in which John F. Kennedy (of whom the mother was the world's biggest fan) died, and (3) the number 2, because that was the TV station that featured her favorite show, *Judge Judy,* which she passed away while watching. This simple, heartfelt tribute—a sentimental and not at all profligate gesture—would be followed by sixteen more tickets involving every permutation of 9, 2 and 63 imaginable, after which the customer would eyeball one of the oranges sitting on the counter, make a comment about how "the fruit looks kinda old in here," follow that with a shocked, disapproving scowl upon learning that the orange costs a whole thirty-five cents, *and then,* in spite of obvious hunger pangs, request another set of tickets involving every possible combination of the numbers 3 and 5. All this would happen, moreover, as the customer stood in the way of the door, blocking other people from entering, while having a speakerphone cell phone conversation for the benefit of the entire store with someone who kept saying "What? *What?*"

Some of the lottery customers are so difficult and demanding that I have nicknames for them: Mumbles, the Screamer, and Toilet Paper (after the material I was once handed that contained a list of scribbled numbers I was supposed to input). However, as much as I dislike seeing some of them, they are our customers. It's the culture of the regulars, that group I encountered in the stockroom with Dwayne, an international brotherhood of mostly middle-aged men who in the evening often lend the store an atmosphere similar to that of an off-track betting parlor. Some of the regulars come in around seven, as the evening rush slows down, and don't leave till after midnight. My first experiences with them have been like that night in the stockroom—ill at ease and mutually suspicious. They wonder if I'm going to kick them out and I wonder if they're going to in some way complicate our arrival in the neighborhood. The younger ones occasionally do their thug routine—*motherfucker this, bitch that, I'm gonna fuck that motherfucker up*—leading me to half-wonder if some of them don't get drunk in our deli and then go rob someone else's. But I've gradually come to realize that, for the most part, the regulars aren't the types to get drunk and knock off convenience stores; they're the types to get drunk and go fishing underneath bridges. Even the younger ones are too old to get in trouble, and besides, if they got hurt in a fight they might have to spend a night at home, watching TV in their own living room, which would potentially necessitate walking more than three steps to get a beer from the refrigerator.

Today one of the regulars, a grumpy old Italian wearing a pork-pie hat and Ray Charles sunglasses, tells me how glad he is that we're keeping the lottery machine, and I don't have the heart to tell him its days are numbered.

"The customer he don' wanna walk all de way down to de Bergen," he says. (Bergen Street is where the next-closest deli with a lottery machine is located.) "My office is right here."

"Oh really?" I remark, trying again to be friendly. Though I've seen him around a couple of times, I didn't realize the old man still worked. "So what do you do?"

"I'm a plumber," he says proudly.

"Oh?" I haven't noticed any PLUMBER signs nearby. "Where's your office?"

"Right there." He points at the corner of Hoyt and Atlantic, where nothing larger than the telephone booth stands. Then he walks outside and sits on our newspaper box. So I ask Dwayne what this could possibly mean—was the old man pulling my leg?

"Alonzo's a street plumber," Dwayne says. "That's his corner. He just stands there all day waitin for somebody to ask him to unblock a toilet. He don't harm nobody."

"Where are his tools?" I ask.

"He used to keep them at home, but that was when he lived in the neighborhood. Now he lives in the projects in Flatbush, so he keeps them in a basement down the block. One of the antique store owners gives him a little space."

"When did he move to Flatbush?"

"I dunno. Ten, twenty-five years ago."

"Ten or twenty-five years ago? That's how long he's been standing on that corner?"

"Like I said, he don't harm no one."

"I didn't say he did, Dwayne. I just wanted to know *what* he does for a living. Is he there every day?"

"Every day, all the time." This bothers me. If the corner is Alonzo's office, how come I never see him there? Sure enough, when I look outside again he's gone.

After that I begin reconsidering the lottery machine. For every

Screamer or Mumbles, there's someone like Alonzo, who's hardly what you would call a lottery fiend. Of course, as soon as I begin having second thoughts, the lottery machine, being the evil, all-knowing creature that it is, seems pleased and emits one of its random robotic belches. (I swear, every time I look at that thing, it smiles at me and whispers, *You know you want to play. Try it!*) Being connected by wire to some central location from which it receives updates throughout the day—numbers, numbers, numbers pouring into its cold blue shell—it will also occasionally hiccup and go off on feverish fugues that I imagine to be telepathic summons to members of the lottery community. That's undoubtedly the worst part of the lottery machine: you often feel like you're hosting an Amway representative or the latest diet guru, a charlatan preying on the feebleminded. The lottery messes with people's heads. It turns them into twitchy, dart-eyed, pattern-obsessed arithmomaniacs—people crazed by numbers. For instance, on January 2, 2003, we had people with dark circles under their eyes and chewed-down nails spilling out the door, desperate to play variations on 1-2-3 before it reached its quota.

"No, you little brats," a lottery customer with a Russian accent shouted at her wailing children, before dropping on the counter what appeared to be change she'd scraped up from inside the couch. "There's no money for breakfast."

But if preying on people's vices is to be avoided, we'd have to shut down the store. Our shelves would be barren. Our cash register would be empty. The regulars would launch an insurrection. Therefore, when Glenda comes back, I tell her we've decided to keep the lottery machine a little longer.

ANOTHER REASON I dislike the lottery machine is that I can never seem to operate it without exposing my incompetence. Anyone can butter a bagel or pour a cup of coffee, but with the lottery there's a whole specialized vocabulary—the daily double, the day-night combo, the fifty-fifty split, box, straight—that tends to out the unversed. Every time I step up to the machine, I have this terrible feeling that I'm going to give myself away and the regulars are going to start calling me Dead Poets Society or Silver Spoon.

Not that I've misrepresented myself. I certainly haven't told anybody things that aren't true. But then again I haven't had to, since no one at the store talks about their personal lives except Dwayne. (Dwayne's personal life *is* the store.) In fact, it amazes me that some of the regulars spend as much time as they do with us and I have no idea whether they're married, single, wanted for murder or Nobel laureates. (Maybe they went to boarding school too: Mumbles of Groton; Toilet Paper, St. Paul's '74.)

But it doesn't matter. There are things you know, things you pick up. The details always tell.

Tonight a young man with one of those unsettling neck tattoos comes into the store. The regulars give him a wide berth, as if he's displaying gang colors I can't see or the telltale bulge of a weapon under his hooded sweatshirt, and suddenly everyone in the store becomes very quiet, except Dwayne, who's having a telephone conversation in the stockroom. Rubbing his hands, the young man announces that he has just gotten out of jail and would like to see someone named Lucy.

"Lucy?" I look at the regulars, but their faces are even blanker than usual. Dammit, it's the moment I feared: my unmasking! I rake my memory for the name Lucy and come up empty-handed. *Was she a clerk who used to work for Salim?*—a thought that for some reason triggers the mental image of a dimpled Rosie Perez look-alike with a glorious derriere. Or might Lucy be the exotic dancer with a receding hairline who lives around the corner and glares at me every time she comes in?

Maybe if I drag this out, Dwayne will sense trouble and get off the phone in time to come to my rescue. "Lucy" sounds like code for something illicit. I've heard about delis with side businesses in things like illegal numbers. Maybe massages? Knockoff handbags? Drugs?! I almost blurt out, "Of course we don't have that here! Are you crazy?" But then I tell myself, *Play it cool. Lucy's not here, man. She's gone. No more Lucy.* Which, of course, relies on the assumption that we don't have Lucy. However, what if we're a Lucy emporium and I'm the last to know? Now half of me wants to say, "sure," just to find out what Lucy is, and the other half is afraid that upon my saying so, a troupe of dancing hookers will appear from nowhere with rubbing oil and hooded towels and then I'll *really* be in trouble.

In the end, however, I just don't want to reveal my ignorance. "Sorry to disappoint you," I say, "but Lucy's not here. *She*"—I have to stop myself from winking—"doesn't work here anymore."

The young man stares at me as if I'm insane, then exits the store shaking his head. At which point Leslie, one of the regulars, comes up to me and, laying his hand on my shoulder, says gravely, "Ben, who's Lucy? 'Cause I really want to meet her." The whole group then bursts out laughing, especially the regular named Floyd, who keeps saying, "Is she *loosie*? Is she *loosie*?"

"What's going on?" Dwayne asks, coming out of the stockroom. Leslie explains, and Dwayne starts heaving with laughter too.

"Lucy ain't a person," he says. "It's a 'loose cigarette.'" He takes a Newport out of his own box and waves it at me. "That guy was asking if he could buy one of these."

"Oh."

"Lucy, Lucy, show us your—" chants Floyd.

"Don't worry," says Leslie. "If you're not a smoker, you wouldn't know."

But I did use to be a smoker. In fact, I lived in New York and smoked a pack and a half of cigarettes every day for almost ten years. How could I not know what a loosie is?

THE NEXT EVENING I decide that it's time to make myself more comfortable in the store. On most days the radio plays during the morning and afternoon, and the television comes on at night. I've been working to the sound track of murder, mayhem and steel-cage matches, or music that somebody else chose, but tonight and from now on we're going to listen to what I want to hear, which will involve at least a modicum of peace and tranquillity. So I arrive early for my shift and change the radio station. From now on there will be no more smooth jazz, no more adult contemporary, and no more crunk; no more Creed, Mystikal, Chingy, O-Town or Parade of the Most Annoying Songs Ever Recorded. Tonight we are going to listen to public radio until the voices of Robert Siegel and Linda Wertheimer make people's ears bleed, and in the meantime, until *All Things Considered* comes on, we're listening to one of New York's classical stations. *Ah, music that doesn't make me want to jump under a train.* It's as if my brain has exited a twelve-lane freeway and is now driving down a sun-dappled country lane, past farmhouses, through covered bridges and next to burbling streams. I feel peaceful and centered, instead of like a character under attack by robots and aliens in a video game.

Then Dwayne explodes through the door.

"Yo, B, what you listenin' to classical music for?" he says. "It ain't dinnertime." This is followed by a burst of static as he jerks the dial from the classical station to Power 105.1, WWPR ("R&B, Hip-Hop and Back in the Day Joints") and doubles the volume.

"Dwayne!" I shout (more to my own surprise than his) and immediately switch back to the Mozart, but it's futile. All night, every time I get distracted, one of the regulars creeps over and retunes the station. Finally I bark at Super Mario, "Who keeps changing the station?"

Super Mario, a goateed Dominican building superintendent from an apartment complex over on State Street, looks at me innocently.

"You mean on the radio?" he says. "I think one of the customers."

"The customers?" I shout, surprised again at the increasing shrillness of my voice. "What are you talking about, 'the customers'? *You're* a customer. Or do you work here and I am not aware of it?"

Super Mario whistles through his teeth and shrugs. I suppose that once you've seen enough overflowing toilets, it takes a lot to get flustered. But over in the pet food section, an older female customer frowns at my tone.

"I have an idea," says Mr. Chow, a kindly parking lot attendant. "Why don't we turn off the radio and watch TV instead?" Mr. Chow is the Mystery Man of Guangdong, a sphinxlike presence who drinks himself into a stupor every night and grins lugubriously even when passed out in the stockroom. He's mysterious in many ways, one of which is that I can never find his empties, even though he drinks four or five bottles of Guinness a night.

"Say, isn't it time for the news?" says Barry, while massaging an apple he hasn't paid for and will soon put back on the shelf. Like many of the regulars, Barry, a nearly blind cab driver, could be in the store during a famine and he would still never spend a dime.

"Yes, it is," I say, grabbing the remote control and turning on *The NewsHour with Jim Lehrer.* "Let's see what's going on in the world."

At the sight of dour, makeup-less Jim Lehrer talking to a panel of guests about foreign policy, the regulars look puzzled.

"Is this American TV?" one of them asks.

"Is he gonna read the lottery numbers at some point?" says another.

I turn up the TV so loud you can hear it through the walls. This will be the first time in New York history that a noise complaint is filed because someone was blasting *The NewsHour with Jim Lehrer*. Nevertheless, despite my efforts to control the environment, by eight-thirty a half-dozen men are hanging out in the store, lounging against the merchandise, holding open the door so they can spit on the sidewalk (and letting in drafts of frigid air) and in general making me paranoid, as there is too much going on for me to notice anything improper. Occasionally a paying customer walks in and does a double take upon seeing so many bodies, wondering if they've stumbled upon some kind of gathering at which they're unwelcome (or maybe too welcome). Someone lights a cigarette directly under a NO SMOKING sign. Bottle caps drop on the floor. More bodies attracts more bodies, including people I've never seen during the three weeks we've owned the store. What kind of person goes out to buy milk and comes home three hours later, saying, "Sorry, honey, there was an *awesome* party in the convenience store, and I just couldn't resist hanging out"? The greater their numbers, the more I feel like an incidental presence, a lonely chaperone on a field trip who the kids only pretend to obey. I want to assert myself somehow, but what if everyone ignores me? What do I do then—kick them out? Would anyone listen?

At nine Andre, a dishwasher at the prison, walks in. Andre is a regular, but he's quieter than the others, a smallish, polite and vanishingly unobtrusive presence. (Dwayne says Andre weighs "a buck seven soaking wet with eight bucks in your pocket," which I can't quite decipher but sounds about right.) He has the look of a guy standing on a corner trying not to garner attention. "Hey, I didn't do anything," his posture says. When he does talk, Andre likes to discuss issues, which also distinguishes him from the regulars, who generally act as if having a political view would somehow taint their manhood. Dwayne once called Andre "a black man with too much education," which confused me. "Andre is a dishwasher," I replied. "I don't think he has much education at all." "Exactly," said Dwayne.

After Andre comes one of my least favorite customers, the unctuous Floyd. A cable TV installer, Floyd is the regulars' lead raconteur, a regaler of riveting tales, such as those about seducing married female customers whose homes he visits. Floyd likes to tease me in front of the regulars ("What's the matter, Ben? Stand up straight and quit acting ashamed of your pecker"), hit on Gab and confuse me about how many wine coolers he's taken from the KustomKool. Tonight he has something rare with him, though: a living, breathing member of the opposite sex. He's on a date. And she's pretty.

"You brought your date to the deli?" says Dwayne. "What, Auto-Zone was closed? The bait-and-tackle store had a velvet rope?"

"Shut up, Dwayne," says Floyd, not laughing. The woman's name is Audra, and not only is she exceedingly lovely, she acts as if there's nowhere else in the world she'd rather be than a sausage party at the deli, and the regulars treat her with respect and adoration. Floyd, in turn, positively glows, and refrains from peppering me with his usual taunts. I let him put two big cans of Japanese beer on his "tab."

Later, after the regulars have finally left, that feeling of poise and tranquillity I experienced at the start of the shift begins to return. Late at night, when Brooklyn is so quiet that you feel like you're tucking the city into bed, back in the stockroom I begin filling a noisy plastic bucket with steaming water and what's left of a jug of Pine-Sol (which, no matter how much you put on, never seems to make much of a difference on those gray tiles, but maybe it would be worse if we didn't at least try to clean them), and as I'm bumping around in the murk I accidentally step on somebody's hand or foot, a body bedded down in the corner among the empty cardboard boxes. After yelping in surprise or pain, a dumpling-shaped old man with a Fu Manchu rises from the recycling area.

"Mr. Chow," I say tersely. "You startled me."

As usual at this point in the evening, Mr. Chow doesn't say anything, just grins, but then he starts making a motion like he's going to leave.

"You can stay there all night if you want, Mr. Chow. I'll leave off the burglar alarm. I just need another jug of Pine-Sol." Using a footstool, I reach up to a high shelf, attempting to coax a bottle that must weigh fifteen pounds into falling, when POW! Something—not the Pine-Sol—hits me right between the eyes, then bounces from my face to the ground, where it shatters. Wincing, and checking my forehead for blood, I hear the distinctly recognizable sound of a glass bottle—another one, not the one that already fell—rolling down a wooden shelf, picking up speed, and then POW! I look up just in time for another direct hit, this time right on the boniest part of the supraorbital ridge. *What kind of barrage is this?* I think, cowering, as two more strikes glance off my shoulder. Broken glass is now all over the stockroom, but not all the projectiles have shattered, and as I look down I see one of them spinning on the stockroom floor: a Guinness bottle, empty. Who would think to put empties in such a place, where eventually they'd be dislodged and rain down like meteorites? Who?!

"MR. CHOW!" I shriek while holding my now-misshapen head in my hands.

But he's already gone, fleeing out the front door faster than I would have thought him capable.

"What is it?" says Dwayne, hurrying back from the register.

Initially he sees the incident as amusing, but after a few days, when Mr. Chow doesn't return, he grows concerned and says that when Mr. Chow finally shows his face I should be nice to him, because "what he was doing he's only been doing for about twenty years."

Mr. Chow, however, never comes back.

WE ARE HAPPY TO SERVE YOU

WHEN WE FIRST MOVED INTO SALIM'S STORE, I WAS TERRIFIED to touch one bag of peanuts or modify the arrangement of Pringles cans, lest we upset our longtime customers. But eventually it feels safe for some minor changes, like shifting the bread rack a few inches to the left so that people standing at the ATM don't block traffic exiting the beer section, and hanging the display of lottery numbers in the front window instead of next to the cash register. These are small changes, trivial changes, the kind of adjustments surely no one will notice.

They notice.

"So," says Mr. Leventhal, a school principal who lives in a

brownstone on Pacific Street, "I see you put your trash to the right of the basement door instead of the left."

"How come you put the Bud Light on the bottom shelf?" growls a half-joking off-duty police officer with his gun still holstered. "Now I gotta bend all the way over to get my beer. Damn!"

"WHERE ARE THE BRAN MUFFINS?" bellows a lawyerly looking man with headphone wires streaming out from his camel-hair earmuffs. "IF YOU PUT THE BRAN MUFFINS UNDER THE CORN MUFFINS I MIGHT NOT SEE THEM, AND THEN I WILL GET REALLY REALLY TENSE. DO YOU UNDERSTAND? PLEASE PUT THE BRAN MUFFINS WHERE THEY HAVE ALWAYS BEEN AND DO NOT CHANGE THEIR LOCATION AGAIN. EVER. THANK YOU."

I'm starting to wonder if we own the store or the store owns us. Nobody cried after Salim departed (and nobody would if we did either), but God help us if we try to change one thing about the deli he left behind.

Certain customers really stress me out, especially a group of RNs from the nursing home down the block. Apparently taking care of their patients isn't keeping these women very busy, because they have time to sit around compiling a database of every price that has ever been charged for any item at any convenience store in Brooklyn, going back to the beginning of time. They use their universal price database to expose us as carpetbaggers and interlopers.

"Seventy-nine cents for a can of tu-NA?! 'Twas only seventy-five cents THREE WEEKS AGO! You raisin' de prices here, mistah?"

The irony of it is, we *aren't* raising prices. Kay hates the idea— she's the sort of person who keeps her own universal price database, and as a store manager her first priority is: How can I keep my prices low? But Salim's prices are from a different era. He charged people nothing, even by Brooklyn standards: two dollars for a cheese sandwich, a dollar for a beer, sixty cents for a cup of coffee. A store can't stay frozen in time any more than a neighborhood can or a city can. Does anyone expect New York to stop changing?

"Don't mind the Rastafarians," Dwayne says of the nurses. "Instead of worrying about what we charge for peanuts, they should be tryin' to figure out how come their patients all look like this." He grabs his neck with both hands and makes a gasping noise while sticking his tongue out.

Of course, Dwayne himself has ideas about what things should cost. For instance, not long after we bought the store, Dwayne told Gab that every sandwich had to have at least .37 pounds of meat.

"Point-three-seven?" said Gab. "According to who?"

"Everyone!" said Dwayne. "Just ask—a sandwich has to have point-three-seven pounds of meat. Otherwise it's not a sandwich."

A third of a pound of meat—Jesus, no wonder Dwayne's sandwiches are so popular. With a third of a pound of meat—plus all the extra layers of cheese, toppings and vegetables Dwayne likes to throw on, all wrapped up in a freshly baked hero—you can feed a whole family, and at our store no one ever gets charged more than six dollars (usually more like five). Moreover, you get the added value of Dwayne's performance. Dwayne likes to make sandwich-making sound like thunder, the way he karate-chops the paper off the roll, slams the refrigerator doors and tosses the serrated knife in the metal sink. His sandwiches look like if you launched them on the East River, they would fail to pass beneath the Brooklyn Bridge. Customers, unaware of the Pavlovian response he's induced, pace back and forth, eyes abulge, peeking tippy-toe over the counter. They're in a trance. By the time they get to the register they've lost the ability to speak and can barely mumble "Howmuchizzit?" Sometimes they don't even get both feet out on the sidewalk before they start tearing off the sandwich paper and eating like grizzly bears, trying to stretch their jaws around that enormous bun. If I were from the neighborhood I'd live on Dwayne's sandwiches, especially now that it's wintertime and the price of everything is going up.

This is something I never noticed before: how much weather affects prices. We're in the midst of New York's coldest winter in a decade. There's a city-wide shortage of long underwear and even, according to the newspaper, rats, which are being driven deeper underground. Since not just New York but the whole East Coast is frozen, the price of orange juice has nearly doubled, and dairy prices have shot up as well, which affects things like cheese and ice cream. This comes during a year in which New York food prices on the whole are going up by 9 percent, three times the rest of the nation. And there's been yet another increase in the cigarette tax (by a dollar) and the city's first property tax increase in ten years, by the largest margin ever. Renting an apartment in New York is also getting more expensive, by 8 percent, double the rest of the country. Meanwhile, wages in New York are actually falling, and for the first time in eight years the transit authority wants to raise the subway fare—by fifty cents, its largest increase in history. New York has always been a cruelly expensive city, no doubt, but even longtime New Yorkers say they've never seen anything like this. No, if I lived in Boerum Hill, I would *definitely* shop at our store.

OR WOULD I?

One day I go to the other deli on our block, a store known as Sonny's. Sonny's is a one-minute walk from us, so sometimes it feels like we're competing with them. We're not. Sonny's owns the market in nondairy milk, sorbet and real cheese. They're the deli for organic, local and handmade food. And whereas our store rarely receives more than a few customers per hour from the neighborhood's young bohemian cohort, Sonny's is always full of people who look like they're on their way to a Weezer concert. The jealousy I experience is like a punch in the gut. The customers carry handbaskets overloaded with expensive groceries and are lost in a quiet state of purposeful browsing, so much so that the only noise is people bumping into each other to get in line. ("Oh, did I cut you?" "No, you go first!" "No, I insist—your basket is heavier.")

Afterward I try to get Kay to go over to Sonny's.

"For what?" she asks skeptically. "To see who?"

"Hipsters."

"Hamsters? You mean from New Hampshire?" She refuses. We argue. I introduce her to sorbet, Havarti and fresh sourdough. She likes all three but remains unconvinced.

This is what Gab means by her mother's business philosophy resembling her driving philosophy: as Kay sees it, if you have a strategy that works—a lane that gets you where you want to go— you stick with it. And what Kay knows is that Americans like a steady diet of soda, chips and sugary snacks—the more processed, the better. She doesn't see the point in being one of those cars that swerve all over the road, changing lanes and slamming on the brakes, which happens to be precisely how her son-in-law drives.

Not that she thinks all food is the same. As much as any shopkeeper, Kay cares about things like how much a product costs and how well it sells. Profit margins are hugely important, and in general, the more likely a product is to give you cancer or a heart attack, the worse its profit margin is. Colt 45, for example, is widely known as a scourge not just on individual consumers but on whole inner city communities, being essentially liquid crack. However, it's also a scourge on convenience store owners, thanks to the fact that the beermaker's highly popular 16-ounce bottles (aka "double-deuces") come with a ninety-nine-cent price preprinted right on the label, leaving the store owner zero latitude for dealing with what may be higher business costs in his or her area. (For us, double-deuces have a profit margin of around 10 percent, compared to

30 percent or higher for most kinds of alcohol.) Other products that employ this form of screw-the-retailer pricing include Doritos, Twinkies and Wonder Bread.

In addition to health food having higher profits than stuff made by the behemoths of the food industry, groceries tend to have higher profit margins than snacks, all of which Kay notices— but again, the idea of not selling Doritos, Twinkies or even Colt 45 seems antithetical to what she knows about American tastes. I need to show her that Americans are gradually learning to eat more than just junk food, because for now the only one she sees doing it is me, and sometimes I think that's worse than no one at all.

BEFORE WE BOUGHT the store I knew Boerum Hill was a mixed neighborhood, but as it turns out, according to the last census, the area around Salim's store is almost evenly divided between whites and nonwhites. One way of looking at this is that we've achieved the American social ideal, a perfect demographic balance, like in the happy pictures you see in college brochures. Another way is that we've placed ourselves in the nightmare situation of having to make a choice between serving one population or the other, without ever satisfying both.

More and more I've been feeling like it's the latter, and wondering why we didn't recognize it as such before it was too late. Everyone says, "Look, Boerum Hill is gentrified," but really it depends what time you're there. During the day, people of all backgrounds are out on the street, having come to work at one of the big employers nearby, like the jail or the Department of Education. Also, during the day, people who live in the neighborhood go off to work in the city. At night you see a more accurate representation of who really lives here, but people tend to cluster—residents of the projects over by the canal, say, and residents of Smith Street in the bars. These groups might not even see each other, except at a place like our store.

We get a sampling of the whole neighborhood because we're right on the way to the Hoyt-Schermerhorn subway station. When we were looking at the store, I didn't pay attention to the housing projects because they're four blocks away, and they have their own row of convenience stores right across the street. But this is the first deli you pass if you're coming from the subway station to the projects, and again, it's one of the only delis in the neighborhood with a lottery machine. There's also Dwayne, Dwayne's sandwiches and the television, all of which ensures that the older residents keep coming.

The problem is that we don't have infinite space and can't stock everyone's favorite products. In fact, we barely have enough space to serve anyone. We could try upgrading the inventory and see if it catches on with the old crowd, but I'm pretty sure our old customers aren't the sort to switch to twelve-dollar bottles of Belgian Trappist beer. They're the sort of people who drink Budweiser from the can—through a straw.

Again, a store can't stay the same, any more than a city can. Things *have* to change.

"Maybe the solution is to go one step at a time and see what happens, not try to do anything drastic," I tell Gab.

This is how I end up trying to change our coffee.

SALIM'S COFFEE IS popular and tastes horrible—to me, anyway. I say this not as someone who refuses to drink anything but Jamaican Blue Mountain or coffee produced on collectively owned farms with ecologically responsible land tenure systems in countries that provide universal pre-K-through-3 education and have no military. I'd like to be that kind of consumer, but I don't have the will or the money. What I am is someone who likes coffee to taste like coffee, whereas Salim's coffee tastes like a scientist's attempt to create coffee without coffee beans, using something weird like flavor crystals. The company that makes it, called CaféAmerica, besides having the inspiring patriotism I love to see in my food, specializes, according to its brochure, in coffee "for large offices and other institutional settings." It's the sort of coffee that is so bad it actually tastes better when combined with the tangy aftertaste of a Styrofoam cup. Teachers' lounges and "breakfast nooks"—that's what the smell reminds me of. Nonetheless, Salim's coffee does have its fans, which may have something to with its cattle prod–like effect on the human nervous system and may also be connected with the fact that when you combine its non-coffee taste with two spoonfuls of sugar and milk, it tastes exactly like . . . sugar and milk. It's also really really cheap, and for us the profit margin isn't bad. But I think I can get us a better profit margin and sell even more cups by replacing CaféAmerica with a Brooklyn-based company called Houston Brothers, which roasts its own coffee using quality beans and offers an inexpensive commercial blend that tastes like real coffee but isn't overly strong and, best of all, will require us to raise the price of a small cup by only ten cents.

Kay isn't enthusiastic. Nevertheless, she reluctantly allows me to go ahead and make the change, perhaps because she knows that before I get anywhere I'll have to deal with Willy Loman.

GAB AND I started calling the sales rep for CaféAmerica Willy Loman because he seemed to have stepped right out of a manual for the Dale Carnegie school of salesmanship. Sixtyish and bespectacled, with a square briefcase and unfashionable trenchcoat, he would often say optimistic, gung ho things that seemed at odds with his humdrum appearance. It was tempting—too tempting—to view him as a figure from a bygone era. Beneath the bland exterior he was all tenacity and fight, and he would claw for every inch of his surely shrinking territory.

The next time he comes in, I'm waiting for him with the bad news: *we're changing the coffee.* However, before I can give him the elaborate speech I've prepared, I have already lost control of the meeting, as Willy Loman grabs my outstretched hand and drags me into the corner of the store for a confidential powwow. It's not clear why he's whispering until I realize that without wanting to be, I've been forced to become his ally.

"So, are your enjoying the coffee?" he asks confidently.

I lie and say yes. I don't have the courage to tell him I hate his coffee. My argument for getting rid of CaféAmerica depends entirely on blaming other people for not liking it.

"Splendid," says Willy Loman, while scribbling on a clipboard. "I've got a whole shipment with your name on it in the warehouse. Is four boxes of Brown Gold too little?"

Brown Gold? Is that the name of the blend CaféAmerica has been sending us?

"Actually, I think you should hold off," I say, my throat tightening, "for now." *Why can't I be forthright? No stomach for conflict! No backbone! Stop being so polite for once in your life and say what you really want to say!*

Willy Loman knows what's up, though, and refuses to acknowledge it.

"Oh?" he says nonchalantly. "Would you prefer something else? I'll just make it Donut Blend instead." Without missing a beat, he scratches out what he just wrote on the clipboard and scribbles, "Donut Blend . . . six boxes."

"No, wait," I say, growing desperate. I can feel Gab watching a few feet away. "It's not the blend," I continue. "It's . . . I think we're going to make a change." *There, I said it.*

Willy Loman puts down his pen.

"Change?" he says. "People don't like change."

"Yes, I know. But sometimes it's necessary."

Willy Loman stares at me, his expression hard but neither as angry nor as disappointed as I had feared. He simply looks determined. He has sized me up and knows what I amount to, and I realize then that he won't go without a fight.

"I get it," he says, "you don't have to explain. But may I ask you something?"

I nod, bracing myself.

"Is the coffee not selling?"

"No, it sells." This is the truth. CaféAmerica makes money.

"Well, then why change? Why change if you've got a winner?"

Now it's time for the speech, which I spent considerable time preparing. Without insulting CaféAmerica or demeaning those who enjoy it, I simply try to tell him what I perceive to be the truth: when it comes to coffee, people's tastes are changing. And they don't want Donut Blend or Brown Gold anymore. Unfortunately, I'm too worked up to speak coherently, and Willy Loman has the good sense to just stand there listening as I exhaust myself flailing around. Finally, when I'm done, he says:

"Okay, let me ask you something else. Are you looking for something higher in quality?"

"Yes," I answer truthfully, and it feels so good to say that, because I think that maybe Willy Loman understands after all, and we can part amicably. "If that's what all this is about," I imagine him saying, "why didn't you say so? Our coffee is terrible! Everyone knows that!"

"Then maybe you want to try our gourmet blend," he says instead, pulling a brochure smoothly out of his breast pocket. My spirits plummet again.

"You have a gourmet blend?" I ask. "What's it called?"

"Gourmet Blend. That's its name. It's made from all imported beans. Highest quality, roasted professionally. I'll just put you down for four boxes and you can decide for yourself if you prefer it or Donut Blend." At that point Willy Loman hands me his clipboard and smiles professionally. "See?" he says. "That was painless."

At this point, seeing me about to cave, Gab comes over.

"How's it going?" she asks cheerfully. Willy looks at her as if a snake has just slithered in.

"Give us a second, wouldya, honey?" he says, muscling a thin smile around bared teeth. "We'll be done in a second." It's his first slipup in an otherwise flawless performance, calling Gab "honey," and Gab, I can tell from experience, has just decided that she is now fully licensed to extract Willy Loman's heart and feed it to him.

"Can I see that?" she asks, taking the clipboard from my hands. "Okay now, let's see here. Hmm, interesting, sixteen-month contract, binding. Hmm, interesting, eight boxes a month, about twice as much as we need. Hmm. Can I see that pen?" She starts drawing big X's though the first paragraphs in the contract, then through the middle ones as well, then finally through the entire document, leaving only a pathetic little clause at the very end entitling Café-America to give us a single complimentary box of Gourmet Blend.

"Here you go," she says, handing the clipboard back and looking at me. "Sign away."

Willy Loman looks at me furiously and departs in a huff. We never see him or CaféAmerica again.

A FEW DAYS later, the first delivery of Houston Brothers arrives, along with a brand-new coffee machine and some new coffeepots. Suddenly I'm nervous. What if the neighborhood *hates* Houston Brothers? What if they don't think it's tasty enough or eco-friendly enough or loaded with enough caffeine? *Change, change, change—*

why change if you've got a winner? Indeed, why? Are we visionaries or merely stupid and greedy? Adding to my anxiety is the fact that other changes are taking place at the store. For example, Kay recently decided to stop selling Colt 45 after deciding that it wasn't worth the trouble. In addition to the tiny profit margin, it was our most frequently stolen beer, and the people who tended to steal it were usually so addled that they tried to run away with it stuffed in their pants, meaning sooner or later there was going to be a horrific accident involving malt liquor and a severed femoral artery.

However, she also decided to reduce the amount of meat Dwayne could put on sandwiches from .37 pounds to .14, and ended a long-standing policy of delivering sandwiches to customers' homes. In addition, despite their excellent names, about half the scratch-off lottery tickets have been eliminated—there will be no more "Cashword," "Cash in a Flash," "Cash City" or "Stacks of Cash." Also, no more "Set for Life," "Stinkin' Rich" or "Money Tree." And on top of that, we have resolved one of the most controversial business issues of our time: there will be no television in the store, mainly because of the distraction it creates for workers. Oh, and one other thing: Kay has, as stealthily as possible, started raising some of our prices, mainly on things that people don't buy very often, like aluminum foil and playing cards.

With all this in mind, I decide that the best strategy is to ease the new coffee in as subtly as possible and hope that no one notices.

Unfortunately, there's no such thing as subtle with the new coffee. Houston Brothers smells like it has the power to stain walls. No coffee brewed in this deli has ever had an aroma this powerful. *Should I open the door? Throw it down the drain? Run the air conditioner? This is too strong. Go away, coffee smell! You smell too good!*

Just then I see Andre, the dishwasher at the prison, standing across the street and waiting for the light to change.

Oh no. Not Andre. Not now. Why him of all people? Andre

probably drinks eight cups of coffee a day. I don't know how he sleeps.

"So, did you hear what the mayor said?" he asks as he walks in. The store is empty.

"No. What?"

"He said New York is a luxury item, like something you would buy at Tiffany's. It's not something you'd find at Wal-Mart or Costco."

"He said that?"

"It's here in the paper, look."

I take the *Daily News* from Andre's hands and nonchalantly pass him his coffee, which I've already prepared the way I know he likes it, with five spoonfuls of sugar. As I pretend to read the article, he takes a sip.

Then he puts the coffee down on the checkout counter.

"Is that the regular coffee?" he asks. "It tastes strong. Did you put in too many packets or something?"

I come clean immediately and explain that we have started brewing a new brand, while Andre stares at me emptily. Meanwhile, the cup sits there on the counter, getting cold.

Finally he takes another sip and says, after a nail-biting wait:

"Tastes a little like dirt. Is that what they call 'earthy'? But I like it. It's not bad." He takes another sip. "I can get used to this."

Massive relief. My first convert. As a show of appreciation, I tell Andre it's on the house, which prompts him to salute me with a kind of mock toast before going outside, lighting a cigarette and heading back to the detention center.

Strange, isn't it, how easy some things turn out to be.

THE NEXT DAY as I'm looking through the window I again see Andre coming toward the store, only this time with a decidedly different expression.

"You changed the price of coffee!" he seethes as he bursts through the door, wagging his finger and practically quivering with rage.

"Whoa, whoa, whoa. Hold on. We raised the price of a small cup by ten cents." I'm caught off guard. Customers are in the store, watching. This looks as if it could get ugly.

"Ten cents?" Andre sputters. "Ten cents!" A vein in his temple is pulsing as if there's an angry worm inside, and his eyes are blinking madly.

"Yes, ten cents. A dime. I don't want to sound insensitive, but what's wrong with that?"

"Don't you know," Andre bristles, "that the price of a cup of coffee in New York is sixty-five cents?"

This is brilliant. Why? Because it's ridiculous. There's no set price for a small coffee in New York any more than there's a quota for the amount of meat on a sandwich, or a law stating that quote-unquote regular coffee means two spoonfuls of sugar and a dollop of half-and-half (something I've been told with absolute conviction innumerable times since we took over the store). Nevertheless, Andre has effectively staked out the position of The Real New Yorker, leaving me to look like some hapless tourist bumbling around Times Square staring up at buildings with my jaw open, asking if the Statue of Liberty is nearby.

"That's crazy," I say, rising eagerly to the bait. "Haven't you ever been to Manhattan?"

Idiot. Manhattan? Why not use Europe as a reference? *Have you not tasted the espresso in the cafés of Copenhagen?* I'm really not good on my feet.

"I don't go to Manhattan," says Andre, "and if somebody tried to serve me a cup of coffee that cost more than sixty-five cents, I'd pour it in the gutter."

"Okay, well, what about a Starbucks? Do you know how much they charge for a small coffee?" This could be seen a mile away, of course. Brooklyn has a couple of Starbucks, but I'd be stunned if Andre has ever ordered a "short." However, he's so mad now he's shaking, and he decides to step out for a smoke. When he returns he seems to have calmed down.

First he looks at me for a long time. Then he says:

"I'll tell you what pisses me off. Salim was in this store ten years, and he hardly changed his prices once. You come in here and start doing it the first month."

Then he leaves, although unlike Mr. Chow or Willy Loman, not for good. Andre still comes into the store every once in a while after that, but not to hang out or for coffee. He comes in and buys cigarettes or a lottery ticket, and barely says anything at all.

LABOR WANTS TO BE FREE

I KNOW THREE RULES FOR RUNNING A BUSINESS. ONE, NEVER go into business with family. Two, never consume your own product. And three, always start out with enough money to get through a rocky period at the start.

It's pretty obvious that whoever coined these rules didn't work in the deli business. The reason people buy delis is because they don't have money; their capital is their own labor and willingness for self-sacrifice (plus the labor and self-sacrifice of family members). That's what makes it a great stepping-stone for people with large, close-knit families and an impatience for success—that is, immigrants. If deli owners had more money when they started out, they'd go into a less taxing line of work.

As our first month as deli owners ends, the toll on us is becoming obvious. For a few weeks we all got by on adrenaline, but now there's no life in Kay's house. We're a family of zombies shuttling back and forth on an endless conveyor belt between our beds and the checkout counter. Kay still hasn't been able to find any decent workers, Edward is still laboring around the clock, and I'm still trudging into the *Review* as often as I can. This level of fatigue is undoubtedly dangerous, both for personal health and for making sound business decisions.

Nevertheless, tonight Gab and I have a long-standing engagement to go out and enjoy ourselves like a regular couple. The occasion: the tenth anniversary of our first date. Gab and I have been together for an entire decade, which of all the things I've accomplished in life is pretty much the only one that unequivocally qualifies me as an adult. Thus we have the night off from the deli and dinner reservations in Manhattan, even if it means spending fifty dollars to come home all the way from the city in a taxi.

But then at the last second we decide that we're too tired to go all that way, and end up at a bar serving buffalo wings and onion blossoms near the Staten Island Ferry.

At the bar, maybe it's just the ambience of year-round Christmas lights and a flickering neon Bud sign, but Gab looks as worn out as I've ever seen her, including during her time at the law firm. She spent her entire day doing accounting for the store and practically has the lines of an Excel spreadsheet imprinted on her cheeks. More than just tired, though, she seems preoccupied and distant. Uncharacteristically, she downs her first cocktail in three unladylike gulps and promptly orders a second.

"Something to eat, too?" the waiter asks.

"Just the drink for now," she says.

I order a cheeseburger, which I find myself looking forward to with disquieting enthusiasm. *How diminished I've become.* Rarely in my life have I worked as hard as I have the last few weeks, and rarely have I deserved to be rewarded more richly. Yet there's nothing I want in the world right now except a cheeseburger, my own second cocktail and a long night of uninterrupted sleep, preferably without anyone counting money in the same room or trying to steal my blanket.

Neither of us has the energy to celebrate. Nevertheless, we have to wring some joy out of the anniversary, do we not? It's great to have longevity as a couple, but what does it matter if you can't enjoy an occasion as significant as this?

"Do you remember our first date?" I ask.

Gab smiles weakly, wincing at the thought. She and I had met as underclassmen at Chicago. We were in our "decadent" phase— that is, both of us were trying desperately to act like depraved college students. But it was a struggle to sustain. We had both been drawn to the University of Chicago (voted that year by *Maxim* magazine "the least fun school in the entire country") for the same reason: pain. We wanted misery and suffering, which the U of C, with its unofficial motto, "Hell Does Freeze Over," was more than happy to provide. What the U of C famously did to its undergrads was work them to death, burying them beneath suffocating, elective-free workloads filled with the Great Books. The school didn't apologize for its lack of fun. It took pride in its reputation as an old-fashioned, heavy-handed, almost monastic sort of place, and therefore attracted a lot of people who took themselves rather seriously, like me and Gab.

But there were differences between us as well. In U of C–speak, Gab was more of a Lockean liberal, whereas I fell more into the Marxist-Rousseauian collectivist camp. Also, even when she was attempting to goof off in her decadent phase, Gab generally went to class, and thus received much better grades.

The most obvious difference between us was our backgrounds, of course. Whereas Gab had been born on the other side of the world, in Daegu, South Korea, I had exited the womb just a hundred or so miles away, at a nice little summer town my parents used to visit in upper Michigan. And whereas Gab was on significant student aid, I didn't even have a clue about the way a Pell Grant worked. These contrasts were important in that they seemed to promise a lifetime of shared surprises. For even though stability-oriented people like Gab and me are probably destined to settle down early and bore even ourselves, marriage needs surprises—although, truth be told, they need not go as far as buying a deli.

Tonight we've agreed not to discuss the store, which means that after the obligatory reminiscing is over, we run out of things to talk about. The store, I realize, has completely taken over our lives.

Then Gab seems to snap out of her funk and pushes aside her glass.

"I want to ask you something," she says. "To be celebrating our tenth anniversary tells us something, right? That our relationship is strong, yes? That despite all the challenges we've put up with recently, you and me, we're holding up?"

I nod somewhat reluctantly, because I have a feeling Gab is about to tell me something I don't want to hear.

"I'm glad you feel that way," she continues, "because as you know, I did some accounting today, and I don't know how to say this, but things at the store don't look so good."

Uh-oh. I knew it.

"How bad is it?" I ask, putting down my burger.

"Bad," she says. "Really bad." Her explanation goes something like this:

We had thought that the store was off to a decent start, because every day we looked at the receipts and saw figures that more or less jibed with what Salim promised us, namely, revenue of around two thousand dollars a day. Sure, some days were disappointing, but if Gab's calculations held up, our debts would be paid off in a few months and we could get our money back and move on.

But the thing about business is that, like anything else, it takes a while to figure out how you're *really* doing. You're like a pilot whose dashboard instruments don't function until the plane has reached cruising altitude—you don't know how fast you're going, how high you are, or how close you are to stalling and dropping out of the sky. There just isn't enough information, and what there is you don't know how to interpret. Furthermore, beginner's errors distort the picture. In our case, the cash register work has been so riddled with mistakes that on some days we essentially have no idea how much business we really did. And ballpark guesses often turn out to be rosy-picture guesses.

Yet no matter how mixed the evidence, to a fledgling entrepreneur the future always looks shiny and bright, doesn't it? You're in business, you have a store, and it has customers, which might seem like modest accomplishments, but it's the beginning and it's hard not to succumb to the delusion that things can only get better. For instance, just the other day we had one of our best shifts—a Saturday in which we made almost twenty-five hundred dollars—and afterward I couldn't help predicting to Gab that by summer the store would be making double that.

That was a Saturday, though, and Saturdays are always going to be the best day of the week for a store that devotes almost a quarter of its space to beer. Sundays aren't bad, either, because of people stocking up on groceries for the week, but Mondays are the worst and also when bills start to arrive, and this being the end of the month, invoices have been raining down like bombs all week—a thousand dollars for orange juice, two thousand for lottery tickets, three thousand for rent. Some of our suppliers, it's becoming clear, have contributed to our misapprehension of financial well-being by giving us steep discounts on our first shipments of ice cream or whatever, and postponing their first bills. Now, however, it's all coming due and adding up to a stupendous debt, on top of the debt we already have.

"We're in a hole," Gab says. "There's no money in the bank, and based on my calculations, we owe our creditors more than I can see coming in. And we have things like tax coming up."

"What do you mean tax? It's only February."

"Sales tax, stupid, not income tax. As a business, you have to pay sales tax every three months. Our assessment is coming in a few weeks, and if my calculations are correct, it will be another few thousand dollars."

"A few thousand dollars?!" The lethargy has worn off. A new feeling has entered my body—not panic or despair, but something more like the shock of being diagnosed with a serious illness. How would we pay off Salim and our other debts if there wasn't money coming in—not now and apparently not for quite a while? *Our business is sick*—isn't that what Gab is saying? We're in danger of becoming one of those stillborn, turn-your-head-away stores that close right after opening. We'd been counting on the deli to pay off our debts, but instead those debts have increased, and now, like any insolvent enterprise, we'll shortly be shutting down.

For a moment I feel almost overwhelmed. Then it occurs to me that *this* is what I had been craving—namely, risk and consequences. The real. Vital contact. And despite the chill in the bar (all of New York seems to be frozen right now, as the commerce-killing cold spell goes on and on), I suddenly feel hot with shame. The folly of it all! The way I invested what should have been a dispassionate business decision with foolish emotions and ideals! But it soon passes, in part because I notice that Gab is staring at me with an oddly composed expression.

"Why aren't you freaking out?" I ask her.

"Because I have a plan," she says confidently.

I look at her in terror. A plan? But of course—I should have known. Gab and her plans. She proceeds to take out a hard copy of the spreadsheet she's been working on all day and outline the sort of brutal austerity program University of Chicago economists used to be famous for imposing on Third World economies. The plan has several components, which she ticks off one by one after ordering another drink. The first is:

We're going to be living in Kay's basement awhile longer. "How long?" I ask. "I don't know," says Gab. "There are a lot of people the store owes money to, and we're at the back of the line." In other words, until we pay off the orange juice guy, Chucho, Glenda the lottery saleswoman, the snack cake thugs and the rest of them, I will not be sleeping aboveground. And since paying them off means fixing the store first, that seems like it could take a long time indeed.

We're going to have to continue working at the store—in fact, we probably have to work there more. This is automatic as long as we're living with Gab's parents. How can we ignore a crisis while it's going on in the same house? Gab will continue doing daily shifts while taking care of things like accounting, and I'll go from four shifts a week to five, primarily at night. There is one change, though: until now Gab has been paying us all minimum wage. Now we'll be working out of the goodness of our hearts—that is, providing free labor at a store we supposedly own.

Also, no more free food. No more eating off the shelves. Consuming your own product may be cheaper than paying full price, but there's a cost to it nonetheless, and once you start doing it, your coworkers do it, and pretty soon your customers do it as well. Yet it's a hard impulse to control. Here you are in a virtual jail cell created by beer and snacks that *you* bought. How can you not feel entitled to a little sampling? (Though I'm not a junk food fiend, I find myself tortured by a desire to sample all the various Hostess and Entenmann's snacks I haven't tasted since childhood—Sno-Balls! Donettes! Guava Cheese Puffs!—a craving I certainly would not feel if I did not have to look at them all day.) In fact, to be perfectly honest, I'm not sure I can carry out this plank of the austerity program.

But it's the next part that really stings. For the last few weeks I have been scrutinizing our customers, analyzing our inventory and gauging the flow of money throughout the day, all the while becoming more convinced that the store *must* radically overhaul its inventory. If we can't serve two populations with different tastes—and we can't, because our space is too small—then we have to go with the one that appears to command the neighborhood's future. That would be the crowd at Sonny's, the people buying sorbet, sourdough baguettes and veggie burgers. It's not an issue of what I like to eat. If Boerum Hill was becoming Hasidic, I tell myself, then we'd find a way to serve kosher food; ditto if it was becoming Albanian or Sri Lankan or Korean, for that matter. As it happens, the people taking over Boerum Hill have the same taste in food as my own, a fact that will truly mark us as boneheaded if we don't adapt to the change.

Gab had accepted this—unlike her mother or me, she was agnostic on the issue of inventory—but requested that the process proceed in a timely and sensitive fashion. An item here, an item there. No more big changes when it comes to products like coffee. If we could afford to get rid of the lottery machine, then it would go last.

Now, though, she insists that the process come to a complete halt until our money woes get resolved. "I'm sorry," she says. "I know this interferes with your plan." Her mother, too, is henceforth to stop making changes. What this means is that Gab and I aren't just stuck in the basement and stuck working as checkout clerks; we're stuck in that scruffy milieu of lottery tickets, wine coolers and penny candy—trapped in Salim's deli, as it were, rather than the deli I had envisioned it becoming. This, to my surprise, I find the most intolerable aspect of the entire situation.

C IS FOR "COOKIE"

DRIVING TO BROOKLYN THE NEXT DAY, I FIND MYSELF ASKING, *When did I get so emotionally invested in the deli?* Was it the moment I stuck my head in the refrigerator, or had it happened gradually, by stealth? This was supposed to be a temporary gig, and a reluctant one at that, to appease my long-suffering wife. At some point, though, deeper convictions had come dangerously into play. Maybe it was ambivalence about my "real job," which was nothing of the sort. The *Paris Review* was not a real place—or at least sometimes that's how it felt. It was fantasy, a make-believe world (poems! stories!) inside a bubble of privilege. It survived by existing in a gravityless world ("society" and "the arts") where the normal laws of supply and demand did not apply.

The deli was an antidote: pure struggle. Which brought about the biggest seduction of all: rash and imprudent action. The Hail Mary pass that rescues us all. There was also a certain Calvinistic tendency to see salvation as coming through work and family, which is something Puritans share with Koreans, and as we look to survive this period of crisis, I find myself clutching those twin talismans to get us through.

THE THING ABOUT an austerity program is that it has to be enforced, but in a family business no one is the boss; or, rather, everyone is. Gab's solution is a voluntary system of fines: screw up at the register, owe the difference. Get a health code violation, pay it yourself.

"This is absurd," I protest. "I refuse to participate in a kangaroo court."

"I thought you were committed to saving the store. I'm doing it. My mother's doing it."

"But you're not the ones getting fined!" Which is true. Whereas the two of them have spotless records, Kay has already reported me to Gab once for accepting a counterfeit twenty-dollar bill and twice for not wearing those ridiculous cellophane gloves for making sandwiches, and meanwhile she's been eyeballing me constantly for signs that I'm sneaking food off the shelves. (Which of course I am. I refuse to give up one of my last sources of pleasure, though technically this makes me guilty of shoplifting in my own store.)

The tension becomes essentially unbearable when we close for renovations. I've been looking forward to renovating since we opened, seeing it as a turning point—maybe *the* turning point—in the transformation from gnarly bodega into trendy gourmet market. My plan is to repair the hole in the ceiling, retile the dishwater-colored floor and rearrange the refrigerators to make walking through the aisles less like squeezing into an airplane bathroom. I'd also like to spruce up the place by installing some lighting that doesn't come from fluorescent tubes and putting in a window so we can occasionally circulate the air. It's a lot to accomplish, but I figure we can get it done in a week if everyone pitches in.

Kay, however, gives us only one day, and this amounts to a bitter concession on her part, because originally she wanted to close the store for only a single shift.

"No time for make pretty," she insists, as if what I want is to paint the store pink and decorate it with flowers. "We need to be making money every day, every hour." She doesn't say this in a greedy way; she says it in a feverish, panicked way. It's not just the bills she's worried about; she thinks that if we close for any significant length of time we will permanently lose more of our regular customers.

Nothing gets on my nerves like Kay's impatience. The second she thinks of something it has to be done, usually by herself. She's a compulsive nonprocrastinator: waiting isn't in her repertoire, and idleness, the act of not doing anything (which many people know by the term "relaxing") causes her actual physical pain. "I do anything not to be the lazy person," she says. "If I'm not doing something all the time, whole body hurt, feel like sick or something. Want to die." And since her internal clock runs somewhere between an hour and a whole day ahead of the rest of the planet (she routinely shows up early for things normal people tend to avoid, like car inspections and dentist appointments; once she got fined by the sanitation department for putting her garbage out too soon), there's no way to keep her satisfied unless you, too, are the kind of person who does all your Christmas shopping in September.

Of course, Kay's not the only one with compulsive tendencies. Where I come from, *not* hurrying is practically an article of religious faith. America's grown-ups don't rush; they throw their arms around the world and try to make it stand still. There's a stubbornness about it, a refusal to give in to the forward motion of time, as if the future itself is just a fad. Nobody drives where they can walk, nobody vacuums what they can sweep, and nobody microwaves (God forbid) what they can cook on an old-fashioned burner. "Fashion" and "technology" are dirty words. Not surprisingly, when it comes to big projects—fixing up a house, say, or the type of renovations we're engaged in at the store—nothing but the most exacting, time-consuming process will do.

On the appointed day, undeterred by Kay's ticking stopwatch, I arrive early with a detailed plan, and things get off to a promising start. Edward, to my surprise, shows up with his occasional partner Ling, a Cantonese electrician, as well as Gab's uncle Jinsuk, who happens to be a professional carpenter. *Wonder of wonders,* I think, *with all this extra manpower, we might actually accomplish some things!* However, as I soon discover—to my horror—these people, all being small business owners themselves, are just as hardheaded and independent-minded as Kay. There's no cooperation. There isn't even a plan. People just start taking things apart and rebuilding them willy-nilly. Soon the store is filled with the racket of a construction zone and a great choking cloud of sawdust. For a while I try to organize things and at least get people to coordinate; but there's a big difference, I realize, between me and the trio of Edward, Ling and Jinsuk: they have power tools and I don't.

Meanwhile, as my dreams for the store disintegrate, through the haze I see Kay standing there with her hands on her hips, hounding everyone to go *faster, faster, faster.*

"Can you please get her to lay off a little?" I ask Gab, feeling as if my stomach is writhing with poisonous snakes that want to come out and bite everyone. "It's stressful enough in here."

"I'll try," she says wearily. Once again Gab is serving as a sort of human buffer zone between two silently warring parties. Kay and I never argue—not directly, anyway. Oh, we clash over just about everything, from coffee to the renovations, and we criticize each other as brutally as any son-in-law/mother-in-law combo, often while standing in the same room, but because of the language barrier there's no need for diplomacy. After all, when we need to communicate and be respectful (something that's especially important for me as the son-in-law), we can rely on Gab to act as a filter.

This puts a terrible burden on Gab, however, and on top of all the other stress she's dealing with, it's beginning to take its toll. We're all strung out, but Gab looks particularly miserable.

As the day goes on and Kay's deadline nears, paranoia creeps in. Gab and her parents are conferring in Korean, and I'm watching them from a few feet away, hoping to pick up a few words. It's indicative of how crazed the day is making me that I consider for a second "accidentally" knocking down part of a wall or cutting some wires to make finishing today impossible. *No, of course I won't do that. That would be sabotage.* But then hadn't I recently discovered Kay deliberately undermining one of *my* goals? After finding an old box of CaféAmerica under the sink, she'd started secretly offering it to longtime customers, brewing a whole separate pot and selling it at the old price of ten cents less than the new coffee.

I was outraged. "Your mother is impossible. I can't work with her anymore," I railed at Gab, who promised to stop Kay from freelancing. But freelancing is exactly what small business tends to bring out. *If I don't do it, no one will* is what you constantly end up saying to yourself. Sometimes the attitude is helpful. For instance, since we opened the store we've been getting extorted by our snack food distributors, Mr. Yummykakes and Mr. Tortilla Chip, who've been trying to strong-arm us into buying more merchandise than we need and "forgetting," if we don't honor their demands, to make scheduled deliveries, or claiming we haven't met their quotas (which are much lower than what they actually want us to purchase). As a result, some of our shelves have gone empty, and customers are asking where their favorite foods are. It's a game of chicken, and much to the consternation of the snack food thugs, who probably thought they could walk all over this roly-poly Asian grandmother manning the day shift, Kay hasn't blinked. In fact, she's banned some of them from the store. My mother-in-law knows all the distributors' tricks, whether it's dumping eight dollies of the new and soon-to-be-discontinued no-calorie beer next to the cash register and driving away before we can open the boxes, or sticking us with a freezer full of ice cream that got too warm in the back of the truck. (Refrozen ice cream has the texture of snow dislodged from the underside of a delivery vehicle.) Besides being fierce, she's paranoid and inexhaustible, a scammer's worst nemesis.

But these aren't qualities that can easily be switched off, and as Kay herself will eventually admit, the stress of the last few weeks has brought out a kind of demonic single-mindedness in her. She's gone into crisis mode, which means that come hell or high water, she's going to get us through this turmoil. As a result, there've been times when she's been almost as fierce with us as she has been with Mr. Yummykakes and Mr. Tortilla Chip. Using all the weapons in her arsenal (the guilt trip, the nag, the tantrum), she's been pressing us to stay focused on survival—making it to the next day, then the next pay cycle—without committing unforced errors like getting fancy with the renovations. No one else in the family has this kind of strength or takes on the same amount of responsibility. Other than Edward, who's not involved in the store every day, Kay's the only one who knows what it takes to get through a crisis. But as I keep telling myself, bullying is bullying, whether it's for a good cause or not.

So after watching Kay browbeat everyone some more, I order

the whole family, plus Ling and Dwayne, out of the store. *Since no one else will stand up to tyranny, I will* is something like the thought going through my head.

"Can you stay here for a second?" I say to Kay, putting my hand on her arm as she's about to leave the store too.

"Me? Why?" She looks surprised.

Instead of answering I close the front door, which, like the rest of us this morning, has come slightly unhinged and immediately wedges tight against the frame.

Now's my chance. I have prepared a speech, something direct but not disrespectful, firm but not inappropriate. *If only the sawdust wasn't so thick and my eyes weren't watery and bulging, and my face wasn't red with exertion and I didn't look like a man who just lost his wits!*

"We need to talk—" I start to say, but before I can finish the sentence Kay screams as if she's in a horror movie and runs for the bathroom. Now, my mother-in-law has the loudest voice I've ever heard. She used to be a wedding singer, and in Korea they train singers to project their voices by making them practice next to waterfalls. Kay's shriek isn't a whole lot less piercing than Uncle Jinsuk's table saw, but luckily her voice is set to stun, not kill, and I may only be temporarily deafened.

The people outside start pounding on the door, though.

"Hey, what's going on in there? Is everyone okay? Open up!" Their alarm is magnified by finding that the door won't budge.

Oh, great. This looks wonderful. I knock on the door of the bathroom, but Kay won't come out. She's locked herself in and is still screaming for help.

"I just want to talk!" I shout at her in a voice that sounds remarkably like Quasimodo's. *What happened to my mother-in-law the bully?* Now she's acting all ladylike and scared, leaving *me* to look like the bad guy. *What kind of person,* I can hear any sensible observer of the situation saying, *terrorizes a defenseless grandmother?* I almost believe she's faking it, playing victim, except she really does seem terribly frightened, and after pleading with her unsuccessfully to come out of the bathroom so I can explain ("Please! I wasn't going to hurt you!"), I give up and do what I can to help the rest of the family open the front door instead.

It takes a while, but eventually we pry it out of the frame, and a few minutes later Gab (after shouting at me, "What's wrong with you?!" on her way in) coaxes her mother out of the bathroom. Shortly afterward, without talking to me, Kay goes home, along with Edward, Ling, Uncle Jinsuk and Gab, leaving me alone to work on the store with Dwayne, who goes home too after a while. *Mission accomplished.* The renovations will not be finished today. The store is a bloody mess, covered with debris, half-finished projects and a thick layer of sawdust. It looks like a bomb blew up inside it, which I suppose in a way one did. So much for family.

AS A RESULT of the fight you'd think I'd be chastened enough to avoid conflict for a little while—and I would, under any other circumstances. Unfortunately, it's just too important to stick to the plan—*my* plan, that is, for turning the store into a gourmet market. Thus while Kay and I make up the next day (or, rather, I humbly beg her forgiveness, and to my surprise she mumbles something about being sorry too), the whole cycle of recrimination, mistrust and behind-the-back criticism starts again almost immediately. Kay sees me doing something she doesn't like and says so to Gab; I see her doing something I don't like and do the same; and Gab, after hearing from both of us, runs out to the street and screams at the sky, "Jesus Lord in heaven, what did I do to deserve this? I'll do anything if you let me escape." (That's the thing about family business, though—there is no escape. You live with the people you work with, and after putting up with them at work all day, you get to come home and listen to them clip their toenails as they hog the television.)

To make matters worse, one morning the mail delivers a sleek, expensively produced catalog from a distributor specializing in gourmet and imported foods. At first I hide it from Gab, who would surely throw it in the recycling bin if she saw it. Then I consider burning it in the backyard, or at least blacking out the company's telephone number, lest I act on some unfortunate impulse. (Remember, Gab just told me no more expensive, nonessential purchases.) But I can't do any of these things. The spreads pictured in the catalog are too sumptuous, the pictures too beautiful. It's like walking past a bakery with the smell of hot, crusty, freshly baked bread wafting out.

"Good afternoon, this is Steinway Gourmet Foods. May I help you?"

Now, let's be clear: this *really* is not your usual brochure. It's more like an art book, something you could leave on a coffee table. The products it offers—a cornucopia of international delicacies, the kind to be found in epicurean gift baskets and crowded window displays at specialty stores in the West Village—have been assembled into still lifes so mouthwatering you can practically taste them. The variety is astounding—who knew there were that many different kinds of balsamic vinegar? And so many delicious little mysteries—for instance, what does hempseed oil taste like? So much wholesome goodness and so little to feel guilty about; this is, after all, the good side of globalization, the flowering of world culture in all its myriad expressions.

Yet as I hold the phone to my ear I feel like I have no soul. The back of my neck is damp and my stomach is knotted.

"Yes," I say, trying not to sound as sinister as I feel. "I'd like to make an order."

"Splendid!" says the female operator in a cool Southeast Asian accent. "However, before we start, I must confirm that you are aware of our thousand-dollar minimum."

A thousand? I had assumed that it was only around one hundred, as it is with most vendors.

"Yes, I'm aware of that."

"Very well, then. What is the first item on your list?"

The first item on my list . . . what list? I haven't made a list. All I've done is go through the catalog trying not to drool on the pictures. My first item? Well, what does our store need (besides everything)? Which products does it *lack* more than any other? *Flip, flip, flip . . .* I should have made a list. But then I would have thought about it and lost my nerve. And what the store needs is for people to stop thinking. It needs inspiration. *Flip, flip, flip . . . Presto!*

"I'll have some Chessmen," I pronounce decisively.

"Chessmen?" says the operator.

"You know, those little butter cookies shaped like rooks and queens?" Doesn't everybody's grandmother keep a package of stale Chessmen in her pantry for visits by the grandkids? *Here, some cookies . . . from the year before you were born.*

"What's the SKU?"

"The what?"

"Product code."

"Oh." *Flip, flip, flip . . .* Now I'm starting to feel it creep up on me: hesitation. Second thoughts. Am I really going to defy my long-suffering wife so I can order some butter cookies?

"And give me some of those chocolate-covered Chessmen, too."

"Next item?"

Now, having successfully fought off self-doubt, I begin to sense a growing freedom. The shackles are falling off. At first I select a few more bland, conservative, New Englandy cookies, but then I move on to the stuff Steinway Gourmet Foods specializes in: world cuisine. Culinary exotica. Gastronomic nirvana. The word "flavor" pops into my head as I peruse the offerings of Indian, Latin American and East Asian cuisine. How did we ever live without it?

Picking up speed and confidence, I order and order and order. *Give me four cases of . . . And yes, a whole box of . . . Okay, multigrain too . . . Sure, throw in the fat-free as well.*

This feels good, I think. I may be useless when it comes to a lot of things at the store, but I know my way around a Whole Foods. And this isn't just regular grocery shopping—it's shopping for the whole neighborhood. What could be more fun?

The only question is, When Gab finds out, will she ever forgive me?

DEATH TOMB

A FEW NIGHTS LATER, SOMEONE TRIES TO BREAK INTO THE DELI. It happens after we close; whoever it is jimmies the lock on the roll-down shutters, then tries to shoulder through the door. Luckily, he triggers Salim's old alarm, which has a siren like the world's loudest smoke detector and can be heard throughout the neighborhood. Frightened, the robber runs off. However, after he leaves, the alarm continues to sound, and as is their custom in New York, the police do nothing about it, while the alarm company attempts to contact Salim instead of us. As a result, we are greeted the next morning by some very tired and upset soon-to-be former customers.

Not the ideal start to a Monday. Yet within a few hours it becomes clear this will not be the worst news of the day, or the week, or maybe even the whole year. For that day the mail, which, as a small business owner I've come to anticipate with horror ("No, take it back!" I want to say when I see the postwoman coming toward us), brings a letter bearing the dreaded return address of the state department of finance—still a bit early for that tax assessment we're expecting. We open it and discover that Salim may have accidentally underpaid his sales taxes for the last few years, and as a result the government is levying a whopping eighty-eight-thousand-dollar fine. Which to my unschooled ears sounds like a problem for Salim, not us. But not Gab. She knows. *We* now own Salim's business, assets and liabilities; therefore, the government wants the money from *us*.

Gab looks like she just saw the noose we're all going to be hanged with. Then, gathering herself, she reads and rereads the letter, poring over each word. When she was working as an attorney, Gab's signature was thoroughness—she would stay at the office all night not to rack up billable hours but because she couldn't bring herself to skim through projects. If she thought she'd been careless, it would torture her every second she was away from the office. Indeed, a point came during the sale of the store when she said to me, "We might be moving too fast." We'd all been in such a hurry—Kay, Gab, me. And now, looking back on that period, Gab realizes that she might have overlooked some red flags.

"I should have waited until the state did its assessment," she says, although if she had, we never would have been able to open by Christmas. "I can't believe how stupid I am."

"Well, we'll just have to track Salim down and straighten this out," I exclaim defiantly. Gab looks inconsolable, however, in part because Salim has already proven rather elusive. Since moving to New Mexico or Arizona or someplace out in the desert, he's changed his number (as the alarm company found out) and failed to send us a forwarding address. We're in contact with one of his relatives, a man in Queens who takes payment on what we still owe from the sale, but who is little help in locating Salim and who becomes impossible to contact after employees of a notoriously aggressive city marshal start leaving threatening messages on our answering machine.

The marshal—in New York, city marshals are a despised class of Old West–style bounty hunters who, despite not being public officials, somehow get to carry badges and guns as they pursue parking cheats and other scofflaws—is named Martin Bienstock, and his quarry are the KustomKools, those sexily purring refrigerators that came with the store. As it turns out, Salim bought the KustomKools last year with a deposit, then struggled to make his monthly installments, causing him to be threatened by the seller with legal action (which we never found out about). As with the tax arrears, this would seem to be a problem for him, not us. However, Bienstock only cares about the KustomKools, which he's been threatening to come over and seize. As a result, since the refrigerators are basically the only valuable thing in the deli, pretty soon all we'll have left is a cave filled with junk food to go with that eighty-eight-thousand-dollar debt to the government. (Maybe we can turn the store into some kind of avant-garde performance space and host readings!) Gab has bluffed Bienstock as well as she can, using her best bite-your-head-off lawyer routine, but Bienstock's lackeys countered by threatening to come over and break down the wall with a wrecking ball. Thus we've been forced to look out the window all day, scanning the block for heavy machinery and ninjas and whatever else Bienstock's posse includes.

Even if Bienstock doesn't knock them down, it feels as if the walls are caving in. What happened to us? I feel like asking. Where did so much evil luck come from? None of our hard work or responsible decision making seems to be paying off. Has it always been this hard to start a modest business like a deli? What law of the universe did we violate, which god did we anger? One day I walk into the store and have this feeling that it is turning into someplace else, a place I visited recently but can't remember. Then it comes to me: with its empty shelves, dirty floors and damp, desolate chill, our store has become the North Korean deli. It has the same atmosphere of decay and despair, the same sadness.

The hardest question is how it happened so quickly. Salim's business may not have been run the way they teach at Harvard Business School, and it may not have been terribly profitable, but at least it had customers—loyal customers—and a purpose. The community depended on it. People cared about it. Somehow, despite selling nothing that was good for you, it had the air of a decent place. And it was not in danger of failing before we took over.

We'd risked more than we intended, I realize. It wasn't just the money we'd borrowed or our careers; it was the store, with its years of goodwill and place in the community. It was Gab's family; it was Edward's health; it was Kay's house, which we haven't made a mortgage payment on now for two months. And it was becoming my marriage with Gab.

OVER THE LAST few weeks, the *Review* has proven something of a refuge from the chaos of the store. George's health isn't great, but as always he seems to be recovering, and the two of us haven't clashed for a while. He seems to have forgotten that I exist, and I'm doing everything I can to keep it that way.

Then one morning, an e-mail slides onto my computer screen at home with the following message, sent from the *Review:*

"We're screwed! Get in here now!"

For the last six months we've been working on an anthology that is due out this spring, and according to a fax we've just received, one of the authors is denying a request I sent to reprint their interview, which is no big deal. *Except the book is already at the printer.* George is going to go ballistic—it's exactly the sort of mistake he'd blame on my being distracted by the deli. He's going to fire me, and then he's going to make sure that no one in publishing ever hires me again, which he can do since he knows everyone, and who would hire someone who got on the bad side of George Plimpton, the most affable and lenient boss in New York?

I rush into the office.

"Does he know yet?" I ask.

Brigid, the *Review*'s managing editor, shakes her head. "He went out early this morning and won't be back till tonight."

Good, there's still time. I get on the phone and start begging the author's agent to reconsider, but they're firm—it's a piece the author has decided not to reprint.

"And if you go ahead, we'll sue you," says the agent curtly, before hanging up the phone.

Brigid is standing next to me as this happens, trying not to look panicked.

"So you're saying we have a choice between getting sued and not publishing this book? We have to do something." After hesitating for a few seconds, she picks up the phone and sends orders to shut down the printing machines, just like in the movies. You can practically hear the machinery come to a screeching, car crash–like halt.

"Now what?" I ask. "Is everything okay? George won't have to find out, will he?"

Everything is not okay. Five thousand copies of the anthology have already been printed and are now going to be sent to a place called the "book crisis center," where they will either be pulped or have the offending pages extracted. Either way, it's going to cost at least ten thousand dollars. Which means George will have to find out—tonight, in a few hours, at a cocktail party at the New York Mercantile Library.

He'll be pissed for two reasons. One, the ten thousand dollars. George may be old money, but the *Review* has a slim operating budget, and ten thousand dollars is one-half of what we pay our authors for an entire issue. It's a part-time editor's salary. It's a couple of parties. It's money that sooner or later George, being the *Review*'s fund-raiser in chief, will have to go out and make up by tapping his network of benefactors.

Two, George didn't want us sending permission requests in the first place. In general, George is rather irritated by the whole idea of permissions, contracts, paperwork, and so on, which is why he put me in charge of it and then instructed me to do as little work as possible.

"It's a gentlemanly agreement when you publish with the *Review*," he once told me. "It's not like we're some cutthroat business making obscene wads of cash. It's for the greater good of literature!"

Most authors seem to agree. Rather than contracts, they gladly accept a handshake or a congratulatory phone call from George, and seem fine with an absurdly puny check and access to comely interns at George's parties.

When George was young, it was easier to get away with a carefree attitude because publishing was filled with people who had, as the expression goes, known each other forever. To pick but one example, when George published his first book, in 1955, a children's fable called *The Rabbit's Umbrella*, his publisher, Viking Press, was owned by the Guinzburg family, and its soon-to-be head, Thomas Guinzburg, was one of George's oldest friends. Now Viking is owned by Pearson PLC, a massive multinational media conglomerate specializing in educational software. It's a different world, and if you don't put things on paper you're asking for trouble.

Thus the staff has been urging George to find religion when it comes to noneditorial aspects of the magazine's business. It isn't just contracts. Overall we want the magazine to be less ad hoc. We want it to come out on time at least occasionally, which means better planning and more accountability. We would like things like marketing to be taken care of by people who actually know what they're doing, so we can concentrate on editing.

In other words, we want the *Review* to be more professional.

However, professionalization is a distinct threat to that spirit of amateur fun so cherished by George. George doesn't want the *Review* to be disciplined; he wants it to be young. He wants it to be taken seriously as a competitor to larger magazines, but without taking itself seriously. Quaint and clubby this model may be, but it's the one he's always adhered to—the idea of publishing as a spirited venture undertaken by a few like-minded individuals—which is the same model that produced the so-called golden age of publishing, when the family-owned houses were churning out one Bellow, Cheever or Roth after another. George's own record of success makes it hard to argue that he was wrong.

Yet all institutions need to mature as they get older, and sometimes the *Review* seems to be getting *older* faster than any magazine out there. Its image—stately, glamorous and painfully Upper East Side—is inescapably dated, no matter how much George tries to act otherwise. Meanwhile, newer magazines have been elbowing their way into the spotlight, partly with different editorial formulas that seem better attuned to the moment and partly by paying attention to the bottom line.

At the Mercantile Library the cocktail party has already started when Brigid and I arrive, along with Elizabeth, our editor at large. Elizabeth tells me she'll break the news to George about the anthology, and that until we see how he reacts I should probably stay at a safe distance, on a balcony overlooking the crowd.

Luckily, the balcony is where the bar is. After downing two quick cocktails, I watch as Elizabeth gradually works her away through the library's vaulted hall and snags George's attention. He seems delighted to see her—*Ha! He's in a good mood.* He listens intently, eyes narrowed, not saying a word as Elizabeth lays out the situation. Then his face seems to darken, and his features seem to elongate, and before my eyes George morphs into a grotesque hawklike bird with a fierce brow and an angry beak. *Oh dear.* He's scanning the room for a face—mine, presumably; Elizabeth must have told him I'm here—and it occurs to me that I shouldn't be spying on him like this. I look again: that angry beak is now mouthing the words (I can see it clearly from across the room) "Where is he? WHERE IS HE?! I want to talk to him now."

"I'm done," I say in quiet voice. There's nothing to do but stand here and wait.

"Don't worry," says Brigid. "We'll defend you. It's not the end of the world, and there was a reason you did what you did."

"Thanks, but spare yourself and don't bother. I've been on his shit list for a while. There's no point in fighting anymore."

Meanwhile George, led by Elizabeth, has stalked up to the balcony. Strangely, I can't help feeling worried for him. He's so furious that he looks like he might explode all over the leather chairs and mahogany desks of the Mercantile Library, and for once in his life you can see that he has absolutely no idea what to say. It's obvious that he wants to say *something,* but George just doesn't express his anger well; he's not enough of an angry person. Yet he has every reason to be upset—in fact, he should be outraged, because this isn't about just one screwup; it's deeper and more personal. Professionalization is just the outer layer of a conflict between George and some of the editors. Yes, we all revere him, but we also look down on him in a funny way, and not just because he's old and occasionally daffy, but because George is an icon of a different era—that clubby era of guilt-free privilege. He's a dilettante (in the best sense of the word), and he doesn't seem to have the slightest inclination to feel bad about any of it. For people who make a fetish of cultivating guilt, that makes him a fraud. Because unlike us, he can never see himself as a fraud—he lacks that power of introspection.

"George, I—"

A glare and I know better than to even apologize. He's actually trembling and, judging by the snarl in his lip, thinking something unpleasant, possibly murderous.

And then, just like that, he storms out of the library, hails a taxi and disappears into the Manhattan night, leaving me to wonder what sort of punishment he will devise. It will have to be pretty imaginative to make me feel worse than I'm already feeling, and I have no doubt it will be.

MONDAY IS ALWAYS the worst day at the store. No one buys anything. They stay at home eating leftovers, I guess, or maybe they dine out, or maybe they just starve themselves. It's one of the mysteries of the convenience store business, like the phenomenon of customer waves, whereby the store goes completely dead for a few minutes—you can hear the cockroaches scurrying—and then all of a sudden twenty customers walk in at the same time, as if they'd been conspiring outside on the sidewalk, huddling in the manner of a football team, with formations and schemes and plans of attack to make sure that not one night will ever go by when I do not commit a huge, pressure-induced mistake.

Today during the day shift we make six hundred dollars, which comes out to sixty-six dollars an hour—*in revenue, not profit*. Take away overhead and inventory costs and you've got less than what a babysitter makes on the Upper East Side, or a dog walker, or a low-level drug dealer. And a babysitter is a damned solo practitioner—our lousy twelve dollars an hour results from the labor of an entire family.

Vultures are circling. Wolves are hovering in the distance. Someone who identified himself as in the market for distressed property stopped by our store the other day and said he'd heard that our store was for sale (which it is not). A few days later a documentary filmmaker dropped in and asked Kay if he could interview her for a film he's making on gentrification.

"As a longtime resident of the neighborhood who's been left behind by privatized hypercapitalist development, your perspective is important," he said. "Huh?" Kay replied. "We only been here two month."

This afternoon, when I trudge up Hoyt Street to start my shift, I see one of our lottery customers, a friend of Chucho's, sitting on one of our milk crates next to some bric-a-brac he's laid on the sidewalk, apparently with Chucho's blessing.

"CDs, VCR tapes, stereo equipment," he says to the crowds passing by. "Women's clothing." When he sees me, he smiles—an expression so foreign and welcome to me right now that it literally stops me in my tracks. Then he asks if I can go inside and fetch him a beer.

"I'm working," he explains. And indeed he is: his crowds—for used shoes, a pair of salad tongs and one yellowing copy of *The Death of James Dean*—are larger than ours. So I go inside and get him a beer.

It is now seven-thirty P.M., and the store has been comatose since the night shift started. This isn't right. It's not natural. Even on Mondays the store has commuters coming in at this time of the evening. Thus I start doing what no store owner should ever do: I stand at the window, anxiously watching people walk by. No one will even make eye contact with me. They know. They can see that the store is empty, because one of my recent "moves" was to declutter the store's facade, thinking that rather than malt liquor ads featuring half-naked nymphets wearing boa constrictors, the public would like to see what kind of store they are walking into before they come through the door. And I think they do appreciate the move. They're saying, "Thanks for letting us see that your store has no customers. I think I'll walk an extra block and go to the deli that doesn't make my skin crawl."

I should at least try to look busy, so I go back to the stockroom and try to burn off some of the fifteen or so pounds I've added since the store opened. Empty cardboard boxes are all over the place—I've got to break them down, fold them up and pack them into bundles, a painful (like ripping phone books with your bare hands) and, best of all, loud activity that serves as a suitable accompaniment to horribly depressing thoughts, until I realize that another human being has come into the store without my hearing and is standing next to me.

"Excuse me. You the owner?"

From my knees, I look up and see a baby-faced Latino kid wearing a weight belt and holding a clipboard.

"Yes?" I pant.

"Delivery."

Delivery? "At this hour?"

"We've never been to your store before," he apologizes. "We had a little trouble getting here."

"Oh. I understand. Do you need my help unloading? The store's empty, as you can see. Put the boxes anywhere."

"I just need you to sign here," he says, passing me the clipboard.

"Okay. Who are you, by the way? Which company?"

"Steinway Foods."

I must look confused because he says the name again, then adds, "You know, gourmet and imported delicacies?"

The name doesn't register with me. Then it hits. "Yes, of course! I placed an order, didn't I?" It was weeks ago, and it's finally here!

"So where do you want us to put this stuff?" the cherubic deliveryman asks. He really looks like he should have wings.

"Where? Anywhere! Right here is fine."

"There's a lot of stuff."

"There is?" I swallow.

"You ordered"—he studies the invoice, counting in his head—"twenty-seven boxes of food."

Twenty-seven?! My God, am I insane? Will our shelves even hold twenty-seven boxes? What could I have been thinking, ordering twenty-seven boxes? Gab is going to go crazy. She'll lose her mind. We don't have that money. We won't be able to pay. We'll get sued. Kay will want to kill me. George already wants to kill me. What am I going to do?

No.

I will not panic. This was the right move. We need this food.

"I'll make room in back," I say, "and in the meantime you can start unloading right here."

Three other deliverymen—much coarser and flabbier than the angel boy—suddenly burst into the store wheeling dollies loaded with boxes. *Boom*—there's another one. *Boom*—another. Stacks begin forming; the door cannot stay closed.

"We'll need that space in back," the choirboy calls.

My God, those shelves of ours won't be empty any longer. It's here! It's finally here! There is a god who listens to the prayers of small, previously irreligious (but willing to be open-minded!) business owners, and today he looked down on us in our hour of need and delivered. I'm thinking of calling Gab at home and fessing up just so I can get her to come over and we can share this joy together.

Meanwhile, the flow of boxes goes on and on.

"Do you want to check what's inside?"

"Huh? Wha?"

"I said, Do you want to check what's inside?"

"Why?"

"I don't know. Most owners just check. Once it's here and we leave, we can't take it back."

"Oh." *What am I thinking?* I'm acting like I've never done this before. Of course I should check. I should make sure that what's inside the boxes isn't damaged, that it hasn't been tampered with, that it didn't fall off the truck. Most important, I should see if it's what I ordered.

What did I order?

Yes, what exactly did I spend all that money on? The phone call is a blur—I got so excited (twenty-seven boxes!) that I wasn't thinking straight and just started calling out SKU numbers. I was in the grips of anxiety and hysteria. It was a frenzy.

"No need to check," I tell the deliveryman.

"Okay, then sign right here."

"I thought I already did."

"No, you forgot." He hands me the clipboard again, and this time I sign very deliberately, and as I'm signing I see the little number at the bottom of the invoice.

It's our total, nearly fifteen hundred dollars.

Never have I seen an invoice so large. Most deliveries cost around one hundred dollars, and with fifteen to twenty of them a week, that expense has been our downfall so far as a business. This is the same as all our deliveries put together.

Just then, as the cherub is leaving, Dwayne walks in.

"New inventory?" he says, weaving his way unsteadily through the stacks of boxes. He's drunk. It's his day off, and he's been drinking all day. Nevertheless, as the delivery truck drives away, he starts helping me open the boxes.

Start small, I hear myself say. Like a little boy on Christmas morning, I need to control my emotions. There is too much drama, too much joy and too much sorrow at the same time. *Pace yourself. Save the big stuff for last.*

The first box is like a cruel joke: one whole case of organic Sesame Street soup. A Brooklyn special. For kids or adults? Not clear, and no, it does not make me warm and happy inside to see Big Bird right now. The only way I'd like to see Big Bird at this moment is if he's *in* the soup.

Next, atop the biggest pile of boxes, is a parcel barely the size of Big Bird's beak. I pry open the cardboard flaps and pull out... four bottles of hot sauce! From Oaxaca! Now, that's more like it. I take out the bottles and search for a temporary place on the shelves, which ends up being next to the Glazed Donut Holes. The bottles look a bit incongruous and lonely there, so I tear immediately into another box, this one big enough to contain Big Bird's head. What will it be? I can barely control my shaky hands as they rip apart the stiff cardboard.

More hot sauce! From Yucatán this time! Which is great, because as everyone who likes hot sauce knows, it's not the heat, it's the taste. You need variety. And now if the store fails, we have enough hot sauce to open a taqueria.

Don't think about it. Open another box. Maybe if I get them all open tonight I can fill up the shelves with new inventory and have the store looking like it had a makeover. That'll win over Gab and Kay, and they won't even care how much it cost. Now, let's see what we have in here...

More sauce! Not hot sauce this time (thank God) but, rather, some new barbecue sauce—a "legendary Texas-style hickory bourbon slow-cooked over smoky mesquite with real old-time flavor" that "goes great with beef, pork, chicken or fish."

Wonderful. Except we don't have any beef, pork, chicken or fish. Unless you want a roast beef sandwich.

"Is this turning into a sauce store?" says Dwayne, peering over my shoulder into the bottomless box of slow-cooked Texas flavor.

"Can it, Dwayne, okay? Just can it. Just because there's no Beef-aroni you don't have to get snotty."

Dwayne belches and grabs himself a Heineken.

Time for another box, and it better contain something of a non-liquid consistency. Fucking sauce store. I did not jeopardize my career and mortgage my future to open a sauce store. I rip open the package and pull out . . . cocktail rounds. *I ordered cocktail rounds?* Jesus. Pardon the sexism and ageism, but I really thought you had to have been a housewife in the fifties to actually buy cocktail rounds. Well, now we're covered in case the Greenwich Yacht Club decides to host a luncheon in Brooklyn.

The phone rings.

"It's Gab," says Dwayne.

Shit.

"Hello?" I say, trying not to sound as depressed as I feel.

"Hi, it's me. I'm doing the bills right now and wondering, did you make a large order of merchandise recently?"

No!

"I'm sorry? What did you say? There are a lot of people here in the store."

"I said, Did you make a large order of merchandise recently? Because there's an invoice here in the mail from—"

"Gab, I'm going to have to call you back. We're getting a customer surge." Dwayne looks at me and clucks, wagging his finger.

"—didn't we agree that we'd spend nothing on new inventory except what we've already been getting? Didn't we? And this is ridiculous. It's almost fifteen hundred dollars. For what? What did you buy? It better be good. Good-bye."

Click.

It's only eight-thirty.

I still have four and a half hours until I can go home and fall asleep.

And when I wake up, it will only be Tuesday.

"This kind of a store is a death tomb," one of the characters says in Bernard Malamud's *The Assistant,* a novel set in a Brooklyn deli grocery during the 1950s. "If you stay six months, you'll stay forever."

Which would be worse? I wonder. Closing tomorrow and having this travesty over our heads for the rest of our lives, or being here forever? I can't decide, in part because I don't want to make choices, so instead of thinking about it I go back to opening boxes, grateful for something to do with my hands.

Back to appetizers, this time creamed herring. To go with the cocktail rounds? Unbelievable. I've gone certifiably insane. I don't know what's worse—the money I shouldn't have spent or the stuff that I was crazy to buy. Maybe I should just eat as much of it as I can before tomorrow. That would be an appropriate sentence, because even I don't eat creamed herring. In fact, I don't even have the faintest idea who I was buying them for.

And then it's jelly—case upon case of Keiller & Son Dundee marmalade (three-fruit, orange, ginger) and Bonne Maman fruit preserves (blueberry, strawberry, cherry, quince, red currant and fig). And spreads (Nutella, organic peanut butter) and some marinades (Soy Vay Veri Veri Teriyaki) and some chutney (Major Grey's) and some salad dressing (*eleven* cases of Annie's Naturals from Vermont) and all this is before we've even gotten to the mustard, which, suffice it to say, spans an entire spectrum of browns and not just the plain yellow stuff.

At the eleventh box I finally take out something I remember ordering: those Chessmen cookies.

"Hey," says Dwayne, "you can get those from our regular Pepperidge Farm distributor—you know, the guy who brings us the devil's food cake and the Goldfish. I think he's got some Sesame Street stuff too—Elmo cookies or some shit."

"I didn't know that, Dwayne," I murmur, sinking into the darkness of thought once again. Only this time it's a more concrete thought: I'm hungry. In fact, I'm starved. What to eat? The space in my belly is like an infant demanding to be fed, wailing its bright red head off, a miserable snot-nosed wreck. And yet even with this new and glorious shipment of food, there isn't a thing in the whole goddamned store that I feel like having. Which brings up a question: What if it isn't food I want?

At that point the door swings open and I reflexively jerk my head to see who it is, expecting Jesus, Buddha or maybe even Big Bird himself (at least a pizza deliveryman), but it's nobody, just another faceless customer. There's nothing to do but get up and serve him, this stranger, while praying he won't be the last of the evening.

PART TWO

PACKS

THEY SAY IF YOU WANT REDEMPTION YOU HAVE TO SURREN-
der something, some piece of your self. It would have to be an
important piece, presumably, one you didn't want to give up; otherwise it wouldn't be much of a sacrifice. But what if the decision to let
go was the easy part, and the challenge was figuring out *which part*?
Every now and then I think of that platitude you hear in graduation
speeches about "stepping outside yourself"—well, great. Sounds like
a plan. But what if you don't even know what "yourself" is and can't
figure out what to step out of? What do you do then?

Of course, if redemption takes place in a memoir, the process
necessarily includes a third step, which is that along the way the

author must stand up to the Nazis or become the first white shaman of a reclusive Amazon tribe—none of which is going to happen here, alas. But the first part, the disassembly of my old self, has been under way now, I realize, since we moved in with Gab's family (how quickly one's identity begins to crack when there are no *New Yorkers* stacked next to the toilet!) and only accelerated after we bought the store. I feel like I've bonded with the deli, sort of the way you bond with your seat on an airplane during an eighteen-hour flight. It's cramped, it's miserable and when you get up you feel like a piece of boiled meat, but you'd fight to the death with anyone who tried to steal it from you. However, I also sometimes feel like a lab rat in some cosmic sociological experiment to judge the effect of precipitous class descent via a kind of Wittgensteinian wormhole of reverse immigration. (Somehow I have started to go native in a foreign country with people who are actually newcomers too, in a country that turned out to be my own, or something like that.) The worst of it is coming to realize that principles I used to believe in as staunchly as anything, like that wide-open embrace of the world and those tried-and-true Strunk and White rules, haven't been of much use during the ordeal we've been experiencing; in fact, if anything they might have been counterproductive.

A WEEK OR SO after the sauce delivery, Mother Nature decides that having inflicted one of her coldest winters ever on the East Coast, she needs to throw in a historic blizzard as well, so tonight I am at the store listening to radio forecasts of thirty-plus inches of snow, hurricane-strength winds and potentially an economic disaster for the city's merchants. Even before the storm arrives the mayor cancels school the next day and calls out the National Guard. Residents are told to stay home at all costs, and judging by the sudden surge in customers wanting candles and bottled water, they're planning to obey.

"Do you think you'll open tomorrow?" more than one customer asks.

"If the roads are blocked, we can't," I reply, surprised at how anxious supposedly tough New Yorkers can get about weather. Spending the day locked up or out in the snow sounds like fun to me. But this storm promises to be different, if for no other reason than that I've never been the owner of a deli during a "cataclysmic weather event." And there is another thing that gives me pause: the older people of the neighborhood who can barely get out of their apartments on a normal day and won't be able to move around at all if the sidewalks are buried. Based on how much food they buy, I would guess that some of them have only enough in their cupboards to last a few days.

If not for the roads (and the bridges, which will definitely be closed tomorrow if the forecast holds, cutting off Staten Island from the rest of the city) I would find a way to make it to the store—for the neighborhood, but also for us, because I know now that Kay was right about the hazards of closing for even one day. When you close, bad things happen. You may not lose all your customers, but you might miss an important delivery, or your food might spoil, or the cat might get angry about not getting fed and pee all over the store. Plus, if you survive taking off a single day, you might be tempted to take off two in a row.

"No way," says Kay when I tell her I'm willing to drive in. "Forget about it. No matter how much we need money, it not worth dying for." Which is a pretty good indicator of how scary this storm is, that even my mother-in-law is counseling restraint.

There's been a lot of sober reflection around here lately. No one has a formula for determining when to call it quits, but if they did I imagine it would be something like: you've made less money than you've spent for way too long (check); even if you were making money, you'd be so deeply in debt that it wouldn't matter (check); not only is your business failing, but your house, which wasn't threatened before you took on the business and which you vowed to protect under any circumstances, is starting to feel jeopardized as well, thanks to your decision to dip into the savings to pay the orange juice company (check); and, finally, *you are miserable!* (check).

That night we sit at the window and watch the storm, which, of course, is not only savagely destructive but mesmerizing in its way. Usually when you look at the Paks' backyard you see a slag heap of spare refrigerator parts rusting amid dead leaves and flapping tarps, but tonight it looks like a miniature version of the Rockies—there's Mount Frigidaire and the Compressor Range, the Luxaire Basin and Great Fan Belt National Park.

The other good thing about the blizzard is that it is so powerful, so enveloping and so fast at piling up snow that early on it forecloses even the possibility of driving, which means that we can all go to bed planning to wake up late. I feel bad for the old folks, but they'll have to survive until at least tomorrow afternoon, which is when the most optimistic forecasts have the storm letting up.

However, in the middle of the night Gab apparently has a different idea from the rest of us. At four in the morning, without telling anyone, she sneaks out of bed and mummifies herself inside about eight layers of winter clothes, and then, hip-deep in wet, heavy snow, she thrashes and stumbles her way across two miles of snow-covered hills to the St. George ferry terminal. It's not a totally out of character thing for her to do. Gab admits that she is the sort of person who "has to do, has to do whatever comes into my mind," much like her never-say-die mother. Lately, however, she's been trying to curb those tendencies, almost as if in the process of trying to match her mother's tenacity and determination over the last few months she's scared herself with how much like her she can be.

This morning, though, Gab is a shopkeeper possessed. After

getting herself to the ferry terminal and crossing New York Harbor at sunrise, she finds that subway service has been canceled, which leaves her no option for getting to Brooklyn other than walking across the Brooklyn Bridge in a whiteout as fifty-mile-per-hour winds lash its exposed pedestrian walkway. For someone who has never been particularly adventurous in a physical way, it's probably the most impulsive thing she's ever done, but then again, how often do you have the Brooklyn Bridge all to yourself? Three hours later (five after she left the basement), she lights up the store's funky tropical awning, and for the rest of the morning she is rewarded with the distinction of being the only store open anywhere in the neighborhood.

That one act seems to bring back a large number of customers, including, I would guess, many who'd been avoiding us simply because we'd rubbed them wrong. (Take your pick how: the siren in the night or the cold coffee? The price increases or the turned-off TV?) New York may be a hard and impersonal place, but people do actually want to like the people they give business to on a regular basis. Today, by showing commitment to the neighborhood, Gab goes a long way toward rebuilding that crucial relationship.

But there's still a long way to go, and this is but one step. In a smaller place than New York they might give a business endless opportunities to get it right, because there's less competition and something better might not come along. Here, a thousand other wannabes are ready to replace us.

JUST AS I'M thinking that Gab, who, unlike me or Kay, has never taken off even one minute from the store, is the one person in this family who's indispensable, in March she gets a call from a friend at her old law firm, the one she quit because it was hollowing out her brain. The friend wants to know if Gab would be interested in a job at a big international bank selling off commercial jets in the bank's midtown office. The friend's husband, who works at the bank, is looking for someone with Gab's qualifications and specifically asked about Gab.

When she tells me this I can't help but laugh, because what could be more ridiculous than going from peddling Slim Jims and Nutrament to selling Boeings? And how could Gab possibly abandon us now, with the store in so much jeopardy? Not even Gab or her mother would try to work at a deli and a bank at once.

Quickly, I realize she's not laughing with me: she's going to apply for the job.

"But you said you'd never go back to corporate law," I cry, suddenly panicked.

"I did?" replies Gab, who has the power to eliminate any traces of doubt in herself once she has settled on a course of action. "I don't remember that."

"You made me promise to incarcerate you in a mental hospital if you even considered it. Don't you remember the long hours and meaningless work—the drudgery?"

Gab looks genuinely baffled. "Even if what you're saying was true," she says skeptically, "this job wouldn't be like that." She explains that it's a contract position, which means they'd be paying her by the hour and therefore she could leave the office every day at five o'clock.

"Which leaves me time to get to the store and work the night shift!" she adds.

Oh God, I moan. Are all Korean women like this? Are they all unsatisfied merely holding down hard jobs while being dutiful daughters, wives and mothers? Do they all have to run extended-family boardinghouses, take classes in flower arranging, start a youth group at their church and master the art of traditional Korean cooking (based on vegan principles, of course) at the same time?

As we're having this conversation I notice that Gab has taken out some of her dour old shoulder-padded jackets and knee-length gray skirts from the storage closet in Kay's basement.

"Well, even if you don't remember how miserable you were, I do. You spent seventeen hours a day in a windowless office reading contracts. At night you came home and ate a scoop of rice in a bowl of tap water. You slept all weekend and went right back to the office on Monday. Your appetite for life seemed to disappear."

"Do you have any kind of evidence for that? Did you write any of that down? Because honestly, I'm having trouble remembering it that way."

I feel like I'm trying to unbrainwash a zombie. Maybe I should sabotage her job application by calling up the bank after her interview to tell them that Gab owns a failing deli. Who would want to hire someone who can't even run a convenience store?

"This is insane. You're being just like your mother."

Which causes Gab to stop unpacking her suits and sit down close to me—very, very close.

"Well, what am I supposed to do?" she whispers. "Turn down a potential job offer? In case you haven't noticed, WE NEED MONEY." She pauses. "*Did you notice?*"

"Of course."

"Well, someone needs to do something about it. My student loans are about to kick in again. And if we're ever going to move out of this basement, we need to stop waiting for the store to pay us back, because at this point I don't know if it ever will."

I stare at Gab and try not to look dumb. *What about it, lazy bastard? What's your plan?*

In my defense, lately I have been trying to pull in more money, but so far not one of my magazine pitches has been accepted. Most of the time I'm not even getting rejections, just dead air. And meanwhile, the way things have been going at the *Review,* I'll be lucky to keep getting my $3.65 an hour, or whatever it is George pays me. *Starting tomorrow,* I vow silently, *I'm going to redouble my efforts!*

Then Gab drops the bomb.

"I want children," she says.

Again, I can't help laughing, because the thought is so absurd. Children, now of all times? Could there be a worse idea? Of course not. Even Gab knows that.

"Okay, now I can say you've really lost it. This isn't you talking. You're driven but not insane. I'm the one with unrealistic tendencies. You're pragmatic. I'm just going to wait—you'll get your senses back in a couple of days."

"No, I don't think I will. Because yes, you're right. I have lost it. Probably I lost it a long time ago . . . But we don't have the luxury of waiting for things to get easier. This is how our lives are and probably how they'll be be for the foreseeable future. Meanwhile, I'm just getting older. So, yes, I want children."

"That's so . . . selfish of you" is all I can think to say.

Before Gab can answer, the door to our bedroom swings open and Kay strides past us toward the laundry room, where the Paks have not one but *two* extra refrigerators for storing food when relatives move in. *Curious,* I think. Is someone else coming?

Kay, sensing the tension, stops, puts down the grocery bags she's carrying and asks if something is wrong.

"Did you tell your mother?" I ask, thinking Kay will put a halt to this nonsense. She's not ready to manage the deli without Gab, is she? What about our personnel issues? What about Bienstock and the sales taxes?

"I've been invited to apply for a job," admits Gab.

"Oh really?" says Kay. "How much they pay?"

Gab rolls her eyes. "Jeez, Oma, couldn't you at least ask me which company it is first?"

"When you start?" says Kay, who doesn't seem perturbed in the slightest.

"I have to be interviewed first. The job hasn't been offered yet."

"I have to start cooking," Kay says, already planning a feast in her head to celebrate Gab's new job. "What you want me to make?"

"Wait," I say, interrupting. "Am I really the only one here who thinks this is a bad idea? The store is in crisis. How are we going to get by without Gab?" I look at Kay. "Aren't *you* worried?"

"Worried?" she replies blankly, as if it's a strange question. "Worried because why? I have *you*. And now Emo coming."

"WHAT?" Gab and I both gasp. Emo is Kay's older sister and lives in Los Angeles. She used to live with Kay; however, the last time we saw her was two years ago, when she and Kay got in an argument and Emo moved out.

"When?" I exclaim.

"She be here Friday. I talk to her yesterday. You go pick her up at airport," she says, before disappearing into the laundry room with the food she'd brought down. As Gab and I stand there, now both struck dumb, I can hear her filling up the refrigerator and singing softly.

THE AROMA STARTS invading our bedroom an hour later. Kay had been to Hanyang, a Korean supermarket in Flushing, and brought home some of the family's favorite dishes: pickled young radishes, salted squid, seasoned cuttlefish and vats of bean paste. When I first moved into the Paks' house, I admit, I had a hard time with the food. Korean cuisine, which largely consists of vegetables like cucumbers and seaweed, with large components of fish and rice, is almost ridiculously healthy and flavorful, and Koreans tend to eat every meal as if a fast just ended, piling their plates with a wildly colorful assortment of food and stuffing themselves till no one can stand up straight. However, one occasionally has the suspicion that in order to protect their cuisine from being overexposed and watered down, Koreans decided to mask it behind some extremely challenging smells, like minced garlic and fermented soybean paste. Now, my enthusiasm for food that is exotic, flavorful and hopefully spicy enough to give you breath that can peel paint runs second to no one, but the tastes and smells of Korean cuisine are so powerful that they seem to permeate everything around them—like milk, if you store it in a refrigerator with Korean food, or me, if you store me in a basement near dried anchovies and pickled cabbage.

Eventually, though, I stopped noticing what Kay's house or, occasionally, my own hair smelled like. Not only did I get used to it; it seemed as if my tendency to scrutinize and judge had gone on a much-needed hiatus. Korean daytime TV, for instance, looks no less dim-witted than the American version, but for some reason watching *Ten Thousand Wons of Happiness,* a popular game show, doesn't depress me the way an hour of *Pyramid* does. Korean junk food looks plenty junky, but Choco Pies, one of Gab's favorite snacks, don't set off the snob siren the way an equivalent American snack like MoonPies ("Oh my God, you're really going to eat that?") would.

Koreans also have a different perspective on what Americans take to be the all-time classic symptom of loserdom: living with one's parents. In America, what Gab and I are doing is considered unspeakably embarrassing. However, every time I watch Korean TV with Gab and Kay, I seem to see a sitcom or a drama featuring a domestic situation that looks scarily like our own, with a multigenerational household living too close together and tearing one another apart over some drama like a shared business. There's no stigma. It's just normal. Kay says that modernization has started to dilute the practice of multigenerational cohabitation somewhat, and of course coming to America introduces all kinds of challenges to traditional living arrangements. However, even after emigrating, Korean-American families tend to go on living the way we do because of the need to enlist family members in labor-intensive businesses like a deli. It's not just that relatives make good auxiliary workers / indentured servants / child laborers; they're also potentially available for household chores, freeing someone like Kay to focus more on business. In Kay's home we're constantly exchanging shifts at the last second, asking family members to fill in and trading favors like "You let me sleep an extra hour tomorrow morning, and I'll do your laundry. Deal?" Living with coworkers provides invaluable flexibility. The house becomes an extension of the store, like a dormitory: you can sense that conveyor belt looping endlessly between the two, shuttling goods and people.

Of course, nothing could be more foreign to my own family, where personal space is guarded as vigilantly as international spheres of influence between rival nation-states. The rule against unannounced arrivals at someone's house, for example, is enforced as zealously as the Monroe Doctrine. After personal space comes *peace* and *silence:* you can share space with someone, but you have to contain yourself, which means not just keeping your personal noise level under control (no gum cracking or scratching, no breathing like a St. Bernard) but not being a "fidgeter" or a "yapper," especially when someone else is engaged in the all but holy practice of *reading.* (Some families, when you get them together, play sports, watch TV or eat. When you get a group of Howes together, you get group reading, not unlike the Puritans and their favorite activity: group prayer.) In general, it's all about control—of your body, your impulses, your emotions, just as Strunk and White advocated.

But perhaps we can change, even after we've allegedly grown up and become set in our ways. Before we moved in with the Paks, I was the kind of sleeper who would be kept miserably awake by someone's whistling nose hair three doors down the hall. Now I sleep like a baby, whether Kay is vacuuming next to my head in the middle of the night or Edward is in the next room singing karaoke. Maybe it's because I'm worn out by the store. Or maybe it's because when lots of people are living together, someone is almost always awake, and it feels like they're standing watch; at some point the brain can't help but relax as a sort of pack instinct kicks in. It wouldn't surprise me: the psychological effect of living with an extended family can be startlingly powerful, especially when the family is struggling together toward a common goal. It can suffocate not just your social life but your whole feeling of autonomy. At some point during the last year I realized that every facet of my life had become intertwined with Gab's family: I had the same doctor, the same dentist, even the same haircutter, a Korean woman at the Staten Island Mall. Maybe moving out won't be so easy after all. And now Gab's got me worried that we can't afford to anyway.

AS SPRING COMES on and we prepare for Emo's arrival, the deli finally gets a taste of stability, one of the most vital conditions for a successful store. Rising temperatures mean more pedestrians, particularly on weekends, which seems to correlate with about a 10 percent increase in revenue. Salim had promised us this would happen, yet for some reason I didn't quite believe him. Maybe because there's an air of unreality to publishing—the work is so much about what goes on inside people's heads; words, sentences, ideas—the idea of being affected by something as elemental as the weather seems almost quaint. In any case, it's refreshing.

Meanwhile, we've also settled into a routine. Now, I am no fan of repetition; I can have an existential crisis if I see the same TV commercial more than once an hour. But routine is essential for a small business—you simply can't start making those teeny-weeny profits that are the lifeblood of your business until you know more or less exactly how much Diet Mountain Dew to order every week, where to find a parking space whose meter you won't have to run outside and feed every hour, and how much change to have ready when Joe Commuter marches into the store for his bagel at 7:06 A.M. sharp.

Another development in our favor is that Gab, after tracking down Salim in Nevada, has negotiated a compromise with him and the government whereby our remaining debts on the purchase will be forgiven in exchange for paying off the tax penalty, which the state reduces by half. Also, her bluff to Bienstock seems to have worked, as for now the threatening phone calls have stopped.

However, new threats have begun to appear around us, including the arrival of two new convenience stores in the neighborhood and a sudden barrage of ambush-style government inspections. This spring we've been visited by undercover NYPD officers trying to catch us selling liquor on Sundays before noon (11:57 A.M., to be precise); Consumer Affairs personnel trying to catch us selling cigarettes and lottery tickets to minors; Consumer Affairs, again, seeing if we pad our scales or use a cat to catch mice; even the Drug Enforcement Agency, looking for contraband sales of cold medicine. No one has caught us yet, in part because Dwayne has an uncanny feel for when an inspection is under way. (It's a sixth sense, and goes with his ability to look at someone and tell if they've been to prison. I have a sixth sense too, but it isn't much use at the deli: I can look at someone and tell if they've been to boarding school.) However, it's only a matter of time before they do. And when it happens, it has the potential to be devastating, because like everything in New York, the city's fines are murderously expensive.

Kay is particularly worried, since a few months ago an old friend of hers from Seoul who owns a deli in the Village called and asked if she wanted to buy his business. No thanks, she said, my hands are already full, but why are you selling? After all, the man owned a successful store, and to show off how proud of it he was, he had given it the kind of name it deserved, like the Garden of V.I.P.'s Diamond Deli, or something along those lines.

As it turned out, the deli's awning, with its boisterous name followed by a long list of products the store sold, caused it to violate Paragraph A of Section 52-542 of the New York City Zoning Resolution, which forbids business from creating "visual clutter." The fine was twenty-five hundred dollars. The cost of replacing the flashy old awning with a more demure one amounted to five thousand more. This, coming on top of endless violations that no one could remember anyone ever being cited for, like having spoons positioned incorrectly in the potato salad (for some reason they're supposed to face down), and others that he couldn't control, like litter outside his door, had convinced the man that it was time to get out of the deli business.

He isn't alone. All spring we've been hearing about store owners hit by obscure and unreasonable fines. New York always increases its collection of things like parking tickets when the economy slows, and with the city now in its second year of recession following September 11, there are fewer tourists and less in the way of Wall Street profits to pump up revenue. Ninety percent of the city's businesses—about 220,000, all told—employ fewer than thirty people, and the government is saying to them, We need you to contribute a greater share.

Puritans and their descendants tend to be pro-authority by nature. They're into structure and consensus; they like doing things as a collective, like group prayer and public stoning. Even when they were taking the radical, ultimately suicidal (for many in the group) step of abandoning Mother England to follow their religious convictions, the Pilgrims did so as a nice, orderly club, spending years meticulously planning their escape. Once they got to

Plymouth, they set up a government that was no champion of individual liberty, either. They liked to intrude on one another's affairs, sending tax collectors and the equivalent of child welfare inspectors into their own homes with onerous frequency. Unlike Thomas Jefferson's belief that a government's job is to do as little as possible, the Puritans were the sort of people who believed that society was at its best when smothered within a government bear hug.

Growing up, I had a vague appreciation for government, because unlike most of the big, abstract forces in America that people talked about—religion, capitalism, mass culture—it didn't seem like much of a threat. But then again, how would I know? It's not like I had any personal experience dealing with the state, other than the six early years I spent in public school. Like most products of the Boston suburbs, I had managed to avoid incarceration in a U.S. prison, was not pressured by my parents' social circle of 1960s-era college professors and hippie musicians to join the military, and had never been in a jobs center, a veterans' hospital or a state-run foster home. The one continuous up-close contact I had with the government was garbagemen, who deliberately spilled trash all over our sidewalk every Tuesday morning. There were also occasional encounters with the toll collectors on the Mass Turnpike, whose dead-eyed expressions made me want to drive away from them as fast as I could. (And for only fifty cents, they let me.) Add it all up and you've got about eighteen seconds of face time with the government a week.

Of course, for a small business owner, it's your duty to hate the government with an all-consuming passion, no matter how big a fan you are of, say, the Corporation for Public Broadcasting. You're supposed to become a rabid, red-faced Contract with America–spewing zealot with a violent hatred of trial lawyers and, above all, tax collectors who think "government" is a synonym for a Mephistophelian leech sucking the hard-earned dollars out of

America's last honest citizens. New York doesn't help matters by never apologizing for taking your money. It's an adversarial city. "Everyone wants a piece of us," says Gab. There's no union or lobbyist to stick up for you. The city itself doesn't care. And with all the adversaries besides the government lined up against you— competition, the economy as a whole, the weather and even something as random and frequent as street repairs—the last thing you have patience for is some multichinned bureaucrat waving a clipboard. And sometimes you just want to know, as Gab said to me recently, "Who's watching *them* to make sure it's fair?"

I DRIVE OUT to Queens to pick up Emo at the airport. She's on the red-eye from LAX, sprinting across the country in response to Kay's summons. After hardly talking for years, the two of them have been on the phone almost every day, and at last Kay had asked her to come out and help with the store. Within days Emo had quit her job, broken her lease and gotten rid of most of her possessions. It makes me wonder: What would someone in my family do if I asked them to drop everything, relocate and come work at a convenience store? Probably resort to the grand old Wasp tradition of installing "difficult" relatives in McLean Psychiatric Hospital in Belmont, Massachusetts.

I look for Emo in the arrivals area. This will be the third or fourth time she and Kay have lived together. Their fighting is so constant and predictable and, above all, so petty ("You think you know about America? You know nothing! I'll show you how to make s'mores") that you would think they really dislike each other. Of course, the truth is, they can't stand to be apart. For the last twenty-odd years, they've both led peripatetic lives, moving every other year, and eventually they've always ended up in the same place, if not the same house. The last time they were in the same city they even worked together at a lunch counter Emo owned in

Manhattan—that is, until they got in an argument and Emo fired Kay (or Kay quit—depends on who you ask), which was awkward given that their bedrooms were across the hall.

"What were they arguing about?" I remember asking Gab.

"I don't know—probably who had the 'real' recipe for turkey tetrazzini," said Gab. After that, Emo sold her lunch counter and moved to L.A.

They don't look like sisters. As I scan the passengers coming out of the terminal, I'm looking for a tall and slender-shouldered former high school beauty queen who jogs, counts calories and doesn't drink or smoke.

"Emo!"

Amid the slumping, shuffling, strung-out-looking crowd (this is the red-eye, after all), I see one person moving at a distinctly faster clip, head erect and eyes focused. She sees me and darts over.

"Where are your bags?" I ask.

"Oh, this is everything," she says in her excellent English, while holding up a handbag that couldn't contain the contents of a glove compartment. "Come on, let's go."

Thinking she means "let's go *home*," we get in the car and I start driving toward Staten Island. But she means *let's go to the store*.

"I didn't come here to sit around," she says, and when I try to protest, she won't hear a word. So we go to Brooklyn, and as a result, Emo, who's nearly sixty (though she looks twenty years younger), works an eight-hour shift at a deli after flying across the country in the middle of the night.

And so it starts, this new phase in the store's life. Emo takes over the morning shift and within weeks has it running smoothly, even to the satisfaction of those finicky commuters. This frees up Kay to focus on things like protecting ourselves against the onslaught of inspectors and adding new products to the inventory.

Meanwhile, Gab starts work at the bank, and, true to her promise, finds energy to hold down the night shift once or twice a week, plus weekends. She does not find the return to legal work mind-numbing, at least for now. Overall, things seem to be settling down, and the summer looks promising. The only one who hasn't found his footing is me.

NAKED WITH DESIRE

AT THE *PARIS REVIEW*, ABOUT A MONTH AFTER THE DEBACLE with the anthology, I find out my punishment: I am being sent to Chicago.

George wants two editors to attend the Chicago Book Fair, a summer festival billed as "the largest book fair in the Midwest." There's an old tradition at the *Review* of attending large open-air book fairs—I think George has this fantasy that away from the hoity-toity confines of Manhattan publishing, we're going to mix it up with everyday Americans, who are suddenly going to develop an insatiable desire for highbrow literature and subscribe to the *Review*. Generally, the staff hates it for the same reason. Not that we don't want everyday readers as subscribers—we do, we absolutely do—but because the act of selling it to them in person tends to reveal just how depressingly unrealistic such aspirations are.

I arrive in Chicago with Brigid on a June morning on which it is simultaneously scorching and snowing—snowing dandelion fluff, that is, or some other kind of white, cottony, intensely allergenic weed. It is good to be out of New York, good to be in the Midwest, good to be on the majestic Great Plains. However, after invading my nostrils, the drifting spores, whatever they are, make my head feel like a giant mound of half-baked dough, just like the goo-covered cinnamon rolls we keep being offered on the concourse of Midway Airport. ("Would you like a gooey slab of uncooked bread drizzled with gooey vanilla-cinnamon-marshmallow frosting?" the employees of the fast-food chain selling them keep jumping in my way to ask. *No thanks,* I say, trying to be nice about it despite my throbbing head.)

Things get worse at the fair. In the morning, after setting up our booth, we sell exactly one subscription—an exchange with the editor of another literary magazine with a name like *Thin Paper.* There seem to be two fairs going on today: one featuring Dan Brown, author of *The Da Vinci Code,* and Elizabeth Berg, author of *Ordinary Life* and nineteen hundred other bestsellers I've somehow never heard of, which is attracting throngs of sweaty, fun-loving, kid-towing Chicagoans. The other fair, the one that Brigid and I are a part of, is a ghetto of literary magazines like *Thin Paper,* as well as some writers' workshops and eco-Marxist publishing collectives exiled to a quiet street three blocks away, near the Porta Potties.

Occasionally someone from the other fair, the one with the crowds, drifts in our direction by accident.

"Did you come all the way from Peeeh-ris?" one woman asks, stopping to look at our booth. She holds two snot-nosed children firmly by the shoulders, not letting them advance to within five feet of us, as if she fears that if they get any closer they will be turned into louche, café-dwelling Euroweenies. Another man, older and wearing a John Deere cap, comes over and announces that under no circumstances will he buy a subscription from us unless we do something about our country's cowardly stance on the war on terror.

"We'll take it up with the prime minister," Brigid sighs.

By noon, beaten down by the midday sun, the pollen and the indifferent-to-hostile crowds, Brigid and I have retreated to the farthest corner of our booth and buried ourselves in manuscripts we brought with us. (The nice thing about working at the *Review* is that you can always lose yourself in a great story and forget what a terrible career choice you've made.) Brigid's pile of manuscripts, incidentally, is five times larger than mine. She has the worst job in the office, maybe in publishing as a whole. Normally managing editors are scary people who specialize in invading other editors' dreams at night and making them feel tiny and fearful: they're the designated ass kickers whose job is to make sure the rest of the staff brings in copy on time and generally meets deadlines. But George has never wanted a magazine that meets deadlines. He wants a magazine that gives him the flexibility to make last-second decisions, fuss over the wording of a sentence and do strange things like send senior editors to book fairs where they accomplish exactly nothing. So he appointed Brigid, an exceedingly fair-minded and somewhat shy poetry fan from Buffalo who would never be mistaken by anyone for Attila the Hun. Her job, amid all the gamboling, towel snapping and other tomfoolery that passes for work at the *Review,* is to somehow put out four issues a year, which sometimes seems a task beyond hopeless.

"I'm quitting," she suddenly blurts out, putting her manuscripts down.

"What?" I say, caught off guard. "Why? When?"

"After the next issue. I can't take it anymore. I'm burned out."

"Is this because of the anthology screwup?" I wasn't the only one who had gotten in trouble. Brigid had taken heat, too.

She shakes her head. "It's not that. It's just time. I've been at the magazine for seven years, and I don't enjoy it as much as I used to. I used to like the fact that it wasn't an uptight place, but now the magazine has a lot of problems that need to be fixed, and I think it's someone else's turn to try."

"Why not stick around and fix them yourself?" I beg, panicked by the idea of the *Review* without Brigid.

"Well, for one thing, because whoever it is is going to have to fight with George, and I'm not up for that. At the end of the day, it's his magazine."

"And a lot of the problems are caused by him."

Brigid shrugs. "We're all so invested in it and think we know better. It's a good time to move on."

"Don't you think you should at least talk to George before you quit?"

Brigid groans. "Have you talked to him lately?" She tells me a story. Recently, an English journalist had called the office and offered to conduct an interview with the heavy-duty French experimentalist author Alain Robbe-Grillet—who isn't the kind of writer George normally likes to publish, but this time, for whatever reason, he agreed. However, he had forgotten to tell Brigid or anyone else, and he had forgotten as well that fifteen years ago the *Review* had already published an interview with Robbe-Grillet (who, evidently, had also forgotten).

"The worst part of it was that George figured it out on his own and felt awful, so he wanted to make it up to the poor journalist with an enormous kill fee, which we fought over because it was way more than we can afford."

Suddenly Brigid's cell phone rings, and she looks at the caller ID panel. It's George.

"You take it," she says, thrusting the phone at me.

"Me? You're the managing editor!"

"You owe me," she says. "The anthology?"

I take the phone from her hand.

"Hullo?" I say meekly.

"Hi ho!" booms the voice at the other end of the line. George is apparently in an excellent mood, vastly different from the last time I saw him. It's hard to make out what he's saying, but he seems to have been out at some posh event the night before and wants to talk about fireworks (his most favorite thing in the world), writers, parties—the usual, in other words.

I interrupt him. "George, it's kind of busy at the fair right now. Is there something I can help you with?"

"Well, I should like to know how it's going," he says, changing his tone.

"How it's going?" I look around our booth, trying to come up with the best way of describing the catastrophe I am witnessing. It is busy at the fair, to be sure; there are certainly plenty of people. But if they are paying attention to us, it's generally to mock us with questions like whether we have any freedom fries or when the last time we showered was.

"It's going great, George," I blurt out. "People here seem . . . really excited to see us."

"Marvelous," cries George. "May I ask how many subscriptions you've sold?"

I try to avoid telling him, but he presses. "Twenty? Fifty? One hundred? Just give me a number."

"Really, George, I can't say. I haven't counted."

"Well, you don't have to give an exact figure, but surely it's more than twenty-five, is it not? This is Chicago, one of the greatest cities in the world, and you've been there all morning! There must be twenty-five people in Chicago who enjoy a good read."

"Yes, George, I'm sure you're right. I don't know how many subscriptions we've sold, but it must be more than twenty-five." And then, to deepen the hole I'm in, I promise to bring home double that.

Brigid's eyes widen while she mouths the words "Are you crazy?!"

"SPLENDID! That's the attitude. I shall eagerly await your return. Bravo, bravo!"

Click.

When I hang up, Brigid practically has her head in her hands.

"Don't worry, I'll take the blame," I tell her. "When he blows up, you can tell him I lost the envelope with the subscriptions in it or something."

"It's not that I'm worried about. He'll be crushed, not angry. Lately he's been depressed. He gets hung up on any little bit of bad news."

We go back to reading manuscripts and wait for the fair to end. What a farce, I think. As if coming all the way out here, not selling anything and being taunted by Dan Brown fans all day wasn't ridiculous enough, now we have to *justify* our failure to George upon our return.

It isn't right. We're here to please George. Why should we fear *his* response if the results aren't what he hoped for? Suddenly I begin to feel frustrated and angry instead of dejected and miserable. The heavy-headedness I've been struggling with since we arrived is wearing off, and I have this compulsion to *do something,* if only to shake things up and not be so passive.

So I decide to get up from my seat, get out of our booth and sell. After all, do I not stand at a counter every day at our deli selling things? So what if selling is embarrassing? My life is a series of bizarre and embarrassing interactions with strangers, and I'm going to make these people buy issues whether they report me to Homeland Security for suspicious Europhilic tendencies or not.

"Excuse me!" I say to a passing woman, after stepping out of the booth. "Who's your favorite author?" She looks surprised at first— *I just wanted to use the Porta Potty!* her expression says—but then she actually stands there. She says her favorite writer is Ian McEwan—bingo! McEwan was the lead interview in one of our recent issues, which I place in her hand.

"Hmm," she says. "I'd buy that."

"How about a one-year subscription," I say, "and I'll give you that issue for free?"

"Deal!" she says. And just like that we've sold a subscription! It was easy. And she wasn't even an editor for a literary magazine. (I know because I ask.)

After that exchange I'm energized to sell some more, which takes some girding of the loins. Selling is practically hardwired into my brain as a no-no, because when you sell you show *desire*. It's like being naked, standing there with your needs exposed ("Buy this—please!"). And unless you're George Plimpton, it's just not okay for a Wasp to be naked.

"What's the last thing you read that made you want to run out to the bookstore and get another book right away?" I start asking people, stepping right in front of them "Are you a reader? Did you use to be a reader? Do you wish you felt like reading more? Is the problem you, or is it the books you're reading? What if I gave you something to read that had the power to make you forget everything else in the world, even your cell phone and your lousy children, and just curl up in some forgotten part of the house where no one can find you? Would you enjoy that? Well, then come over here and take a look at our table, because this story is going to blow your mind . . ."

The thing about selling, of course, is that most people don't need this much persuading. For instance, if they've come to a book fair, it's a pretty good bet that they're going to buy some books. You just need to give them a reason to overcome *their* inhibitions. So as surprising as it sounds, this lame shtick actually works. People stop, they visit our booth, they pick up actual copies of the magazine, and then out of pity for the poor fool standing there sweating and shouting like a lunatic, they buy subscriptions—some of them, anyway. Enough.

"Free back issues with a one-year subscription—take your pick of a collector's edition featuring Hemingway or Faulkner. I also have V. S. Naipaul, the Trinidadian Troublemaker, in his American debut."

"You sound like a carnival barker," Brigid whispers. "But don't stop, it's working!"

"Get your half-baked goo-covered cinnamon buns with any large serving of Toni Morrison," I almost shout. "Don DeLillo comes with a side of bread sticks." It occurs to me that for all my entrepreneurial adventures over the last half year, I haven't really sold anything—not actively, at least. That's because at a deli you don't really try to sell people things; instead, you act as if you want to kill them, throw their shit in a bag and glare at them until they leave the store. But selling is the logical next step, and it's also one of those unexpected intersections between George Plimpton and the store, like the amateur ethos. With things like book fairs, George is always trying to get the staff to embrace the job of selling rather than coast on the expectation that something intrinsically noble like "literature" will succeed on its own. He cajoles us to get out there and hustle, while showing by example that even the self-sell can be liberating, rather than a defilement of one's modesty, because in order to do it you simply can't take yourself too seriously.

By the end of the day Brigid and I have sold well over fifty subscriptions, far more than we expected. Having barely broken even with our expenses, we're hardly what you would call a raging success. But as the crowds dissipate and a giant black thunderhead builds behind the Sears Tower, we sit there for a little while and bask in the warmth of the late afternoon.

"Let's count the money," Brigid says eagerly, taking out a fat, greasy wad of bills from an envelope she's been carrying in her back pocket. Then we repack our boxes of back issues—which for once seem noticeably lighter than they had been on our way to the fair—and jump in a rental car before the clouds explode in an epic downpour.

ABOUT TWO WEEKS later I go into the *Review,* where things seem to be falling apart. Given the normal dishevelment of the office it's hard to tell, of course, but the stacks of unopened mail seem to have reached a new height, the sink seems fuller than ever of dirty dishes and I dare not check the answering machine for fear of the angry messages it contains. Our fall issue is even more behind than usual—the printer's deadline is a few weeks away and we have no idea what the contents are going to be—and the office is completely empty while the staff is on summer vacation.

Completely empty, that is, except for George, who is sequestered upstairs, starting on a new book, a memoir, *le grand report.* That is, if he can get started. Like all writers staring at a blank page, George would gladly sell one of his lesser organs for an excuse to do something else. Oh, he tries, as the desperate noises coming through the ceiling attest. *Get up, get down, sink heavily into creaky wooden chair. Then get up a few minutes later and walk anxiously to window, then sit down again. Turn on* SportsCenter. When the office phone rings, George lunges for it before I can even get a hand on the receiver.

"Hullo?" he says. "Hullo? Hullo?" Disappointment—it's only

the friend of a staff member, not even an angry author demanding payment for a story published years ago.

Ever since Chicago I've been fearing a moment like this. Sooner or later he'll come down and—will we talk about the state of the magazine? Will I tell him about Brigid? Others, too, are leaving, I know. Is it time for a frank discussion or should we go on skirting the issue? What will his reaction be if I tell him that the magazine seems to be falling apart? Will he be angry? Sad? Indifferent?

At ten-fifteen George practically tackles the mailman on his way into the building. Then he drops into the office.

"Don't mind me," he says with concentrated seriousness, holding under his arm a copy of the *New York Post* opened to Page Six. "Just looking for the, um, *galleys* I left here last night." *Shuffle, shuffle.* George starts rummaging through the mounds of paperwork on Brigid's desk, destroying whatever semblance of order it might have had.

"Can't find a damn thing in here. This office is a bloody mess! Where in tarnation is everyone? Why is this office always empty?"

"You told everyone to go on vacation last week, George. Remember?"

George looks briefly at a loss. "I did?" That was before George started the memoir, when he was still in a good mood. "Yes, of course," he says, his voice immediately softening. "Well, good for them. All with their families, I hope." As for George's own family, they're out in the Hamptons till the end of summer, along with nearly all of George's friends.

"Very well, then, carry on," George says, lifting up his chin. But I don't hear the door shut; instead I hear the tortured machinations of a man dying for companionship. More papers shuffle, magazine pages flip, and now and then comes a small, helpless sigh. Finally I sense a presence immediately behind me and catch a whiff of stale Scotch and last night's veal piccata at Elaine's.

"George!" He's leaning over my shoulder.

"What are you working on? If I may ask."

"I'm trying to *read*," I huff, wheeling around. "The fall issue is due in a couple weeks, and there's almost nothing in it. Doesn't that worry you?"

"Of course it does. Of course. How long did you say, three weeks?"

I nod.

"That's no time at all. Still, we can squeeze in a drink, don't you think? Why don't you come upstairs and I'll fix us both something—"

"George, it's not even noon."

"—while you call up the girls."

"George!"

"What, you don't know any girls? Well, come upstairs anyway and have some lunch. We'll order sandwiches from the deli." He pats me on the shoulder. "Not your deli, of course."

Upstairs, the Plimpton apartment has been transformed. The de Koonings and Warhols are still in place, plus the mounted water buffalo and other trophy kills, but with George's family out of town, an aging, dilatory frat boy appears to have moved in, leaving the townhouse covered in Chinese food cartons, half-empty cocktail glasses and dirty clothes. A late-night pool game is in evidence, an ashtray, a crumpled pack of Marlboro Reds.

"So," says George, his mood rapidly improving, "I have been thinking about the next issue, and who we should interview."

"Oh really? Who?" Last week there was an editorial meeting devoted to this very question. Interviews are always the centerpiece of an issue, and for the fiftieth anniversary it is vital that we come up with a heavy hitter. The names floating around include Solzhenitsyn, Eco and Murakami.

"Niminam!" George shouts triumphantly.

Niminam? Is that an African author? I am not a connoisseur of world literature like others on the staff, but neither is George, and I am a little surprised to hear him suggest a name I've never heard myself. Then I realize who he really means.

"You mean Eminem?"

"Yes, exactly, the freestyle vocalist. Can you call his people and set something up? I should think you might want to do the interview yourself."

"Yes, George."

"Incidentally, given the success of your foray into the Midwest, I'm thinking of sending you to another fair later this fall. How do you feel about Akron?"

The phone rings, and George picks it up.

"Hullo?" It's George's agent, evidently calling for a progress report on the memoir. "Yes, things are going swimmingly." George winks at me. "The words are flying out so fast my fingers can barely keep up! You've disturbed me mid-sentence! Oh, and you might be interested to know that our next issue, the anniversary issue, is going to have an interview with the great rapper, Numnum! Ben is going to do it."

Feeling increasingly tense, I wander off into George's living room. If Brigid is going to quit after the fall issue, then we're running out of time. There might not be another opportunity to tell him the ship is going down. But what if in his current fragile health that pushes him over the edge?

It all goes back to George's vision. Brigid is right: ultimately it's his magazine, and you have to respect what he's built. But for the sake of the future, can't it be just a bit more serious now and then? Why does he always have to resist being responsible? Is the fun-plus-youthfulness formula such a crucial element of the magazine's identity, or is it merely an excuse for George to divert himself when he doesn't feel like writing?

"Ah, there you are," says George, padding into the living room. "Our sandwiches have arrived."

We return to the kitchen and sit down at the table, where George begins regaling me with the kind of story he seems to draw no end of pleasure out of telling, no matter how many times he has told it before:

"... and then I said, 'My God, man, get us out of here,' but the door to the cave was locked and it was so bloody hot that I had no choice but to take off my pants ..."

As he's talking to me, I become preoccupied by George's ever-fascinating bird's nest of white hair, which occasionally attains Warholian dimensions of unruliness. Today, however, the style is more that of a foppish prep schooler, bangs hanging droopily over the corner of one eye, and as I look at it I can't help thinking, *Don't we all have to grow up sometime? Even George?*

"... I'd never seen a pair so large. It was unspeakable. You couldn't peel your eyes away even if you wanted to ..."

"George ..."

"*Snakes everywhere,* flicking their tongues and hissing, while the helicopter tried to drop the ladder just a few more inches ..."

"George ..."

"Yes, Ben, what is it?"

George's eyes are surrounded by folds as thin as parchment, and he can't keep his jaw from hanging slack, or his chest from heaving when he gets this worked up. *Don't we all have to grow up sometime?*

Suddenly George gets a serious look on his face and shoots up from the table.

"I've got something to show you. Will you wait here?"

Two minutes later he returns carrying a cardboard box full of magazines, which he hands to me proudly.

"What are they?"

"Take a look."

I open the box and pull out an ancient copy of *Sports Illustrated* with George's byline on the cover.

"One of my first articles," he says.

I glance at the piece, about a foray of George's into the world of sports as a "professional amateur," the role that characterized so much of what he does, whether it's writing, publishing or acting. The next magazine I pull out is an ancient edition of *Harper's,* also with a story by George—the whole box is filled with George's early writing. He's been rereading his work as a young journalist, trying to jog old memories.

"I hadn't looked at these in forty years," he says, leaning back. He's hardly touched his sandwich and is now eyeballing the bar in the kitchen.

"Why not?"

"Because I dreaded the embarrassment. I was terrified that if I looked back I'd be forced to admit that I can't write at all, that I'm a fraud."

"And were your fears . . . justified?" I can't believe George has such fears. I've never seen him show any insecurity at all. "Were the pieces embarrassing?"

"Some of them, yes. But others—" He stops short. I know what he wants to say, but self-praise doesn't come easily to George. It goes against his wiring. However, it's important for him to talk about this, so I encourage him to muscle it out.

"Some of them weren't bad, if I say so myself," he manages between gritted teeth.

The lunch is becoming strangely emotional. George is turning me into some sort of stand-in psychologist. However, not only am I totally unqualified for this role (shouldn't he call Charlie Rose instead?) but the fact that it's George makes it all the more intimidating. George is the master interviewer: he's conducted hundreds, if not thousands of interviews onstage and in print, and knows just which questions to ask (or, perhaps more important, not ask). With his encouragement I've done a few interviews myself for the magazine, but my style of interviewing couldn't be more different. George is subtle and delicate. I give the maxim "there are no stupid questions" a backbreaking workout. And I'm not happy in the slightest about George witnessing this firsthand. Nevertheless, wiggling out is not an option. The task of summing up his life is obviously causing George distress, and he needs a sounding board.

"Do you feel like a different person now than when you started writing?" I ask. George looks at me curiously and frowns. *Too vague,* I think. Who wouldn't feel that they'd changed over fifty years? But then he surprises me by answering.

"I am a different person," he says sharply. "Being a writer didn't come naturally. I had to coach myself, learn little by little."

"Did you have any mentors?" Better: a concrete question. George muses about the influence of Paul Gallico, a sportswriter and novelist who had been his model for the "professional amateur," but the question obviously doesn't engage him.

"What about how to write sentences, that sort of thing? Did you imitate anyone?"

Again George answers somewhat indifferently. I'm missing the mark. There's something else he wants to talk about—his insecurities are elsewhere.

"Well, what's the hardest part of your job, George?" I ask, deciding to be as blunt as I can.

Suddenly he lights up. *At last!* his expression seems to say.

"Performance," he says. "Performance is the part that I dread. Getting in front of an audience, having to speak and entertain . . ." He shudders. "I get so bloody nervous."

This gives me a bit of a chill, because for George to even talk about "performance" means he's stepping out of character, which, either because he's incapable or because he refuses, he simply does not do. George onstage, George regaling guests at a party, George holding court among autograph seekers at a restaurant, are all more or less the same person as George in the office or at home. The mask doesn't fall away. But everyone who knows George has at one time wondered how happy he is about being "George" all the time, and whether he's ever wanted to say "Enough! I'm tired of being charming."

"You really don't enjoy performing?" I ask incredulously.

Frowning, he shudders again. "Sometimes I hate it," he says, another shock—George never uses the word "hate." "I get so bloody nervous and worked up. 'How am I going to do this? I have no idea what I'm doing! Why am I here? What if I fall on my face?' Oh, it's absolutely terrifying."

George has none of his usual spirit as he says this. He simply looks tired. And now I'm reeling, for not only does this upend my image of George as someone with zero inclination to look inward or engage in self-doubt, but it challenges the whole notion of him as a kind of overgrown child. After all, why would someone do something he hates except out of a sober sense of duty?

"George, I have to tell you, I never thought you were doing anything but having fun."

"Well, then, you see, I am a fraud." And as if it pleases him just to say that, the faintest smile touches his lips.

Thus ends my session as amateur psychologist, to the relief of both of us, probably. Whatever the moment was—George revealing something of himself or me just imagining it—it's over. We talk for a while longer; then, inevitably, the phone rings ("Hullo, Sunny, is that you? Yes, the memoir is almost finished. Just a few more pages. Actually, yes, I am free tonight . . .") and his attention drifts off. I sneak out of the apartment and make the long trip back to Staten Island.

ALIENATION OF LABOR

NEW YORKERS SPEND A LOT OF TIME IN DELIS. IT'S NOT uncommon for us to see the same customers walk through the door five or six times a day. Some people act as if our store is part of their home and come in wearing pajamas or stroking an iguana; some stroll through the aisles for an hour while having an intimate phone conversation at the top of their voice. The way these people act has a desperate adolescent "look at me" quality, and at the same time there's a certain haughtiness, an attitude of "What, you didn't hear? This is New York. Get over it." And, of course, they're right. What would New York be without bad behavior? And where would people exhibit it if not in delis?

To New Yorkers a convenience store is essentially a public place, more like a park than, say, a private restaurant. Not long ago a customer came in and asked me to throw away an empty soda can. Then she started giving me garbage from her purse, and then she went out to her car and started bringing me fast food wrappers and coffee cups. I was starting to feel like I had a Department of Sanitation sticker on my forehead and was thinking about saying something nasty, but I held back. It's better, I've learned, to just take people's trash when they hand it to you, because the alternative is to pick it up yourself off the street later.

Similarly, it's always hard to say no when people ask to use the bathroom, especially if they come in grimacing and clutching themselves in agony, as they usually do. If you're not motivated by sympathy to say yes, then you're at least concerned about the possible effect on your store of saying no. The problem is that after using the bathroom, people tend to skip the requisite courtesy of purchasing even a token pack of gum. If I were a better person I'd look at them and think, *I'm glad they're feeling better now*, but cleaning bathrooms tends to shrivel one's reserves of compassion, so instead I glare and resist the temptation to ask, "Did you smile for the hidden camera in the ceiling?"

The most annoying thing customers do is a move I call The Placeholder, which happens when a person walks into a store, grabs an item and puts it on the counter before going off to do the rest of his shopping. When he finishes, he comes back to the register and inserts himself at the front of the line by virtue of having left that item as a kind of proxy—a Placeholder.

There's no logic to this system. If we all used Placeholders, every checkout line would devolve into chaos and people would end up bashing each other in the head with cans of kidney beans. The move is so brazenly antisocial that would-be critics find themselves sputtering with stupefaction, and usually looking to *me* as the ostensible authority to sort it all out. (Which I rarely do, because typically the person who used The Placeholder is also the sort of person you do not want to get into a confrontation with.)

Of course, there's a flip side to annoying customers, and that's annoying deli clerks. Not long ago I went into a fancy Korean deli in SoHo, looking for a snack. The store happened to be empty when I walked in, which didn't prevent the puckish middle-aged woman standing at the register from ringing up every item I touched, even when I was still ten feet away. Not liking to be rushed, I began randomly picking up items and putting them back, but it didn't seem to faze the woman at all. On the contrary, to let me know she was waiting, she jingled my change.

Sometimes New Yorkers take it too far—the pushiness, the constant, unnecessary hurrying. But sure enough, her technique was working; I had this urge to keep moving or leave the store. As a result, when I finally approached the register I was agitated and had a hard time getting my wallet out of my pocket. I hated her then, but of course instead of giving her just one of the fresh, crisp twenties I had just withdrawn from the ATM, I gave her four.

"You try to tip?" she cackled.

I was ready to pass it off with a casual remark about the winter dryness numbing my fingertips, but for some reason I tensed up and couldn't speak. The woman looked at me curiously, standing there with no sound coming out of my mouth. *Why are you still here?* her expression said. *Go outside and think about Mommy! I gave you change—move on.*

"I'm not a tourist!" I almost shouted at her then.

But it was too late. Outside, I stood on the sidewalk feeling humbled, wondering when my next opportunity to prove myself to the city would come.

My mother-in-law, I've noticed, has a similar effect on people. She's the archetype of a certain New Yorker who, whatever her actual story, is assumed to have sacrificed so much and worked so hard just to be here that it almost makes you defensive. *Why are YOU here? What's YOUR story?* It's not only people like Gab who struggle to live up to their parents' example, in other words; it's all of us. New York never lets you just sit there and relax. So many people are dying to get in, and willing to do almost anything to stay once they get here.

A MONTH AFTER Emo's arrival I go with Kay to Jetro, a grocery wholesaler on the Brooklyn waterfront. Jetro is the deli mother ship, a giant warehouse filled with cat food, Cheez Curls, phone cards to every country in the developing world, and a few dozen middle-aged men wearing clothes they've obviously slept in. It's like Costco or Wal-Mart but dirtier and without frills like air-conditioning or pest control. The aisle signs are in English, Korean, Spanish and Arabic, although reading them can be difficult no matter what your nationality, because Jetro skimps on lighting, too.

We have with us our official Jetro member's ID, which identifies us as deli owners. (As if by looking in our half-closed, bloodshot eyes you couldn't tell.) The general public is not allowed in. Jetro's prices are a cut below what you find at most wholesalers, but what attracts deli owners from all over the city is not its discounting, which isn't all that remarkable. The reason Jetro exists is to cut out deliverymen, the short-range truckers who haul goods from the storage centers to the convenience stores. Deliverymen cause headaches; in addition to bullying the store owners (as in the case of the snack cake thugs), they always manage to bring that emergency shipment of toilet paper you paid a premium express delivery rate for two days after you run out. And of course they charge a percentage. Jetro not only eliminates the percentage, it gives deli owners the "freedom" to fill their own shelves with whatever they want, whenever they want it. Meaning, of course, you get to be your own deliveryman.

Whether this is a good idea for the deli owners is an entirely separate matter. Small business people would always rather do things themselves. That's their nature. But a deliveryman has a truck—that's one thing you pay him for—and a deliveryman also gets paid to sacrifice his lumbar discs and groin muscles. Jetro knows exactly how its independently minded clientele thinks, and its attitude is *You want to do it? Here's a shipping container—unload it yourself, and try not to get run over by a forklift.* The result is like a reality game show—*Shop to Death!*—in which contestants try to navigate an obstacle course seeded with challenges intended to maim and/or humiliate them.

When we arrive at the waterfront I attempt to park as close to the entrance as possible, so that afterward we won't have to haul our "U-boat" (what Jetro calls its industrial cast-iron shopping carts) across Jetro's pothole-riddled lot. But there are no spaces except in a loading zone, which Kay, sitting in the passenger seat, nudges me toward.

"That just waste of good space," she says. "Go on. Don't be scare."

This is the beginning of my morning's humiliations—being called a sissy by my fifty-five-year-old mother-in-law. Shopping with Kay is never good for my self-esteem. I'm either hiding my face in my hands, hoping nobody I know sees the candy wrappers and cold coffee casually flung from our vehicle as we cruise down Fourth Avenue, or rebuking myself for being such a lightweight. At Jetro, Kay always seems to get in confrontations with other deli owners as she bumper-cars through the aisles, and I have to play peacemaker before things get physical. She bargains, she haggles, she nags, and I have to stand there and smile while people look at

me like, *Is this woman for real?* Kay exhibits no fear or squeamish-
ness, no recognition of physical or psychological pain. What it
boils down to is that no matter how much more of a man I am as
a result of this deli experience, I will never be as much of one as
my mother-in-law.

This realization comes after deciding I'd had enough of beating
myself up. The Puritan tendency is to dig ever deeper for sources of
guilt (which, given the iniquitous history of the Puritans' descendants, the Wasps, tend to be ever plentiful), but lately I've run low
on the necessary fervor for self-carving. All I want is to continue
the store's success.

However, Kay's tendency to throw herself at things is our next
big issue. We have to find a way to stop my mother-in-law from
working herself to death, whether that means reducing her load
generally or specifically targeting the damage she inflicts on herself doing things like going to Jetro. Kay's body has been altered by
the physical strain of the last seven months. On one hand, she's
leaner and even stronger than before. The other day, looking through
the store window and watching her smoke a Parliament out on the
corner (one of those rare moments in which she stopped moving
long enough that I could actually look at her) in her favorite sleeveless T-shirt, I could see new definition in her biceps. Kay has always
had thick shoulders and arms, thanks to the years she spent sewing
in sweatshops, but now they look young and sinewy again. On the
other hand, she's been injuring herself constantly, whether it's dropping a case of Chunky soup on her foot at Jetro (thanks to which she
now has an eggplant for a big toe) or reaggravating a damaged rota-
tor cuff from the sweatshop years. Thus my presence here on the
waterfront at nine A.M., shopping for industrial-sized boxes of pine-
scented car freshener trees and El Bubble chewing gum.

"What is better, studded or ribbed?" Kay asks, holding up a box
of Trojans. "Which one customer like more?"

Mortified—doesn't she realize that I, of all people, have no idea, having been in a relationship with her daughter practically since the onset of puberty?—I snatch the condoms out of her hand and fling both boxes on the U-boat. "Let's keep moving," I say. Kay shrugs and we roll on. The next section is pet food. *Nothing to be afraid of here, right?* Except that when my back is turned, Kay deadlifts a couple of enormous bags of kitty litter onto the U-boat.

"Hey, that's my job!" I protest. Those kitty litter bags are as heavy as wet rugs, and they don't have a thing on them you can grab. They're the worst menace to lower backs since the eighty-pound sacks of rice Kay lugs home from the Korean supermarket.

Too late. "Job done," Kay says. She asks me if I can run back to a previous section and fetch some paper towels instead. *Sigh.* Jetro sells blocks of Bounty that look impressive when you lift them over your head, but the truth is, they're as light as marshmallows. And while I'm distracted she hoists some more heavy merchandise (What do they put in cat food, anyway? The stuff weighs more than lead) onto the U-boat. I'm not amounting to much help.

This sort of scene gets repeated any number of times each day. Rather than wait even thirty seconds for help, Kay will invariably move the oppressively unwieldy racks of produce and soft drinks inside the deli herself. She's as much the compulsive nonprocrastinator as ever. The family has tried to restrain her, but without physically stopping her it's simply impossible.

"What if we make the store so successful that your mother doesn't have to work there anymore?" I asked Gab the other day. She shook her head. "She'd still come in and kill herself. When it comes to work, she doesn't trust anyone else, not even me or Emo. She wants to do everything herself."

I think about that remark a lot, because it suggests that self-reliance is a compulsion, not a skill you acquire because you or your parents thought it would be good for character development. You acquire it by being scarred, and becoming incurably suspicious that if you don't take care of a job yourself, no one will. Which is a harsh statement, if true, because how many of us are lucky enough to be immigrants, war refugees or single parents? (Maybe being a shopkeeper comes close?)

In order to convince Kay to slow down, I need to know what makes her tick. But how do you even begin to understand someone whose origins are so distant? Sometimes I look at her the way I look at a musician or an athlete and think I could never do what they do.

Don't get me wrong—I'm not suggesting that Kay's an automaton. In Korea, her generation experienced some awful things during the Korean War—massacres, aerial bombardment, forced relocations—which she doesn't talk about. And as immigrants the Paks went through plenty of other dramas, which similarly aren't discussed. The sum of those experiences, I'm certain, tended to numb as well as focus the mind.

After the paper towels and the pet food, she and I move on to the personal hygiene section, above which Jetro's corrugated steel roof, now popping in the late morning heat, has sprung a leak, resulting in a flood that even a lifetime supply of Bounty can't soak up. Naturally, Jetro's management acts as if the thigh-deep puddle isn't there. Kay and I look at each other. Should we have brought our own inflatable canoe? The Black Pond of Aisle Seven is filled with pigeon feathers, floating Optimo cigars and other crud, and as I wade in I worry about it carrying some electric current too. But since the warehouse is now roasting like an oven, it actually feels refreshing, and with the cases of tampons and Huggies perched on my shoulders as I make one sortie after another into the muck, I can easily imagine the studio audience for *Shop to Death!* cheering in appreciation—not to mention the denizens of Boerum Hill. Of course, wet pants become something of a liability in Jetro's frozen section ("Gotcha!" the producers scream), and as I run around frantically fetching frozen logs of baloney while icicles of sweat form on my eyebrows and pneumonia develops in my lungs, the studio audience breaks into nervous laughter. I would laugh too, if only these sorts of tasks weren't the ones gradually killing Kay.

AFTER JETRO ONE task remains, a brief stop at Jetro's little cousin, a Yemeni-owned place called Screaming Eagle.

Unlike Jetro, I look forward to going to Screaming Eagle. It's smaller and even grubbier, but its young owner, Walid, is right down there in the squalor with you, and it's one of those obscure but integral parts of the city whose existence I would never even have known about had we not gone into the deli business. Nevertheless, as soon as we get there, I always have to fight the urge to run. The place is forbidding. You park on this lifeless industrial block of truck bays and warehouses without a pedestrian in sight—just different shades and textures of concrete covered with broken glass. One of the truck bays belongs to Walid, though I can never figure out how Kay knows which one, since there's no sign. After parking next to a car with no wheels, we approach and, finding a half-open side door, enter without knocking.

"Yoo-hoo!" says Kay, stomping out a Parliament before waltzing blithely into the darkness of a crumbling stairway. "It's me, old Korean lady. Anybody home?"

There's no buzzer or waiting room. You just feel your way along (unless you're Kay, in which case you barely slow down, despite the gimpy leg) to the next door, which feels as if it could open to a dungeon, an arsenal or an opium den. Suddenly you find yourself inside a dim, low space full of men wearing ankle-length tunics, with devout-looking beards and faces that always convey surprise and displeasure no matter how many times we come. Middle Eastern music plays in the background, but shuts off as soon as we walk in. Seeing Kay, some of the men walk out. Then Walid comes out and greets us, and while still stealing nervous glances at us, the remaining men go back to their work, which involves slicing open an endless heap of cardboard boxes containing all manner of small electronics and personal hygiene products, plus tobacco and baby formula, then setting out the boxes on shelves for clients like us to rummage through.

Given the way you enter, Screaming Eagle doesn't feel like a legitimate business, but instead like part of an underground economy where much goes on that is sketchy. Essentially, Walid is a middleman who dips his hand in the torrents of consumer goods flowing about the globe. Things like razor blades, teeth whitener, iPod headphones and batteries moving around peripatetically between the factories where they are made and the shelves where they are finally sold, and sometimes getting hijacked. Take baby formula, one of the most expensive items in a grocery store. The underground retail market loves almost nothing more than a twenty-five-dollar can of Enfamil because it has a constant worldwide demand and the price is consistently high. In fact, illicit sales of Similac and Enfamil are thought to reach hundreds of millions of dollars globally, and attract the likes of—yes—Al Qaeda and Hezbollah. It's laughable but true, and though Screaming Eagle isn't an outlet of the terrorist baby-formula-and-teeth-whitening market (every time government inspectors have raided our store, their stuff has checked out), lots of places just like it in Brooklyn are.

This is one reason I have the urge to leave—the feeling of being an intruder. Walid's employees, who have the jumpy air of newly arrived immigrants, stop working so they can stare at us. Maybe they're offended; after all, most of Screaming Eagle's clients are Middle Eastern shopkeepers like old Salim, who got us into this place. There aren't many mismatched couples like the clean-cut white guy and the Asian grandma wearing a skin-tight T-shirt and red lipstick, trailing cigarette smoke.

It testifies to Kay's character, courage or whatever you want to call it that she appears to be the only woman to set foot into Jetro or Screaming Eagle. At first that struck me as odd, since you always see women at Korean delis. You see men too, but less frequently, and often just in their golf clothes at the beginning or the end of the day. At many Korean-owned businesses, a husband's job is to bring money to and from the store and open the heavy steel shades (leading to the moniker "shutterman") before heading off to the driving range. Many also pick out the store's inventory at a place like Jetro or the Hunts Point produce market in the Bronx. However, with Edward running his own business, Kay does this part, too.

At Screaming Eagle she avidly sifts through the cardboard boxes. She's in her element; this is her kind of shopping. It takes brass to come in here and a merchant's steely eye to find the good stuff, and at the end Kay gets to jujitsu with Walid over prices. The discounts end up being worth it, but even if they weren't I think Kay would come in here anyway. Afterward she always wants me to tell her what I know about Yemen and the Middle East, which isn't much. It may look like Kay's all business, but she's curious, just like anyone else. *Who are these people? What are they doing here?* and *What do they think of us?* Which are, of course, the same questions I have about Kay.

GAB'S COUSIN JUNG comes over that Sunday for a barbecue, and while chatting with him in the backyard I confide my struggle to understand Kay. "Good luck," he chuckles. "It's a generational thing. Her generation is special. They don't even understand themselves."

"What do you mean?"

"Okay, I'll give you an example." Jung says he was watching Korean TV recently and saw a show about Korean housewives of approximately the same age as Kay undergoing therapy for what you might translate as "hyperadvancement syndrome."

"These were women who grew up when Korea was barely even the Third World—it was almost the Fourth World," he says. "I mean, we're talking outhouses, drinking out of streams, livestock in the yard." Since the 1960s, however, South Korea had developed from one of the poorest countries in the world into what many call the most technologically advanced nation in history, with its futuristic communications infrastructure and world-dominating tech firms like Samsung. Jung, who has just come back from visiting Seoul, says the country makes the United States look old and backward ("We're ten years behind"), and those women experiencing "hyperadvancement syndrome" had, like all Koreans, seen their world change about as much as humanly possible in one lifetime. They were suffering from future shock.

Gab's father is a good example. The rural village he comes from, called Dogae, was home to his ancestors for sixty generations, according to family lore. When Mongol hordes invaded Korea in the thirteenth century, Edward's relatives were there. And when the Japanese first started marauding Korea three hundred years later, they were still there. And when the Russians and the Americans divvied up Korea after World War II, things were still more or less the same. But this last generation had been different. It had cut the cord. And when Edward left, he didn't just wind up in a neighboring village or Seoul—he went to the other side of the world.

In Kay's case, her background was more cosmopolitan; her parents were successful merchants from North Korea who imported goods from Manchuria. Their estate was supposedly so big that it had eight gates leading up the driveway. Even as Korea endured famine and foreign occupation (Japan annexed Korea in 1910 and held on to to it until the end of World War II), Kay's siblings went to school in a chauffeured car, had a radio in their house and enjoyed other luxuries. However, when North Korea turned Communist in 1948, the family lost everything. Kay's father, targeted for his fortune and his anti-Communist political activity, was arrested and sentenced to the gulag. His family won his freedom only by ransoming their estate and cashing in on a personal connection to the uncle of the future North Korean dictator Kim Il Sung, then fled to South Korea, where Kay was born.

Kay's parents were educated; her siblings attended high school (a privilege reserved for the elite) and even college, but the family's reduced circumstances in the south forced her to earn money instead. Blessed with that powerful voice, she joined a singing troupe that performed at weddings and baptisms, and while still a teenager she met Edward, who was serving in the South Korean navy.

Edward had also been affected by Korea's tumult, but if dramatic ups and downs shaped Kay's childhood, displacement shaped his. During World War II Edward's parents went to Japan, where his father became a laborer in a tin mine and eventually died of lung poisoning. An only child, Edward was dealt another blow when, upon returning to Korea, his mother married a petty tyrant who made home life unbearable. As soon as he was eligible, Edward joined the navy and headed abroad. When he met Kay (she was working as a receptionist at a YMCA in Seoul) he was on shore leave, and immediately after their wedding he went back to sea, setting a pattern for the rest of their marriage.

Kay was left to live in the household of the tyrannical stepfather Edward couldn't stand, serving her in-laws (as per Korean tradition) as a virtual slave. Their house, a former Japanese hospital that had been converted into a general store, was haunted by the stepfather, a cripple who began drinking every morning at ten, when the day's shipment of *makkali* (unrefined rice wine, also known as "farmer liquor") arrived. By lunchtime the tiled walls would ricochet with his hateful haranguing. Whenever Kay's mother-in-law left on an errand, her father-in-law jotted down the time, and if she returned a minute later than promised, he would haul himself over to the doorway and sit there with his stunted legs folded beneath him muttering, "I'll kill that woman someday" while beating his palm with a ball-peen hammer. Kay's job was to cook, clean and mind the store. She cried herself to sleep each night, accompanied by the sound of hissing, the old man's favorite meal being snake soup, which he forced Kay to prepare using live snakes caged outside her room.

"You think you have it bad living with my parents and working at a deli?" Gab says to me one windy afternoon during a rare walk we're taking, alone, along Staten Island's industrial shoreline. "At least no one makes you cook snake soup."

Eventually Kay managed to get herself kicked out of her father-in-law's house for disobedience. On the street, she was aided by customers from the store, who took up a collection, enabling her to move into a flat. Soon afterward Edward quit the military, having recently completed an elite training program for engineers sponsored by the U.S. Navy, and from maintaining engines aboard destroyers he now attempted to shift to factory work. Kay went back to singing at weddings and baptisms, then got pregnant, and the two of them tried domestic life. However, within a year Edward went right back to sea, this time circling the planet for various commercial shipping companies. For the next decade he would be essentially absent, usually as far from South Korea as physically possible.

Kay decided she needed a more lucrative career than wedding singer. Although Edward sent home checks from Gdansk, Valparaiso and Seattle, she had little idea when they would come or how much they would be for. Luckily, her older sister Sook Ja had just opened a bakery in downtown Seoul and was finding herself unable to handle the job alone. Kay volunteered to help and soon was running the place.

Managing a bakery meant waking up at three in the morning every day, not the sort of work that fits well with raising young children. Fortunately, Kay had help—Edward's stepfather had recently passed away, and Edward's mother had moved into their apartment. With her babysitting, Kay was able to turn the bakery into one of the more popular eateries in Seoul.

The bustling bakery was in a trendy part of the city favored by South Korean celebrities. It had small coffee-shop tables and a large young staff, some of whom lived in what was becoming a sort of dormitory in Kay's apartment. Within a few years it had become so successful that Kay decided to expand, so she bought a restaurant that specialized in tripe soup, which Koreans typically eat for lunch. And she bought a bigger apartment to accommodate all the workers she was taking care of, and a Hyundai Pony, which, according to Gab, made her very proud.

"She used to get in the Pony and open the window so people could see her at the wheel, then drive it one block to change parking spaces," Gab once told me. At night she went out with friends wearing flashy jewelry and European shoes. Korea as a country was now fully immersed in hyperchange, the negative effects of which included abominable pollution and great political instability (coups, strikes, assassinations), but so far Kay was enjoying it all just fine, thank you very much. Twenty years earlier, she and Edward might have gone back to Dogae and settled into a thatch-roofed farmhouse, and Kay might have spent the rest of her life washing clothes in the river and growing her own food. Instead, she had a career *and* security for her family that she herself provided, plus the resources to indulge herself. What's more, she had the satisfaction of making it up as she went along, of standing out. Her own mother had been a strong woman and a partner to her father's businesses, but she was nothing like Kay. For what Kay was doing, there were no role models.

But then Edward had enough of shipping and came home, and everything changed. He would never have insisted on Kay staying in the kitchen—he was both worldlier and not nearly cruel enough. The question was more, How would *he* fit in? Where was *his* place now? What would *he* do? You have to feel for Edward—he'd spent the better part of a decade toiling in one of the world's most dangerous professions, and upon his return he found his home filled with strangers, his country in the midst of an industrial revolution (not to mention a brief but severe recession at the end of the 1970s), and his own children barely able to recognize him. As he looked for ways to establish himself, his marriage with Kay began to fray.

For all the confidence Kay had earned as a single parent, this struck surprising terror into her. As a woman in a male-dominated society, Kay could never shake the feeling that by stepping into a "man's role" she was violating some natural law of the universe. "My mother is a very complicated person," Gab says. "On one hand she's a sort of feminist, believing women ought to be assertive and independent. For instance, when I was growing up she used to tell me that the sort of woman she admired was an 'inteli,' which comes from the English word 'intellectual' but in Korea means an educated, independent, career person. However, she also believes that women should cook, clean and raise kids, and anything different from that freaks her out. In her mind a woman should stay at home, because anything else will eventually break up the family. It's unnatural, she thinks. And since she's also very superstitious, these things really bother her."

So when Edward came home and found himself uncharacteristically idle, Kay decided she would give up her own independence in order to restore the "proper" marital balance. She came up with a plan. "My mother knew my dad would never be happy in Korea," Gab explained, "so she offered to move to the U.S., because that was a country he knew." (During his time in the U.S.-sponsored engineering program, Edward had been stationed for a few months on the West Coast.) Of course, the fact that Korea as a whole was experiencing a fit of *migukpyong*—America fever—nudged her along as well. Twenty years earlier, there had been almost no Korean immigration to the States, but since the Hart-Celler Act of 1965, which ended the de facto policy of accepting only white immigrants, Korea had sent more émigrés here than any country except Mexico or the Philippines. Kay, who had never been outside Korea, had zero interest in America. She disliked the food, didn't particularly care for the culture and had heard too many stories of Koreans in the United States who ended up working twice as hard for less money. (They used to say that at Kimpo Airport you could spot the immigrants coming home from America because they all looked like *guh-ji*—bums. Kay was also disturbed by the ubiquitous stories of immigrant parents being abandoned by their Americanized children.)

Approximately a million people of Korean ancestry now live in America, and the sheer size of the group is a factor contributing to its success. There are Korean radio stations, Korean newspapers and Korean business associations with considerable lobbying power in cities like New York and Los Angeles. Korean businesses tend to work with other Korean businesses and depend heavily on networks built around social organizations such as churches. However, Gab's family always seemed to unconsciously avoid places with large Korean populations, starting out in Houston for a couple of years, then moving to rural Ohio, and finally in Staten Island (which at the time had fewer Korean residents than any other borough). This made the struggle of adapting to a new country even harder than it could have been. As Kay had feared, the family suffered a steep drop in its standard of living—everything they'd brought with them from Korea, all the proceeds from selling Kay's businesses, went into founding a family-owned air-conditioning company, which, like all start-ups (particularly those in a country that the owner has just moved to), struggled at first and went through years of ups and downs. Until Edward became established, the Paks were forced to live in trailer parks and a brutal succession of blighted condominiums overlooking highways and cemeteries. Kay had no choice but to work in sweatshops and as a night cashier at stores, and meanwhile she still had to raise three kids and open her doors to an endless stream of visitors, including me and Gab. Despite her attempt to restore the "traditional" balance between a husband and wife, there was no switch from breadwinner to full-time housewife.

But of course there was a happy ending: the family stayed together. In that sense, things have worked out. And now, with the store getting on its feet, there is finally the potential to restore what had been lost.

On that day when I stand at the window watching Kay smoke in her tank top (never has the name for that particular shirt style suited its wearer more appropriately, by the way), it feels as if we are in some kind of golden moment, and it almost looks that way, too. For one thing, the sun is setting, and at six o'clock on a July day the light filtering through the industrial haze of New Jersey is nothing if not peachlike. (To my mind Brooklyn is always at its best during a long summer sunset, when it is still a city and still dense with neighborly interaction, but when the volume and pace are at a humane level and you don't feel literally overshadowed by the sheer bulk of New York's money and ambition.) For another, inside the store a few feet away from me, one of our new workers, an eagle-

eyed college kid named Kevin, is meticulously unpacking a shipment of inventory in front of a startled frozen food deliveryman.
After failing in our initial attempts to hire people other than Dwayne
who don't share TV time with us every night, in Kevin we've developed a competent, able-bodied employee who craves as many shifts
as we can give him. Kevin has an especially useful talent: he makes
a sport of sniffing out the deliverymen's tricks and is essentially a
one-man stop-loss squad, probably saving us hundreds of dollars
a week. And with Emo making the morning shift into smooth sail-
ing and Dwayne thwarting the narcs, it feels like we're actually cov-
ering our bases for once, instead of constantly being caught out of
position.

Meanwhile, a group of Mexican busboys stand in back, boister-
ously but not offensively getting smashed on cases of Corona Light
sold to them at a special regulars' discount. Residents of one of
Chucho's overcrowded rooming house–style apartments upstairs,
they've been doing this now every Wednesday since the start of the
summer. Other regulars—I'd say we currently know about a third
of all people who come into the store by name—keep coming in and
lingering by the checkout counter, some for a few hours. They
bring their lizards and their dogs, their mothers in Nebraska (via
cell phone, of course) and all their annoying habits, like the Russian limo driver who always starts shouting lottery numbers at me
when I'm in the middle of talking or counting someone else's
change, or the woman in neon pink spandex who can never decide
what sandwich to order and stands there at the counter slowing
down the line. Some of the regulars have come back—Super Mario,
Barry the half-blind cab driver, a soft-spoken Haitian waiter
known as "the General" who stands in the snack section every
night for two hours and doesn't speak. I'm not sure why they've
returned. At one point back in the spring I think we all realized
how miserable we'd become, and it could be that since then we've

made an effort to be friendlier. Surely success brightens one's attitude.

Speaking for myself, the biggest change has been a kind of
loosening of that legendary clenched-sphincter Puritan uptightness.
Even with a store as small as ours you can control almost nothing—
except maybe the environment. And I had tried. Imposing my will
on the music or the coffee was a way of making me feel like we were
also capable of influencing bigger things, like our fate as a family
or my marriage. However, it was even worse than I feared—in
addition to all the things about a streetside business that are fundamentally chaotic, there was Dwayne, and there was the built-in
instability of our neighborhood, and there was all the arguing at
home, which made decision making of any kind all but impossible. Gradually, I began to surrender some of my own ability to
control—a decision here and a decision there. Nothing since then
has happened that I can directly attribute to my new, Zen frame of
mind, and yet I'm almost sure that it has helped. For one thing, the
inventory (which is essentially the store itself) has attained a kind
of equilibrium: we're no longer the junk food bazaar we were when
we took over, but we never got more than halfway to being the
gourmet market I wanted to be, either. The store is a mutant, a
hybrid. It isn't coherent in the slightest—the first time people come
in, they often get that "Huh?" look on their faces as they struggle
to process the mixed signals sent by a lottery machine and tofu
jerky, or by Olde English malt liquor and Belgian Trappist beer. But
I learned to accept this and so did most of the customers, maybe
because our lives weren't coherent. New York wasn't coherent. Why
force it to be?

The reward has been that after being a spaz my whole life—I'm
a socially nervous person and always will be—I have an almost
greater comfort with strangers than I do with people I know well.

Standing there all day not knowing who's going to come in next or what they're going to say, you have almost no choice except to become a bit more easygoing, and to trust more. It's a good thing. Everyone should work at a checkout counter for some part of their lives.

PROBLEM EMPLOYEE

AFTER SIX MONTHS OF WORKING WITH DWAYNE, I STILL CAN'T decide if he's the store's biggest asset or worst liability. On the positive side, you have an employee who shows up for work on time six days a week and frequently comes in on his off day as well. You have an employee who when he's at work rarely stops working, whether he's washing refrigerator doors or assembling Sunday newspapers. You have an employee who's essentially a foolproof government sting detector, a discouragement to would-be troublemakers and the convenience store equivalent of Daniel Boulud or some celebrity chef, all rolled up into one.

On the other hand, you have an employee who is a constant

headache, whether he's openly disobeying instructions, second-guessing his bosses in front of customers, barking at the customers themselves or merely dropping jaws with outrageous behavior and lewd commentary. You have an employee whose friends and family come into the store and do everything possible to distract him. You have an employee who's almost as much of a magnet for trouble as he is a deterrent.

And you have the gun.

I have long worried, without telling anyone, that Dwayne brings a gun to work. One day, early on, Dwayne was carrying on with his usual stories of wildings and carjackings (he had just finished telling me about the time he stabbed a man in the cheek with a fork) when he asked me:

"So what do you carry?"

"Carry?"

"To protect yourself."

I was taken off guard (not to mention still getting over that image of the fork in the face). We had been in the store only a week or so, and self-protection was—somewhat bizarrely, in retrospect—way down my list of priorities. I had bigger things to worry about at the time, like remembering the price of Coors Light tallboys and finding the stamina to stay awake. But I didn't want Dwayne to think that I was so naïve as to have not given the issue thought. So I muttered something I hoped would be indecipherable, somewhere between "I forget" and "a salad fork," which Dwayne rightly interpreted as "nothing."

He was apoplectic, of course. The way he made it sound, brown-stone Brooklyn was still an urban combat zone, despite the peaceful changes gentrification had wrought. The store would be robbed sooner or later—it wasn't a question of *if* but of *how many times.* And it was a question of how you responded: submissively or Dwayne-style, which would send a message to the United Convenience Store

Stickup Men's Association, or some similar organization, and determine whether you became a frequent or merely an occasional target. Not preparing yourself wasn't an option.

"Well, what do *you* carry?" I asked.

With his usual attention to detail, Dwayne cataloged an arsenal that would have given Travis Bickle the willies:

"... blackjack, throwing star, bolo, chain whip, nunchuks, pepper spray ..." By the time he got to the gun he owned (some kind of pistol), it seemed almost like an afterthought, though firearm licenses in New York are hard to come by (obtaining a carry permit is next to impossible). If Dwayne had a gun it was almost certainly illegal, and as someone with a criminal record (I know that Dwayne went to jail when he was young, though I've never had the courage to ask what he did), he could do serious time. And we could get in a lot of trouble, too.

Personally, I hate guns. Not on principle, mind you, but out of fear. I've never gotten over the suspicion (planted in me by some after-school special, no doubt) that guns go off by themselves all the time and bullets ricochet off walls until they find a nice, innocent non-gun-owning victim's forehead to land in.

So I told Dwayne to leave his weapons at home, which seemed to astonish him at first. Eventually, he relented. Of course, as I was soon to find out, Dwayne made up his own rules at the store, and unless I was going to frisk him every day, there was no way to stop him. Nevertheless, if he had a weapon inside his baggy overalls (or his mysteriously heavy backpack), he didn't tell me. And sometimes I wondered if we were better off that way, with a sort of "Don't ask, don't tell" policy for gats and Glocks. There would be times, I would eventually realize, when maybe having a weapon around would not be a categorically awful thing. The pertinent question was whether it should be in the hands of anyone but Dwayne.

✳   ✳   ✳

ONE THURSDAY AFTERNOON I'm sitting at my desk at the *Review* talking to Jack Kerouac's lawyer in Boston when the line goes dead. *Did I say something wrong?* I wonder, staring at the receiver. We *seemed* to be having a perfectly friendly conversation. Why did Jack Kerouac's lawyer hang up on me? Oh no, have I done it again?

Then I realize that all the computers in the office have also gone dead, and the air conditioner too, which was laboring to keep up with a ferocious heat wave. "Power outage," someone says, though this being only two years after September 11, everyone is also acutely aware of that other possibility.

It's hard to say which would be more frightening, I think, as I get up from my desk and move outside to the Seventy-second Street Esplanade, where crowds have gathered to see if anyone else knows what's happening. The rumor is that it's a blackout, although no one's really sure. The last time New York had a citywide power outage, during the infamous Summer of Sam, arsonists and looters terrorized the city, and the power didn't return for days. Here on the Upper East Side, probably the most target-rich neighborhood in the whole city, we'd be sitting ducks. Not in the least bit eager to find out what that's like, the staff of the *Review* starts packing up and heading home.

"Nonsense!" George thunders, having come down from his office. "If the mobs come, we'll invite them upstairs for a drink." I can see it: as gangs of rampaging teenagers pound on the door of his townhouse, George leans out his window with a tumbler of Scotch, shouting, "Tally ho! Do you happen to have any ice?" The man simply has no fear (not to mention infinite good-natured trust).

George wants us to come up to his apartment and make ourselves comfortable, but I grab my backpack and wave good-bye. Not only do I want to be in a different neighborhood by nightfall; I want to make sure the deli is locked up and fortified as tightly as possible, to ward off looters for at least a couple of days.

I start walking toward the subway, but the trains aren't running, so I walk across the Queensboro Bridge with a few thousand other jittery (literally—the bridge is wobbling) souls. Once I've escaped Manhattan I feel better, but now it's almost five o'clock and the light is starting to fade. Never has the long summer sunset felt so ominous, like that point in a horror movie when you know that the eyeball-less monsters with blood dripping from their mouths are about to emerge from their lairs. And I have yet to see a single police officer.

In Brooklyn, I come across a pack of anxious, sweaty commuters standing on a corner listening to a battery-powered radio. *"It's a blackout,"* someone says, *"not a bomb. The mayor just said so."* The crowd issues a collective sigh of relief, but are we really supposed to feel better? Apparently the whole eastern seaboard is without electricity. Nearly one-fourth of the entire country! It's the biggest blackout in history! Now I'm really starting to worry—how many days can the store's steel shutters hold up in case people try to break in? Would it be wiser to move all the merchandise to Kay's house? Does somebody need to stay behind and stand guard? I have images of myself barricaded inside the darkened store, holding off a siege with . . . stale sandwich rolls? the deli slicer? I wouldn't even be able to defend myself with hot coffee, since the coffeemaker won't work. Then again, maybe the store will smell so bad after a few days that the mobs won't even want to come in.

That's not likely. As any petty thief worth his salt would know, a convenience store would contain thousands of dollars in phone cards, scratch-off lottery tickets and tobacco. Moreover, after a few hours looters wouldn't come just for the high-value goods—they'd do it for the thrill, or the beer, and then after the food runs out and New York begins to starve, they'd come for the cat food, which in our dawning *Mad Max*–style future *will be just as valuable as gold.*

The more I worry, the more I want to get to the store, but it's getting harder to keep going in the direction I keep telling my legs to move in—namely, forward—because thanks to the peculiar bend of my journey, from the Upper East Side through Queens and then back toward downtown Brooklyn, I'm now going against the crowd of commuters exiting Manhattan, which is sort of like trying to reenter Yankee Stadium just after the last pitch of the ninth inning. And this isn't even the thickest or sweatiest part of the horde; it's the minority that was undaunted by the prospect of walking eight or ten miles in record heat and started as soon as the blackout began, rather than waiting to see if the power came back on. Any second now I'm going to get trampled by a much larger wave of workers exiting the Financial District. And how many would there be? Half a million? A million? In this heat, a million people constitutes a veritable Bataan Death March. There would be people coming over the Brooklyn Bridge who got winded climbing a single flight of stairs, people in suits and high heels, people freaked out if not for themselves then for the family members they've been unable to contact, as the city's cell phone network is currently overloaded. *What good is a cell phone if it doesn't work in an emergency?* they'd be wondering, and *Why did the city have to get rid of all its pay phones?* Next they'd be cursing the city for removing its park benches: *Where exactly is a tired person supposed to sit? And what happened to the drinking fountains? And where are all the police officers? And how come downtown Brooklyn doesn't have street vendors anymore, somewhere to at least buy a soda?* They'd be getting angrier, more frustrated and more desperate as they trekked down Boerum Place, a forbidding and seemingly endless street of unapproachable courthouses connecting the Brooklyn Bridge to Atlantic Avenue, and then as they turned east on Atlantic they'd be thinking, *Finally! A normal street with stores!* But then they'd have to walk two more blocks, past the jail and the parking lots, just to get to their first convenience store since they left Manhattan, in all probability well over two hours ago.

That store would be ours.

Walk faster! Suddenly I have this feeling that the store has not been shut down. We've never actually talked about what to do in a public emergency. Would Kay be tempted to stay open and use this opportunity to make money? Of course she would, you moron! *Hurry!*

Minutes later I see our distinctive awning, and with a tremor I realize that the store is indeed open and utterly besieged. Thousands of people are trying to get through our door.

In their way stands Dwayne, who is partly succeeding at managing the flow, but this is a societal breakdown, and these are dehydrated people in the grip of mass hysteria, or worse, women who need to pee.

After fighting my way in, I see Gab and Kay behind the counter.

"What are you doing?" I yell above the roaring crowd.

They look at me as if this is the stupidest question they've ever heard. What would be the proper response? Serving a line that starts back in Manhattan? Making money faster than we've ever made it before? There is something that does sort of require explanation, however: Why are Kay and Gab both wearing money, as if it were some kind of fashion statement to cover yourself in damp bills?

"We can't use the cash register," Gab shouts, "so we have to store it on our bodies." She points at herself: she has fives tucked into one rolled-up, sweat-soaked shirt sleeve and tens tucked into the other, and twenties under her collar. All smaller denominations she has in her hands or on the counter, although it's clearly becoming impossible to count loose change as the store gets dark.

As if what's going on outside the store—the crowds trying to get in, the growing mayhem—weren't enough, this is a complication I hadn't even considered, and yet another reason to close down immediately.

But Gab and Kay won't have any of it. People aren't just buying refreshments to cool off; they're grabbing anything off the shelves they can get their hands on. Meanwhile, the temperature inside our refrigerators is rising (and every time somebody opens one of the doors, it rises even faster). By midnight the milk and orange juice will have spoiled, the ice cream will just be cream, and the cheese will be Cheez Whiz. In the morning the cold cuts will have to be tossed out—and basically that's half the store right there. Who knows when we'll get any of it back. Even if the blackout ends tonight, tomorrow is Friday and the deliverymen might not come for almost a week. Then we'll lose the bread, fruits and vegetables; plus, each night that the city is without power is another night with a big LOOT ME sign spray-painted on the facade. At last I understand the situation. We could be facing losses that take us into going-out-of-business territory, so why not get rid of as much merchandise as possible? It would seem foolish not to.

If only the store weren't so vulnerable and exposed. Money is everywhere and getting harder to keep track of. As I join Kay and Gab behind the counter, it occurs to me that we're conducting an elaborate charade wherein we *pretend* that people actually have to pay us for the merchandise they take from our shelves, as if there would be consequences should they not. In truth, anybody can do anything they want to us right now: take our stuff, steal our money, burn us to the ground.

Just as I find myself wishing I hadn't told Dwayne to leave his weapons at home, a police officer comes to the store, the first I've seen since this whole episode started. He approaches Dwayne and says, "It's crazy out here. You got your piece?"

"'Course!" says Dwayne exuberantly.

"Good," says the cop. "You need any ammo?"

"Nah, I'm square," Dwayne says. And the cop goes off, probably to hide in his car.

It's finally getting dark outside now, and inside the store, where it's been dark already for a while, we're establishing a system that will allow us to remain open for a few more hours: holding candles or flashlights in one hand, we individually escort customers using the other hand to the places in the store where the items they want are located. Since many of the customers we're getting now fall into the straggler category—the old, out of shape, and barely ambulatory—a lot of the hands tremble as you hold them, and the voices heave with exhaustion as they tell you things like:

"Ain't walked this far in twenty-five years, still got ten more miles to go. I'm going to pick up some groceries now and carry them home, because I don't think there's going to be anything left in all of Brooklyn by the time I get there."

It's an intimate interaction: you and this stranger whose face you will never see walking hand in hand to the canned vegetable aisle, and ultimately it's the sort of moment that this blackout will be remembered for, for that night the city does not erupt into lawlessness. On the contrary, it breaks out in rooftop parties, impromptu midnight parades, civilians taking on the role of traffic cops, and other abnormal acts of neighborliness. At the store, we empty our shelves and refrigerators by ten o'clock, then drive back to Staten Island, where the lights blink on at three A.M.

The next day (and for years afterward) I refuse to believe that I really saw what I saw between Dwayne and the police officer, but one day I ask him and with a laugh he confirms it was real. "Hell yeah," he says. "Hell yeah."

✳   ✳   ✳

THE GOOD DWAYNE—a courageous, loyal and street-smart watch-keeper—is almost always followed by an appearance of the scary Dwayne, however.

On another hot night around the time of the blackout, a man walks into the store while Dwayne and I are on duty and starts taking off his clothes. It's always sort of surprising how popular the practice of shedding one's garments in convenience stores is. This is our second naked customer of the evening. However, unlike the previous one, this person is ripped with eerily twitching muscles, has a look on his face that suggests he just finished chewing on a high-voltage wire, and refuses to get dressed or leave until we provide him with a bottle of Heineken.

"Friend, you better get out of here before you get in trouble you can't get out of," Dwayne growls. To which the man only laughs in response—a ghoulish, soul-chilling cackle. Then he lifts up a dirty bandage wrapped around his shoulder and shows off a gaping, blood-encrusted bullet hole above his heart that could not be more than a few hours old.

"My friend, can't you see?" he says with some kind of Slavic accent. "I come from trouble."

At which point Dwayne bolts for the stockroom, where he keeps the mysteriously heavy backpack.

"Please leave," I beg the naked man while he's gone. "Just get out of here."

"I want beer," the man states firmly, holding his ground.

A few seconds later Dwayne returns holding not a gun but an aluminum bat known around the store as "the Thunder Rod." He's about to take a swing when I jump in front of him.

"Wait!"

Dwayne looks at me as if I'm crazy.

"It's not worth it," I say. If they start fighting, I reason, the best that can happen is that Dwayne somehow subdues the naked man, but even if he does we're likely to end up with a crime scene, a bloody mess, ambulance chasers and one big hassle. Better just to give the naked man what he wants.

"Listen," I say, turning to him. "If I let you have one beer, will you promise to leave?"

He nods solemnly, looking almost sane. So I start toward the beer refrigerator in the back of the store, until I get to Dwayne.

"You can't," he growls, blocking the way. "That's not how it's done." The Thunder Rod is still over his shoulder, but now Dwayne's stance is rotated in a different direction: toward me.

"Come on, Dwayne! Give me a break." He just stands there, though, clogging the canned goods aisle and glaring at me. Finally, after five or so excruciating seconds, he inches aside ever so slightly.

I dash to the beer refrigerator and remove the first bottle I see, then pass it to the naked man. "Now leave," I say. "You promised."

However, he just stands there in his nakedness and looks at his beer. In my haste to avert a bloodbath I had given him a Rolling Rock, I realize. "I asked for Heineken," he says.

"LEAVE!" I shout, grabbing the Thunder Rod from Dwayne. "GET OUT AND NEVER COME BACK, YOU CRAZY BAS-TARD!" I chase him out of the store and stand there on the side-walk, trembling, until he's disappeared.

When I come back, Dwayne is still seething, and for the rest of the night we don't speak, pretending to ignore each other while I try to forget that image of him standing in the aisle with the Thun-der Rod cocked toward my head.

DO WE HAVE to fire Dwayne? It's a question we've been asking since the day we bought the store. Kay and Gab have their own objections to his conduct. Personally, here I am trying in various ways to upgrade the image of the store, and there he is (despite admonitions to behave otherwise) commenting graphically on the appearance of female customers, or yelling at people for calling the store a "bodega" ("This ain't no Puerto Rican store, amigo. Go down to the projects to get your *arroz con perro*.") or screaming at his daughters over the telephone, promising to practically toss them out the window when he comes home. There are the X-rated phone conversations with his numerous girlfriends ("We gonna do it tonight? 'Cause I ain't puttin my ass on the train to Far Rockaway if you ain't puttin' . . .") broadcast to crowds of mortified customers as he casually spreads mayonnaise on a hero.

But we can't fire him, for a very simple reason: the neighborhood would go nuts, which Dwayne understands as well as anyone. This is why sometimes I wonder if we own the store or the store owns us. After Salim left, the neighborhood saw Dwayne as the one and only legitimate thing about the store, not only because he had stood behind that cold-cut counter for seventeen years, but because he embraced the role of neighborhood advocate, whether it was on behalf of the kids coming out of jail, Alonzo the street plumber, Mr. Chow or the lottery customers. He's beloved for being an old standby during a time of change, and also because of his own personal story of redemption, which apparently the entire neighborhood knows. Everyone is aware that Dwayne has struggled with addiction and violence, that he had two children at a young age by different women—none of which makes him so out of the ordinary here. What is exceptional is how hard he has fought to crush his demons and buck the stereotype of young urban deadbeat dads. Everyone knows that Dwayne waged a long and ultimately successful battle for full custody over his seventeen-year-old daughter Keisha, whom he's been raising on his own now for seven years. The store was integral to that turnaround. It is his anchor, and from his pulpit behind the glazed honey ham he preaches the gospel of self-sufficiency, involved parenting and honest work.

As with all preachers, though, you can often see vanity coming into play; Dwayne *needs* that pulpit. Yet you can also see that he doesn't rest on whatever laurels he earned as a thug. He doesn't portray himself as someone who *used* to be hard. On the contrary, he takes pains (especially for the benefit of the male members of his audience) to establish that he is *still* whoever he used to be, maybe more so. Thus the cringe-inducing treatment of women, the frightening displays of rage and, well, the gun.

In a store as small as ours, you don't really have the luxury of keeping someone at arm's length. Can you share the space and share lives without becoming co-opted one way or the other? And what does Dwayne want from us anyway?

One night Dwayne asks if I can do him a favor: he wants me to drive him somewhere after work. Since Dwayne never asks for favors, not only do I say yes, I don't even ask where he's going. The question occurs to me only after we get in the car and start driving.

"Bed-Stuy," he mumbles, pointing vaguely toward the heart of Brooklyn.

Bedford-Stuyvesant: one of the biggest, poorest and scariest neighborhoods in Brooklyn. Kay would not be pleased. We have a rule about coming straight home with the proceeds of a shift, and right now I've got two thousand dollars in a paper bag wedged under my seat.

"Any place in particular?" I continue, trying to sound relaxed.

"Just drive," Dwayne says coldly. His mood has changed since we got in the car. Usually I can't get Dwayne to shut up, but now all of a sudden he won't talk. He just sits there in the passenger seat and fidgets with his phone.

At first the landscape we pass through is familiar, and I pretend we're on an ordinary supply run to pick up diapers or cigarettes. When you work with someone like Dwayne every day, it's easier than you would think to pretend, and forget that he or she may be a violent sociopath—until you get in a situation where you feel utterly exposed and vulnerable.

Now the question *What does Dwayne want from us?* comes back to me. Because until recently I thought I was starting to get an idea what it was. Trite as it sounds, he wanted the store to be about more than just work. He wanted that connection with the neighborhood, that loyalty and sense of purpose—and from us he wanted the same thing.

"I want you to come to the Founders Day picnic," he had said to me in the spring, then asked and asked again. Before that it was "Let's go down to Baltimore and eat some rock crab this weekend" and "How about we go to Pennsylvania and hit one of them Dutch kitchens?" Maine for lobsters, Chinatown for the late-night all-you-can-eat buffet, even his annual Mother's Day party.

Somehow I managed to turn them all down.

In part this was because as I saw it, Dwayne and I didn't need to go on any extracurricular bonding expeditions. We were already doing the equivalent of a cross-country road trip every week. Dwayne's efforts at bonding cross some sort of invisible line. He just wants the job to be about more than work, and all I can think of is, *Hasn't anyone told him that it's a just shitty service job paying $10.50 an hour?* He should be pushing for health insurance, not to have me come taste his barbecued chicken.

Gradually, as the rejections have piled up, his sociability has cooled. Dwayne has also been having a difficult summer within that sliver of his life that falls outside the deli. His rent recently went up, and he's juggling more girlfriends than ever, it seems, while coping with the material demands of two teenage daughters who happen to be on summer vacation. At least the turmoil at the store is over, the possibility of it closing or being sold, which threatened to turn his life upside down as much as it did ours. But I wonder if Dwayne senses that his days at the store are numbered—after all, the neighborhood might throw a fit if Dwayne ever got fired, but what if it didn't matter? The neighborhood isn't what it used to be. Given how rapidly things change and people move in and out, it's arguably not even a neighborhood anymore.

Maybe he's plotting to get some of his blood and sweat back, I think as we drive deeper and deeper into Brooklyn. Earlier in the evening Dwayne's friend Monty the low-level drug dealer had come in the store, and he and Dwayne had an argument out on the sidewalk—about what I'm not sure. Dwayne's been hanging out with a more Monty-like crowd recently and quelling whatever tension he's feeling with multiple six-packs of Heineken consumed over by the projects in the early morning hours after work. When we first got the store, Dwayne told me he avoided the projects. Could the old Dwayne be making a comeback, I wonder? Could he be drifting back toward his thuggish old self? And what does that have to do with this crazy joyride we're on?

"Dwayne, how long is this trip going to take?" I shout at him. We're now so far into Brooklyn I don't know what neighborhood we're in, or if we're even in the borough anymore. We keep passing dark, windowless buildings, weed-filled lots and derelict storefront churches with patently inappropriate names like Bright Horizons and New Beginnings.

He still won't answer, and internally I'm starting to freak out. What could possibly be out this way, and why won't Dwayne tell me what it is? I wish I had called home and told someone in Gab's family what we're doing. Actually, I wish I'd just said no to his request. And I wish he wasn't inside my head with all his loyalty-and-community-ties BS. I wish you could just coexist with Dwayne and not have to be continuously challenged by him—but of course none of that is possible. Dwayne changes the store just by being in it. And he changes us.

"TURN! TURN, I SAID!" he suddenly shouts, as if he's just woken up.

It's an awkward spot for a turn. Dwayne wants me to make a left, which would require cutting through three lanes of opposing traffic. What's more, since we're going fifty miles per hour, there's no time to slow down—we'll just have to go up to the next intersection and make a U-turn.

But Dwayne won't wait—he reaches across and grabs the steering wheel, guiding us right into the oncoming headlights.

BA-BRUMP!

The car makes a horrible metallic scrape as it rides up over the sidewalk. Whatever Dwayne was heading for, we missed it, and probably flattened one of our tires as a result. But we missed the cars heading toward us and somehow ended up in a parking lot. The question is where.

"Dwayne?"

Dwayne is laughing. "Who taught you to drive like that?"

"Dwayne, where are we?"

Dwayne, however, has already gotten out of the car and started walking away, leaving me to either follow him or hang out alone in a dark parking lot with two thousand dollars in a damp paper bag. I look around. We seem to be sitting directly beneath some kind of pulsing neon light, almost as if we'd arrived at a midnight carnival in the heart of Brooklyn.

Then I get it. He won. By kidnapping me, he'd finally gotten me to go on one of his trips.

"White Castle?!" I yell. "You dragged me all the way out here so you can get some food?"

But Dwayne's already inside making an order. For both of us.

I LOVE YOU, TOMORROW

THE FIRST TIME I WALKED BEHIND THE CHECKOUT COUNTER I felt a little buzz of excitement, and nine months later it has yet to wear off. Who'd have thought that being a checkout clerk would have such addictive properties? Maybe it's the Puritan upbringing and the absence since twelfth grade of any real psychotropic agents, other than the occasional Men's 4-Pac, that makes me susceptible. But that buzz is real, and for that reason most of the mistakes I make occur during shift changes.

Buzz. I just started the evening shift, and Kay and Gab are telling me at the same time what to do and what not to do when vendors stop by to collect bills tonight. Meanwhile, the lottery machine is chattering away and a dozen or so customers are milling about the store, having their own conversations, listening to ours or, in one case, sighing loudly in protest when a customer pays for her groceries with a stocking full of pennies. I can feel my brain being pulled in eight directions at once, its awareness reaching out like octopus tentacles to snatch bits of information from all corners of the store. Some organizational genius, some supreme cognitive database, is taking in all that information, processing it and making appropriate choices about how to respond, and I almost don't feel like it's me. After all, if I tried to do eight things at once, I couldn't. But somehow, since I'm not trying to, I am. I'm in the fabled "zone," a state of equipoise wherein I become my environment and my environment becomes me: *I am a convenience store.* I'm even dimly aware that *outside* the deli, where it's getting dark, a group of men and women have been loitering on the corner as if waiting for something to happen.

"Did you get all that?" asks Gab, standing there looking doubtful with her hands planted on her hips. "I said there are three envelopes inside the safe, one for the garbage people, one for the bagel man, one for . . ." I nod at her and smile: Gab knows that I'm just as fast as her at the register now, and no more likely to screw up. If she tells me something, I usually remember to do it. This almost seems to irk her—she's competitive, after all—and so now she's trying to throw me off by hitting me with an extra data stream.

Meanwhile, two men walk into the store at the same time, one old, one young. They proceed directly to the checkout line, the young one first. What I notice about the young one: he's clean-cut, taller than me (and I'm standing on a three-inch-high platform) and fidgety. What I notice about the older one is that he's faded, disheveled and kind of lumpy—maybe a bum who after buying himself a beer intends to stand outside and harass the customers?

". . . and don't forget to turn off lottery machine at ten o'clock," says Kay, "otherwise big problem happening. Okay? Come on, let's go." She and Gab leave the store for the night.

Less than a minute later, the young man arrives at the counter and asks for a pack of Newport Lights, "please." Now, regular smokers don't say "please." They say "PACKANEWPORTS!" and flick a crumpled tenner on the counter. Therefore, I will now verify that this person is of legal age to buy tobacco products in the city of New York, even though the law states only that I have to card people who *look* younger than twenty-five (as if no one ever looked seven years younger than they really are).

However, just then Old Lumpy starts coughing obstreperously. In fact, he sounds as if he's having some sort of asthma attack.

"Are you okay?" I ask.

He waves me off and seems to recover. I go back to the customer buying Newports, who's waving a twenty at me and standing half-way through the door. Customers are shuffling their feet again, rolling their eyes at the delay.

"Can I see your—" I begin.

Old Lumpy then starts barking and flapping his arms.

"Is there a problem?" I ask. Lately there have been a lot of prob-lem customers. I even had to call the police for the first time after a youngish fellow with annoying chin hair refused to stop scream-ing at me or leave the store because I made him show me ID for a pack of American Spirits. He said I was guilty of "age profiling" and threatened to expose me on his blog.

Again, Old Lumpy quiets down. But now the customers have rightly become annoyed, and one person has already put down their groceries and left. So I decide to take the younger man's money with-out carding him (it doesn't matter, I think, because if he's under eighteen, then so am I), and as he's walking through the door toward that knot of people I saw on the corner, I have one of those small moments of insight that usually get forgotten in the daily chaos of a store. It occurs to me that the back of the neck is a really revealing part of the body: something about the combination of posture and muscle tone tells you as much about a person as their face, if not more. And as I watch the exit of this particular fellow, who's wearing what I now recognize as the sort of overlarge blue oxford only a teenager would wear, I'm thinking, *Boy, he looks a lot younger from behind. I may have just dodged a bullet.*

The next thing I see is Old Lumpy's hand holding up a detective's badge. Almost immediately I get an out-of-body feeling, as if I'm watching this whole scene not through my own eyes but via a shaky handheld camera. And in my head a song begins to play—I can't quite identify it at first, though I know I've heard it a thousand times.

Bad boys, bad boys, whatcha gonna do? Whatcha gonna do when they come for you?

It's a sting, and we're busted.

"Didn't you see me signaling you?" Old Lumpy—Detective Lumpy, I should say—asks.

"Signal me? You mean with all that coughing and hand waving?"

"I was trying to tell you, 'Don't do it. Ask for ID. That boy's under eighteen.'"

"You distracted me, that's what you did." My world is deflating, collapsing, running out of oxygen. That omniscience I felt a minute ago is morphing into fishbowl-head, wherein I feel uncomfortably aware of peripheral phenomena I can't seem to focus on. It's the same sweaty, off-balance, my-arms-are-too-long, the-world-is-moving-too-fast dysphoria I experienced during my very first shifts—combined with anger: hot, pulsing fury.

Detective Lumpy shrugs and hands me a sheaf of papers that I have to sign either admitting guilt or requesting a hearing before a judge. I can't decide what to do, but as I'm flipping through I see a page with the vital statistics of the patsy, the customer who bought Newports. He's not eighteen, it's true. But he will be in four months.

"What, you couldn't find someone whose eighteenth birthday is tomorrow?" I snap. "How about the center on the local high school basketball team? Just give him a cane and a fake beard and some orthopedic shoes."

"What were you expecting?" Detective Lumpy snaps right back. "This is New York."

He's right: did I think they were going to send in Dorothy and Toto? Little Orphan Annie sucking a lollipop? Harry Potter?

"Besides," he adds, "I didn't need to do any of that. You were easy." He tosses me the sheaf of paper and leaves. Out on the sidewalk, I watch him take out a Newport from the pack I just sold the boy in the oxford. Against the cobalt blue light of Brooklyn at dusk, its orange ember makes a brilliant contrast.

FOR YEARS NEW York has had this ridiculous rule about not carding people unless they look college age or younger, but now I understand it. In a sense, everyone in New York is adept at visually processing strangers' faces in a matter of seconds. We do it in the subway, we do it on the sidewalk, we do it in bars and restaurants. What's the difference between those situations and the couple of seconds you have at the register to decide whether someone falls into that eighteen-to-twenty-five threshold?

One difference is that if you screw up while selling cigarettes, you can wreck your business and lose your livelihood. Because in keeping with its treasured image as the city that makes nice to no one, New York City metes out merciless punishment against businesses caught selling tobacco to minors: the first violation costs a thousand dollars or so, which for a deli owner can easily amount to a week's profits. The second, if incurred during a two-year probationary period, costs a few thousand more plus the loss of the tobacco license *and* potentially the lottery machine, which will wipe out most stores like ours.

Of course, nothing could be more honorable than preventing children from smoking. But if the goal is so important, why not simply force everyone who buys tobacco to show their ID, which would eliminate innocent mistakes?

Maybe because such a system would be *too* effective. Convenience store clerks will never card everyone unless they have to, because it slows down the checkout line and incites a surprising number of people to raise trouble (apparently because they resent being told they look young). However, since they don't want to make a deadly mistake, either, clerks come up with elaborate rules for who and who not to card, like *Has a walker. Talks about grandkids. Buys denture cream.* Now, call me cynical, but something tells me this is exactly what Big Tobacco would want, to have the convenience store clerks of America deciding who does and doesn't get access to tobacco. Such a system would be designed to fail at least part of the time, would it not? And who would benefit? The tobacco companies, for one, and the agencies giving out fines, for another, both of which get to make money from tobacco sales while looking rightfully concerned about teen smoking.

One late night after the sting, in a fit of conspiracy-minded pique, I do some heavy-duty Googling to see if my theory has merit. Unfortunately, I can't say that I find a smoking gun proving that Big Tobacco induced the government of New York City (or anywhere else with a similarly self-defeating law) to knowingly create flawed regulations. However, I can tell you that since at least the mid-1990s tobacco companies have been enmeshed in the crafting of legislation governing youth access to tobacco, and one of the things they've pushed hardest against is mandatory age verification. Not surprisingly, they want to appear as if they're deeply concerned about teen smoking, so they publicly support "retraining programs" to "educate" retailers on how to prevent underage sales. Rather creepily, in fact, Philip Morris and the tobacco companies actually administer "We Card," "It's the Law" and other programs that are part of the punishment for getting caught selling tobacco to minors in many states. Meanwhile, many retailers' associations actually support mandatory age verification, because the so-called retraining programs and the associated laws cause so many inadvertent mistakes.

"You're arrogant," the guy with the bad facial hair who wouldn't leave the store had shouted at me. "You're judging people based on how they look." And he was right: deciding whether to card someone is a kind of profiling. Unfortunately, I'm just not very good at it.

AROUND THIS TIME there's a change in New York City's official rules for street vendors, the people who sell things like hot dogs and roast nuts on the sidewalk (who presumably do it not because of a passion for the great outdoors but because they can't afford actual stores). Since we're not a street vendor, the change doesn't affect us, but it's worth mentioning because of what it says about the mentality of small business owners.

The change is an increase in the city's fines for violations such as not wearing paper hats, standing a few inches (literally) too far from or too close to the curb, and leaving carts unattended while making bathroom visits. Overnight, the fines go up from two hundred and fifty dollars to one thousand, and since most vendors receive an average of seven violations a year—often three or four at once—many are facing ruin. (The kind of sudden and capricious ruin that the cart vendors, many having fled despotically run Third World countries, know all too well.) No public hearings or debates in the city council have been held on this calamitous change for twelve thousand or so of the city's most economically challenged families. And the only way to fight the tickets is for the vendors to go to an obscure court called the Environmental Control Board, fill out forms and wait for hours while losing more money—this for people who epitomize the embattled yet scrappy New Yorker everyone claims to love. Some street vendors earn as little as thirty-five dollars a day.

Dread is the nature of small business. You're gnawed by fear that something is going to come out of nowhere and flatten you before you've even had a chance to shout, whether it's a blackout or a government inspector. The urge to seize control of your own destiny, even if it means doing your own precious business harm, can be difficult to resist.

"You cannot survive without tobacco, trust me," says Habib, one of our cigarette suppliers, when I go to pick up smokes a few days after the sting. "It will be the end of your business."

"Yes, but what are we going to do?" I reply somewhat desperately. We haven't decided yet if we're going to contest the violation or plead guilty. I ask Habib if he has any suggestions, and he shrugs. A leather-faced old man with an Abe Lincoln beard the color of a tangerine, he's standing inside a steel cage lined with probably a hundred thousand dollars' worth of tobacco—Mores, Vantages, Lucky Strikes, Virginia Slims. If you want to buy something you have to accompany him inside, where it's actually quite comfortable— you can sit on a couch, watch TV, and get yourself something cold to drink from the refrigerator. (No smoking, though—a little fire could turn Habib's cage into a tobacco-flavored human barbecue in about three seconds.)

"Why don't you transfer the business to a relative?" says another deli owner who's been standing there listening to our conversation. "Have the relative get new licenses for the tobacco and liquor, wait for the one-year probation to end, and then have the relative transfer the business back to you. Whenever people have trouble with the city that's what they do."

It's not a crazy idea. Of course, by law you're not allowed to sell a business for the purpose of evading punishment, but is the law ever enforced? According to Kay, until recently the city barely enforced any of its regulations governing the business of a convenience store, in contrast to now. And in a way, that approach benefited the city: being somewhat hands-off made it possible for immigrants from places where informal, off-the-books, underground economies were the norm to find their niche and replenish the city's entrepreneurial spirit generation after generation.

Instead, though, we decide to stop selling cigarettes altogether, voluntarily surrendering a hundred dollars a day in earnings, or about one-third of our daily profits. Maybe it's the small business person's pigheadedness that motivates this decision, the feeling that "I'd rather put myself out of business than let someone else do it." Or maybe it's forward thinking. After all, if we get caught again, which seems inevitable, given the tenacity with which the city is stalking us and its penchant for ruthlessness, we'll eventually lose the tobacco license anyway and have to make the same adjustment. This way we'll at least get to keep the lottery machine! (What a statement—being desperate to hold on to a device that drives everyone crazy and earns only three dollars an hour.)

Either way, suddenly everything is jeopardized. The summer is over. For the last few months, I realize, I've been looking forward to each day rather than counting off the hours. Every morning, the first thing I did was check the logbook in the kitchen where the profits from the previous day are written down. Tomorrow was our friend—not that the numbers were *so* stupendous; it wasn't like watching a portfolio of Google stock. It was just a sense that we as a family were doing our jobs and making good choices, and the future would turn out okay—all backed up by the apparent reality of numbers. Now it's over. We're headed back into survival mode, and I'm the reason we're there.

A RARE CAT

AT THE BEGINNING OF THE FALL GEORGE STORMS INTO THE office, directly after returning from a month-long vacation in the Hamptons, and with his suitcases still in the hallway and sand still stuck to his shoes, he summons the staff for an emergency meeting right there next to the luggage—no cocktails, no sandwiches, no merry round of storytelling to get things started.

"I've just finished reading the material you all gave me to consider for the next issue," he says, waving a pile of manuscripts, "and it is dreadful. In fact, it's the worst pile of submissions I have ever seen." Then he looks directly at me. "Ben, would you care to defend this?" He starts reading from one of the stories I gave him, a very solid piece from a reputable literary agent. The young female author had written a sort of McEwanesque horror story about a young woman being absorbed—consumed, really—by pregnancy and marriage into a libidinous and depraved upper-class family. George, reading it in the most lugubrious voice imaginable, gives it the sort of treatment no story could survive.

"You call that writing?" he sneers after a few paragraphs. "Tell me why. I want to know."

I falter, unable to respond, in part because I know that despite what he says, George does not really want to know. He's not interested in a debate. He wants to make a point, and he knows that if he fights dirty, none of us will do so back.

He continues reading, making more and more of a mockery of my selection.

"How could you call yourself an editor and fall for that?" he taunts. "Really, it's shameful."

Then, seemingly becoming aware of how vicious he's being, he steps back. "I don't mean to put you on the spot this way, but I just have this feeling that . . . things are not right here. We've gone astray, and we have to get back on track. Everything is on the line! We must do *something*. I want to shock you all into action."

Then he goes upstairs, and the staff confers.

What to do? To some of us, this isn't about the magazine per se or even just the fiction; it's about George showing us who's boss after being away for a while. Or it's his way of coping with the distress that his memoir is causing him, a display of bravado intended for himself as much as anyone. He just needed an audience.

That night I stay up late writing a defense of the story George rejected, a passionate appeal for reconsideration, which I've never attempted before. It will be the opening move, I've decided, of a larger campaign to talk with George about the magazine before it's too late.

SCARCELY A WEEK later, I get a phone call at Kay's house from the *Review* at an oddly early hour. I know everyone claims to experience this at such moments, but something really does tell me not to pick up the receiver, that bad news awaits at the other end of the line, and that if I don't answer the news will reverse itself or simply go away. But the phone rings and rings—someone seems to have turned off the Paks' answering machine—and eventually I have no choice but to pick up.

It's Brigid, who'd gone into the office early because she was fretting over some last-minute detail concerning the fall issue, which she and George had just sent to the printer. As she was coming down East Seventy-second Street she saw an ambulance pull to the curb and paramedics rush into George's townhouse, and when she stepped inside George's sister was already there, and she stoically reported that George had not woken up that morning. The rest of his family was upstairs. Soon afterward the paramedics came down and quietly went back to their vehicle, and people started going up to George's bedroom to say good-bye.

On the express train to Fifty-ninth Street I sit numbly, waiting for the flood of emotion. It doesn't come. I don't feel like I'm in denial—not after watching George's health decline over the last year and worrying about him as much as we all have. Yet it doesn't seem possible that George, of all people, is gone, and part of me truly believes that when I get to the office it will turn out to be one of his stunts, an elaborate hoax for some magazine piece he's writing.

Of course, the fantasy crumbles as soon as I walk into the office and see the faces of the staff, a moment that unleashes the flood I had been expecting. As I sit there at my desk, a basket case, I think of the last conversation I had with George, up in his kitchen, and wonder if he was in even worse shape than I realized. This fills me with regret for not doing a better job of helping him, and for probably making him worry about the *Review* a lot more than he needed to at the time. It's hard to feel too much gloom and despair upon the death of someone as essentially lighthearted as George, yet there really was a melancholy tinge to his being, and it was something I now knew he wished he could have expressed more openly. Most of all I just feel an implacable sadness at the idea of not seeing him anymore.

That morning, without George, no one in the office has any clue what to do except cry. Eventually we decide to call all of George's friends (a job that would literally take days were we to be even halfway successful) and tell them the news before it reaches them via some impersonal medium such as the Internet. They, in turn, of course want to know what the cause was (which in a day or so we'll know to have been a heart attack) and whether anything had happened to George, a trauma of some kind. However, as far as we can tell, George had had a normal evening, wandering the city and drifting from party to party. It was the way he lived, alone but out in the world, totally private and public at the same time. He must have had fun (didn't he always?) because he came home late, then died peacefully in his sleep, a fitting end for a life like his, except that I really think he would have preferred to fall into the polar bear's cage.

Over the next few weeks the shock wears off and is replaced by a period of collective self-examination. As if George's loss isn't a big enough tragedy, the *Review* has to answer all sorts of fundamental questions about its own existence and whether to go on without him and, if so, how. What did George mean to the *Review,* and can he be replaced? Is it enough to have his genes embedded in the institution, or does it require his touch, his instincts? Maybe the magazine died with him; maybe it died a long time ago. Essentially these are academic questions suited for a biographer or a symposium on little magazines, except that jobs are on the line, not to mention one of the great names in American letters.

George himself had long resisted thinking about the future, despite his exhortations to us, the staff, and his own occasional morbid tendencies. He didn't groom a successor, and every now and then he hinted that should he pass suddenly, he would like the *Review* to shut down. No one believed him, though, one reason being that he had recently assented, at the urging of his lawyer, to the creation of a board of trustees that would do exactly the opposite—namely, ensure that the *Review* survived in his absence. The board consists entirely of George's friends in the publishing industry, writers, editors and arts patrons who could be counted on to open doors and sign checks if needed, but who would otherwise stay out of George's way. They were not supposed to be involved this soon, but now with George gone they must decide how to move forward. And for those of us on the staff who've long been frustrated by George's quirks as a boss (which is to say, nearly everyone) their presence is a huge relief, because they of all people—outsiders from the real world—should grasp the need for *professionalization*. In fact, one board member tells us right away that the *Review* needs to "grow up."

The irony, of course, is that because of the deli, my appreciation for whatever you want to call George's approach—amateurism, dilettantism, Walter Mittyism—is much keener than it was a year ago. Now when I think of book fairs, the slush and having all these twenty-five-year-olds do jobs they're patently unqualified for, I see something positive and altogether rare: the ability to remain small, open and full of passion. But it's not an easy philosophy to articulate. You end up sounding like you're arguing against progress or success. And after years of wishing that George would let the magazine "grow up," I'm not about to hinder that process anyway. Not without solid, well-defined reasons and a coherent strategy.

In any case, there isn't time. As soon as George dies and the decision is reached to go on without him, there's a feeling that a statement must be made quickly. Literary magazines are so ephemeral that missing even one issue would, in the board's eyes, jeopardize its existence. Unfortunately, this rush forward distracts us from the personal struggle to come to terms with George's death. We spend so much time thinking about what he meant as a mentor and a boss that we don't really think about him as a friend and a human being.

But of course when someone is gone, you continually find yourself bombarded by little reminders of his or her presence. George had presence to burn—the shock of white hair, the old Boston face, the extra few inches in height. He had everything needed to draw attention. What I realize now that he is gone, however, is that George, like my father-in-law, was one of those people who entered a room so quietly you didn't even notice. All you'd hear was the soft groan of a door hinge and the padding of socked feet. Then the rustle of paper, a vigorous scratch of the belly. *Are you busy? Don't mind me. I would hate to . . . You are? Well, then, come upstairs and let's shoot a game of pool. Come on, put that book down.*

More than once in the weeks after his death I sit in the office and listen to his desk chair creaking over my head, the way it did when he was really struggling. And once I hear his voice coming from the next room, with that inimitable accent and all its trademark locutions. ("Phooey!" "Drat!" "I should say!" "What a rare cat!" "You've made me cross again.") It turns out to be his son, Taylor, paying a visit.

I'd noticed during the last year that George didn't just make work look easy, which of course many successful people do. Easy wouldn't have been enough. George had to make it look like he was having fun, which of course he often was—great, guilt-free fun that was possibly unearned. But now I know that George's fun-loving persona was part of his job, and that he really did work at it, as opposed to just reveling in it. After all, why make a career out of being "fun" if it was often an effort and wasn't, strictly speaking, financially necessary? Maybe you do it simply because you're used to doing it, or maybe you do it because you need to prove to yourself that you aren't just coasting with what you were given—that you're trying, and justifying, and improving, which wouldn't be that different from outrunning a vague form of guilt, would it not? Maybe George and I had more in common than I thought.

FEAR FACTOR

LIKE MANY CAREER-MINDED WOMEN, GAB HAS ALWAYS WOR-
ried about waiting too long to have children. Being the sort of
hyperorganized, goal-oriented person that she is, she even had a spe-
cific age as her deadline: thirty-two. Thirty-two was the year because
thirty-five was when the increased risk of birth defects kicks in,
and she wanted enough time to have at least two kids before then.

If only her husband would comply.

During the summer, after things settled down at the store, we
started trying to initiate "the plan" amid all the, uh, complications
that result from having a potential audience of family members in
close proximity. Knowing that one's in-laws are upstairs and capable

of barging in at any second can make one fatally fearful and hesitant; however, it also has the potential to inject an element of danger and excitement! After all, here we were, a married couple in our thirties, a period during which physical romance often loses its adventurous thrill, having to tiptoe around and be secretive. It was like being teenagers again, except that when you're young you're in the mood all the time, so you don't mind running out to the gardening shed on a moment's notice (as opposed to thinking, "Right now? But *Fear Factor* isn't over yet"). Also, when you're young you heal faster after falling with your pants around your ankles into a box of gardening tools.

So we spent the summer being adolescent and wishing our bodies would follow suit. However, our attempts at reproduction have failed, boosting Gab's impatience to a Kay-like level of intensity. Among other risks, she's been leaving Pottery Barn Kids catalogs and how-to-get-pregnant books all over the place, which is alerting Kay to our efforts.

"She go to doctor *again*?" Kay asked me the other day while Gab was at the ob-gyn. Part of me thinks that Gab wants Kay to find out, because when she does she will drag Gab to her herbalist in Flushing, who will give her praying mantis ovaries or some such concoction guaranteed to get results. This scares me, though, because what if instead of Gab she focuses on me, and makes me go on a diet of rhinoceros horn or wolverine testicles? Or what if she just decides this is the last straw? "American man, he can't do nothing, not even make beautiful wife pregnant!" (Donald Barthelme: "What an artist does, is fail.") Maybe she'll conclude that I'm not worth wolverine testicles.

Then one morning I pull myself out of bed and, as usual following a night shift, wake up with only half a brain. I'm dying for a cup of coffee, but as I drag myself into the kitchen I realize it won't be necessary, because before she left for Manhattan, Gab stuck a little present on the refrigerator door that provides all the jolt I need. No, it's not a sonogram showing that at long last she is with child; it's a note from her ob-gyn with the name of a male fertility clinic and some handy advice on masturbation, titled "PATIENT INSTRUCTIONS FOR COLLECTION OF SEMEN SAMPLES."

After ripping the note down and checking the house to see if Kay or anyone else has seen it (thankfully, I'm the only one at home), I call Gab at her office and demand to know what she was thinking.

"Well, we've just been having so much trouble," she says. "I thought it was time for you to get some help."

"Time for *me* to get some help? How do you know it's not *you*?"

"Don't worry," Gab says calmly. "I'm getting tested too. Fair is fair."

"Well, it doesn't seem fair to me that I have to have my 'struggles' broadcast to the whole family." ("Must-see TV tonight! Find out if Gab's husband is shooting blanks!")

"Oh, you know my parents. They don't read what's right in front of them."

"But the refrigerator door is where your mom puts all her vital information." This is true: everything from employees' telephone numbers to shift schedules and delivery receipts are posted on the refrigerator. And now, I'm afraid to say, so are guidelines on self-lubrication, plus tips on which particular lubricant to use (as if any male over the age of eleven needs to be told this. Who's coming in for male fertility testing anyway—second-graders?).

I hang up the phone and sit down in the living room of Kay's empty house. Maybe Gab is right—maybe I should get tested. Should I get it over with right now? I am still in my pajamas, after all, and there's no one here . . . *Oh, for Christ's sake!* I have to be at the *Review* for a meeting in a few hours, and it wouldn't be very "professional" of me, would it, to run late because I was doing *that*?

That's the sort of thing George would have understood. ("That's why you're late? Of course it's not a problem. I was doing the same thing!") But of course George is gone.

Part of me thinks that the problem is just my wife's impatience; six months is not actually that long for a couple in their thirties to have to wait for conception to take hold. But part of me can't help wondering, *Is it us?* Could we be somehow mismatched, like those couples you occasionally read about in which one spouse turns out to be allergic to the other? Could it be that on a spermatazoic level a battle of personalities is being waged, pitting my sensitive little overthinkers against Gab's overachieving go-getters? I've begun to worry that my squad of little Bens, with their tendency toward reflection and process-mindedness (*Who gets to ascend the fallopian tube first,* I can see them wondering, *and how does that "privilege the narrative" of the fallopian crossing?*), are getting distracted from their job. Can a terminally ambivalent and self-questioning personality turn one's own progeny into the equivalent of a Massachusetts politician's presidential campaign?

I'VE ALWAYS BEEN an involuntary mimic. I pick up not only people's accents but their hand gestures, their speech impediments and, eventually, since language determines our perception of the world, their whole outlook on life. In everyday situations this is problematic enough. However, given the random assortment of characters you meet at the checkout counter of a New York deli, working at the store sometimes makes me feel like Sybil, or at least as if I'm auditioning for a flash improv troupe. *Now be a French diplomat! Now an Albanian hit man! Now a garbage-truck driver from Bayonne!*

The key to involuntary mimicry is a feeling that your personality has become unmoored, that you're an actor in search of a part, that you have no core—which isn't an uncommon feeling in a deli late at night. Sometimes things slow down and hours pass without a single familiar face coming through the door. During these stretches you're in the same place you always are—behind the checkout counter, looking at the door—but there's a dreamlike quality to it all. Did a shriveled old woman in a camouflage tube top really just spend fifteen minutes talking in Spanish to our selection of cheese? And is there really such a concoction as "whipped-cream-flavored ice cream," which someone just asked me for? At these moments *anyone* could walk through the door—the president; Donna Ledbetter, my sixth-grade girlfriend; a man clip-clopping on goat legs—and I would not be surprised. I myself could be anyone; I could try on a new accent or give myself a completely different persona. Chemical enhancement of reality doesn't even begin to approximate the sense of *Why am I here? Where did I come from?* that I feel on some nights. And while I can fight the undertow pulling me into a vortex of trippiness, resistance usually just makes it worse. It's like *A Nightmare on Elm Street,* where the characters are always saying *Don't fall asleep! Don't fall asleep! Don't* . . . and then a burn victim missing his face walks into the store, taps the counter with his claw—I mean car key—and calmly asks for a bran muffin.

Of course, for some people the identity crisis at the root of an unmoored personality is a bit more fundamental. Immigrants, for example, have to navigate between the increasingly distant and mysterious world they come from and the just-as-confusing place they come to inhabit. In my case, where I come from isn't exactly a mystery. Going back centuries I can find out almost anything about my ancestors—where they lived, how many children they had and, most important of all, where they went to college. And these people had a definite *identity.* They were, if not entirely uniform as a group, far more like one another than not. For starters, their ancestors came from England (East Anglia, for the most part) and made the voyage to America as families, rather than as individuals. That's important, because the settlers of New England were almost disgustingly pro-family, to the extent that they actually outlawed single people and forced them to move in with other families if they couldn't form their own. They were also middle-class—tradesmen, artisans, ministers—and superbly educated. But the most important thing they shared was similar worldviews, like that stubborn loyalty to the past and a certainty that old ways were better than new ones. One of the more eye-opening facts about the descendants of the Pilgrims is that after going to all that trouble to get away from the Church of England—you know, prison, exile and crossing the ocean in a leaky ship—many of them converted *back* to it within just a few generations. Some of my relatives even fought on the English side in the Revolution. The point is, despite their newfound freedom to be anything they wanted in the New World, despite the atomizing tendencies of democracy and despite having almost half a millennium in which to change, my family didn't. Puritan culture remained strong, even after the Puritans themselves vanished.

So how could someone like me possibly have an identity crisis? How could someone so anchored to history feel unmoored, especially after growing up in *Boston*?

At least to some extent, Boston *was* the problem. Ethnically, Boston is many things—Irish, Jewish, black, even Armenian. But what it is above all is Puritan. Puritan values ooze from the city's institutions, its way of life, its customs. No city in America "looks back" with as much ardor as the city with a historical plaque commemorating something on every corner. No city sees itself as constituting "the elect" the way the Puritans did, unless there's another outlying, midsized city in America I'm unaware of that calls itself "the Hub of the Universe." No city is as consumed by education, and very few have the same overall climate of harsh sobriety. Growing up in Boston means that you see things like a hostility to fashion, an aversion to self-promotion and the name Caleb as, well, normal. In order to realize how peculiar such things actually are, it's better to be displaced, and the more violently the better.

In that sense, the experience I've had over the last two years has been a lucky one. First came the disassembly of self, the softening up of an already tenuous psyche. Then came exposure to values—potent ones—that were the opposite of those I grew up with, from the way immigrants tend to look forward and care more about results than process, to the way small business isolates you from the rest of the world, as opposed to being embedded in all that family and history. What I've been experiencing, in other words, is not just displacement but a clash of fundamentally conflicting outlooks, that of the immigrant entrepreneur and that of the Puritan: someone moving up and anxious to move up even faster versus the chaperones, the people trying to put the brakes on God's country of the future.

Which is all a roundabout way of saying that I've gained some perspective, I suppose. And perspective is an important thing; it may even be *the* thing. But some conflicts can't simply be left at a standoff. Some values, if taken seriously, can't be reconciled with other values—not in the same body. You have to make a choice. One side has to win, doesn't it?

IN NOVEMBER, GAB and I travel to Denver for a friend's wedding—our first real trip together since the deli opened. And our first night in a hotel. I'm as happy to be in a room drenched in disinfectant and featuring a highway beneath our window as I was as a child. But the best part is that Gab's fertility cycle, which she's graphed onto her weekly planner with minute-by-minute precision, is due to hit its peak the day after the wedding ends. So I've delayed our trip home by twenty-four hours and secured a rental car for the purpose of making a romantic getaway to the Rocky Mountain resort town of Steamboat Springs.

In a way, just being in Colorado might help along our efforts. I spent a few years of my life here, and this is my territory, so to speak. The land is sensual and rugged, and this journey up the mountains feels like a chance to conquer this whole issue of overthinkers versus overachievers. There's something virile about it, a hint of danger and recklessness, or more than a hint if you consider that snow season has just started and some of the notoriously avalanche-prone mountain passes leading to places like Steamboat will soon have to be closed, if they haven't been already. As we drive up into the clouds and the first of several snowstorms, I feel like I could catch a few wolverines on my own, while Gab looks smaller and smaller, hunching nervously in the passenger seat. *This is even better than I planned*, I think.

We arrive at our hotel with six hours to kill until the Magic Moment. Since ski season has yet to start, Steamboat is devoid of interesting activities other than afternoon drinking at one of the many local bars offering green-chile enchiladas and endless reruns of Jimmy Buffett's greatest hits. So on the advice of the concierge, we end up making a mad dash before sunset for some irresistible-sounding natural hot springs half an hour outside town.

And that's where the trouble starts. The hot springs are located at the end of a county road that would have been eminently drivable if snow hadn't once again started to fall—heavy snow, with flakes so big they seem to have their own gravitational orbits. And now the sun is disappearing behind the steeply bowled wall of the Yampa Valley. At around six o'clock, in conditions that could be described as either whiteout or blackout, we arrive at the hot springs' drive-way, a series of muddy, unpaved switchbacks proceeding more or less straight up a steep ridge.

"Do you see that sign?" Gab says, pointing to a sharply worded warning to *not* attempt to reach the hot springs under *any* conditions without four-wheel drive, which our rental does not have. She also points out that the car's insurance will be invalidated the moment our tires leave the pavement.

"I don't like this," she says. "We should go back."

She's right. After checking my cell phone, I see that we're out of range. And there hasn't been another car or house along the county road for miles. We could walk the rest of the way, but even if we could get to the top of the switchbacks in our sneakers and light coats, the springs could be closed. All in all, it seems like an extremely bad idea to proceed.

However, when you're trying to psych yourself up to consum-mate an act of passion, to *create life,* after flying across the country and driving up into a black and stormy sky, what choice do you have?

So we start traversing up the switchbacks, and as we do I wonder if I've already made that other choice between the values of the immigrant entrepreneur and those of the Puritan. I'm tired of thinking, and thinking about thinking, and being "hung up on the eternal," as one of my coworkers at the *Paris Review* recently called this ultimately self-defeating point of view. Inwardness can be a good thing, until it becomes involuted and can't turn itself around. The Puritans were inward, but they were also exemplary when it came to engaging with the world.

And then we're at the top, having traversed our way to the sum-mit of Mount Switchback, Destroyer of Rental Cars. (Ours is no longer white, but it is still running, thankfully.) Below us, on the other side of the ridge, lie the hot springs, roiling and steaming in all their bubbly glory. (They're open, though we're the only ones here.) We clamber down as quickly as we can and immerse ourselves, soaking for a good hour, which feels even better than I imagined. I'm no New Ager, but if you'd told me that all the stress we've experienced over the last year, from buying the store to the cigarette drama and now the pregnancy issue, had turned into solid masses that lodged themselves painfully inside my joints and now are melting away, dissolved by the 104-degree heat, I'd have believed it. Because that's how good it feels, and heck, in 104-degree heat I'd believe anything. After all, what part of the body does not love being wrapped up in 104-degree heat?

As it turns out, Little Bens do not. There's little need to worry about Little Bens overthinking or being ambivalent after they've been subjected to 104 degrees—they're cooked. Boiled alive. Or so flaccid with heat exhaustion that they can barely wiggle their tails. (The management should really put up a sign warning people about this. It could even be fun, an enticement, particularly at a hot spring. "Hot springs are an excellent way to reduce your chances of an unwanted pregnancy, especially for you men who can't seem to get the job done anyway.")

At the time, though, we don't know this, and we won't until Gab gets back to New York and reads it in one of her pregnancy books. Which is good because in Steamboat Springs we were able to enjoy ourselves for once without hiding it, like the grown-ups we used to be and someday will be again.

ON THE FLIGHT home from Colorado I'm looking out the airplane window at the great checkerboard of farms across mid-America when suddenly I realize I'm seeing a different checkerboard—the one in our deli formed by all the dishwater-colored tiles spreading out before the cash register. It occurs to me then how much I'm looking forward to getting home. Our three-day trip has taken me and Gab away from the deli for longer than we've ever been, and during that time I've been thinking about it more or less constantly. I even made Gab call her mom twice a day to find out how much the shifts had made. Gab also misses the store, but she's too busy thinking about babies to let it distract her. For me it's the set of pleasures I most look forward to—for instance, the satisfaction of beholding well-stocked shelves after the deliveries have come. Or the anticipatory buzz of a busy weekend starting as soon as I wake up on a Friday morning. Best of all is when the store gets so overloaded with customers that extra people are needed behind the counter and everyone is communicating telepathically, a human assembly line with seamlessly interacting parts, and the customers are happy and the whole store hums with energy. During times like those it feels like you're thinking not with your head and not even with your hands but with someone else's hands—Gab's, Kay's or whoever's—and you almost get the sensation of being one big organism behind the counter. It's glorious and mindless and probably weird, but most of all it's collective and communal.

Unfortunately, our experiment in running a tobaccoless convenience store is not going well. It isn't just the loss of revenue, devastating as that is, or the defection of customers who used to buy cigarettes *and* beer, groceries or the newspaper. It's the message it sends, the tone it sets, the seemingly high-handed attitude it broadcasts. Even some nonsmokers are offended by the idea of a convenience store that doesn't sell tobacco. And there's no use explaining when you've had, as we have, customers actually throw things at us in anger or drop their groceries and walk out. Smokers and their ilk feel persecuted enough in this city—they've had so many changes imposed on them in the last few years. "And now I have to feel judged here too?" as one customer put it. "Screw you."

What makes this even more tragic is that over the summer the store had finally found its way, acquiring a form that suited the neighborhood. It had a kind of double or triple life, but so, after all, does the quintessential New Yorker, with a day job as a waiter and a night job as an actor, or an economic existence here and a family somewhere else. Our store had all these different and painfully particular customers, yet somehow we had found a way to reconcile all their various needs. And it was a beautiful thing. Someone once told me that small business is "is putting your faith in the world. Your risk your reputation, your family, your future, and essentially trust that you'll be rewarded." For a while in the summer of 2003, that's how it felt.

COSTA RICA

ONE MORNING A FEW DAYS AFTER WE GET BACK FROM DENVER, Gab and I are sleeping in after a late shift when Edward comes down to the basement, which he rarely does when we're home. Something he says to Gab in Korean causes her to bolt out of bed.

I sit upright, wondering what the fuss is about. Did we over-sleep? Did something happen at the store? If so, why did Edward summon Gab instead of Kay, as he normally would? Maybe Kay had a bad night again; lately she's been anxious about the cigarette problem and unable to sleep, and then the next day she passes out while sitting at the table or counting money on the kitchen floor. She's in a state of nervous exhaustion, and her mind isn't working right—she's been making very un-Kay-like mistakes with money and scheduling, forgetting things she of all people never forgets. The other day while cooking she almost lit herself on fire, and apparently this wasn't the only kitchen accident she's had recently, because her hands are covered with burns. Of course, the more strung out she gets, the more she smokes, and as a result she's also chronically sick. So when I hear her in the living room coughing after Gab has run upstairs, I'm again pondering what we can do to make Kay take better care of herself.

Then, a few seconds later, a new level of urgency: I hear Gab pleading with her mother to "open your eyes, just say something," so I run upstairs, where I find Kay on the floor, sitting but slumped over, as if she's performing a yoga move that involved pressing her forehead to her knees. Gab is sitting next to her, plainly distressed, and Edward is pacing nearby, looking even more worried.

"What happened?" I ask.

"I don't know," says Gab. "My father says she took some cold medicine for her cough, and now she can't wake up. Oma?" She shakes Kay's shoulder, and nearly knocks her over.

"I'm . . . fine," Kay finally mutters, in English, which is a good sign because it shows she's hearing us talk. She's slurring, though, and her voice has none of its usual force.

Gab rolls her over and puts a pillow under her head. Squinting at the dimness of an overcast morning, Kay looks to be in searing pain.

"I think we should call an ambulance," I say.

Gab and Edward look at each other. No one in Gab's family likes doctors or hospitals, and they always wait till the absolute last second to seek medical help.

"No ambulance," Kay gasps. "Too expensive." Which is such a Kay thing to say that for a second I think, *Okay, this isn't such a big deal. Everyone's going to be fine.*

I convince Edward to let me take her to a hospital five minutes away, though, and as Gab and I are driving her there, her condition starts to deteriorate.

"I can't tell if she's breathing," Gab says, holding her mother's head in her lap in the backseat. "I don't like this. Why is she losing color?" We race to the emergency room, and at the entrance to the ER I convince a nurse with a stretcher to help us get her out of the car.

"What happened?" he asks us.

I helplessly confess that I don't know. The nurse then checks Kay's vital signs and, apparently startled by what he sees, whisks her away from us, plunging her into the depths of the hospital, which Gab and I have always regarded with trepidation because newspaper reports say it is broke and many of its buildings seem to have been abandoned.

Hours pass. We sit in the emergency room watching as a car accident victim hobbles in, followed by an old woman writhing in the agony of an apparent stroke. I think then about something that happened to Kay not long ago as she was coming home from the night shift. After leaving the store she drove down Atlantic Avenue to the Brooklyn-Queens Expressway, where the entrance ramp is little more than a stop sign and you have to merge with traffic going sixty miles per hour. Accidentally, Kay cut off a livery cab driver in a town car, and instead of honking at her once or flashing his headlights, he kept his hand on the horn for what seemed like forever, then chased her to the elevated portion of the Gowanus Expressway, where he cut in front of her and slammed on the brakes. Kay wouldn't get out of her lane (of course), and as a result found herself trapped inside a maelstrom of honking, rushing traffic at the mercy of a psychopath, sure that she was going to die. Yet she couldn't help noticing how peaceful it was up on the Gowanus, six stories over Brooklyn, looking down at rooftops of enormous nearby buildings like Jetro, while the Statue of Liberty and Wall Street winked at her on the horizon. She waited for the town car driver to come back and smash her window, but instead he stayed in his car, as if he too were paralyzed by the beauty of the setting. Then with a harrumph his car roared off, lurching in and out of his lane as he sped toward southern Brooklyn. Kay's heart rate returned to normal, and she somehow managed to steer herself back to Staten Island. This had happened last summer, and since then she had been living in fear that she might see the livery cab driver again, either on the road or at the store, but she didn't tell us because she was afraid that we would criticize her or try to stop her from going home by herself.

After hearing about the incident I felt shaken. What other secrets does my mother-in-law keep? I wondered. Particularly, what else about her own suffering has she not been telling us? Given that before we bought the store her health was not the greatest, it can be hard to judge the store's overall impact—her body went from broken to more broken. "Before we make opening at store, I be okay. Now whole body not work," she would claim. But "okay" to her meant those thunderous physical breakdowns, which were often the result of cleaning the house too hard (Kay's method of cleaning leaves the house looking like it got jostled by an earthquake, pictures askew, appliances nonfunctional, mop handles snapped in half) or cooking marathons (five hundred handmade dumplings in thirty-six hours, say) or something more mysterious and implacable, like suddenly growing old after a life spent pushing yourself twice as hard as everyone else.

And then, of course, the other possibility was that Kay was not being secretive at all, but that we chose not to see how much damage the store was inflicting.

"Are you relatives of Kay Pak?" a nurse finally comes over to ask us. It's evening, and we've been at the hospital for the entire day and still don't know what happened to Kay or what her condition is. Gab is a wreck. "You can come in now."

In a busy hallway, a kindly male doctor who seems to be either Pakistani or Indian sits down with us. He says—jolt number one— that Kay had a heart attack and is lucky that we insisted on taking her to the hospital. "Heart attack?" Gab and I sputter, barely able to mouth the words. "But . . . she didn't say her chest hurt . . . and she's only fifty-five . . . she's never had heart trouble before." With seasoned patience, the doctor waits for us to adjust to the new reality before administering jolt number two, which is that as far as he can tell, this wasn't her first heart attack—she's had one or two before, possibly a few years back.

"Your mother is strong," he says, smiling a little, as if without knowing Kay he can tell exactly what kind of person she is, "but the way she's living, no one can survive for long." He says the tests they've taken so far indicate flashing red lights across the board, from dangerously high blood pressure to emergency sugar levels. "She needs to eat better," he continues, and she needs to start exercising and stop smoking.

"What about work?" Gab says.

"What kind of work does your mother do?" the doctor asks. Gab tells him about the deli.

"She needs to stop immediately," the doctor says. "That kind of stress is the worst thing for someone with her risk factors. I suggest six months of continuous rest, and then she can go back to work gradually, but in a different kind of job."

Gab and I nod solemnly, stunned by the news and frightened of what it all means, but relieved that we've found out in time.

Jolt number three has yet to be delivered, though, and it comes when we ask the doctor if we can talk to Kay and tell her how lucky she is.

"She's in a coma," the doctor says. "We had to put her there so she can recuperate, and I think probably she will come out of it soon, but I can't be sure."

A coma? I think. *Of course: the one way to get my mother-in-law to settle down and stop doing things.* I'm sure if she were awake she'd be ripping the tubes out of her arms and trying to get out of bed, demanding that Gab fetch her a Parliament, which she'd try to get away with smoking in the hospital bathroom. And then she'd run to the store, yelling at us for abandoning it on a Saturday, of all days. (Emo and Dwayne have actually been holding down the fort just fine since this morning.)

"Well, can we see her?" Gab asks. "Just for a second?"

After making us promise not to disturb her, the doctor assents and takes us to the most dismal of all possible hospital rooms, an underlit windowless space with stains on the wall and disused machinery stacked in the corners. As much as I like the doctor, I have the urge to yank Kay out of here and put her in some swanky Manhattan hospital, whatever the cost. But then the nurse pulls back a curtain, revealing Kay's spent-looking body, and I realize that with all the machines she's hooked up to a move would be impossible. She's been stripped, gurneyed and intubated, and her life force is so deeply buried in the coma that all her facial muscles have gone slack, to the point where she's become unrecognizable. *It's not her!* I feel like saying. *She's somewhere else in the hospital, somewhere the situation is less dire. We should find her and see if she's okay!*

But then I see draped over a vinyl chair what I know to be Kay's signature article of clothing: that sleeveless orange shirt that shows off her arms and touts a place she's never been to, and I have to leave the room so as not to disturb her while my emotions get the best of me.

✳   ✳   ✳

THREE DAYS LATER Kay wakes up, and after the doctors have checked her out and she's eaten, the family stages a kind of intervention while she's still stuck in bed, informing her that for the sake of her health, we have to sell the store. Lying there somewhat stunned, my mother-in-law has an expression on her face that I've never seen on her before: she looks helpless and resigned. She doesn't rip the tubes out of her arms and walk away. She doesn't pshaw everyone and say, "Please. I make my own decisions." She just sits there and listens without resisting. *Finally,* I can't help thinking. Ganging up on her doesn't feel good, but with a woman as strong as Kay, what choice do you have? And since we are helping her, whether she sees it that way or not, it is important to be strong ourselves. After we explain why she's here in the hospital (she herself can't remember anything from the day she came in), I think she does understand how close to killing herself she has been. That look of acquiescence would seem to indicate a recognition that it's time to let go, though later it occurs to me that, knowing Kay, it could just as easily be shame at not being stronger, shame at not being able to work and dread of the physical pain that idleness will cause.

Nonetheless, she agrees to come home and rest, and for a few days we take turns watching her to make sure she doesn't slip outside for a cigarette or try to clean the house. It feels ridiculous to be babysitting a grown-up that way, especially someone as independent and vital as Kay. I don't like it and I hope I never have to do it again. What something like that does to your own dignity makes you question whether it's worth the cost. However, partly as a result of her confinement, Kay's strength, if not her health, returns quickly, and soon she is begging to be let outside. It starts with a few errands—picking up her own medicine at the pharmacy, for instance—and soon she is ready to visit the store. As her jailer on that day when she first goes back, I make her swear that after dropping off some money she will come home immediately. "Oh, I promise," says Kay, crossing her heart dramatically. The next time I see her it's nine hours later, at the end of the night shift. The following day she slips out once more, and after that it is right back to the old schedule, and so much for our plans to close the store.

D.I.Y.

EVERYONE WAS AFRAID THAT THE *PARIS REVIEW* WOULD FOLD without George, but once the collective concern for the magazine became clear, folding was no longer the issue. The issue was who would run the place. The board wanted to bring in someone from outside right away and already had several candidates in mind, as we learned from the newspapers. At first it looked as if the long-time editors wouldn't even get one issue to prove we were up to the job. However, with some clever convincing from the staff, the board members realized they had to at least give us a try if they expected anyone to stick around and help them keep the magazine going. The search was thus suspended while the board "reassessed." No one thought they were seriously thinking about letting us run the place, but maybe, we thought, if we do a good enough job, they'll have no choice.

Thus there's been a change in atmosphere: with something like a year to prove ourselves, we've dropped the slacker routine. No more wandering into the office late or missing deadlines. No more extended absences for the sake of skiing or finishing a novel. Painfully, about half the staff has voluntarily departed or been let go, resulting in hugely increased productivity from the remaining editors. All in all, it's considerably less "fun" now than George would have liked, but it's also a lot more efficient. Years of accumulated errors are being purged, and one of the results is that we've put out some of the strongest issues in a long time.

Yet we still don't have a circulation manager, a contracts specialist, or an IT professional. The office is still located in the Manhattan medialand equivalent of Nunavut, and we still let twenty-three-year-old nobodies edit Nobel laureates. There may be less pool playing and fewer business trips to the Playboy Mansion, but the office still feels like that of a college newspaper rather than arguably the most famous literary magazine in the world.

This is dangerous. As long as the *Review* clings to its amateur past, another fiasco is inevitable. And this time it's going to matter.

WE ALL HAVE new roles at the *Review* since George's death, and one of the responsibilities that has somehow ended up in my lap is overseeing the anthology series that the ten-thousand-dollar mistake came out of. Truly, it's the sort of thing that could only happen at the *Review*. Not only does the ten-thousand-dollar mistake strongly argue against giving me this particular job, but overseeing the anthology means coordinating an important nationwide reading series, and as someone who once had a calendar from the wrong year hanging over his desk for eight months and couldn't figure out why he kept missing appointments ("What do you mean my doctor's appointment was two days ago?"), I should be banned categorically from any sort of job that involves booking people's plane tickets or anything as logistically complicated as staging a public event.

The most stressful part of the job is dealing with the authors themselves. Some writers are nice, ordinary people you wouldn't mind living next to or allowing your daughter to date. Most, though, have the sort of large and colorful personalities you expect from artists. There are the flakes who, having devoted every cell in their brain to penetrating the unconscious, have forgotten how to do mundane tasks like getting themselves to a bookstore for a reading by seven P.M. And there are the social misfits who, as a result of cutting themselves off from the world outside their own head or spending too many years trying to climb through a blank computer screen, have a tendency to show up drunk, pick a fight with an audience member, make a pass at the person introducing them or not show up at all. In short, readings are scary, because you never know what's going to happen when you unleash writers on the public.

On that Thursday in late July I have an evening reading with Robert Pinsky and Jamaica Kincaid scheduled at the Harvard Book Store in Cambridge. I'm supposed to work at the deli in the morning, then jump into the car and drive up to Cambridge in the afternoon. However, Dwayne, who's never even a minute late for work, inexplicably fails to show up when his shift starts. Half an hour passes, then an hour. I call him, and no one answers. When I finally see him coming down Atlantic Avenue, his gait is unsteady and his face looks mangled and swollen, as if he's been in a brawl.

"What happened?" I say.

"Had a toothache," he says woozily. "But it's over. I got it out."

"You went to the dentist?"

"Hell no. I ain't gonna pay no hundred and fifty dollars."

"So who did it for you?"

"I did it myself."

"With what?"

"Pliers. Then I passed out. That's how come I'm late." He rubs his jaw with bloody hands.

Hearing this I almost pass out myself, but there's no time—I have to get on the road. I'm running at least an hour late, and by the time I get on the highway, the afternoon congestion has already started to build. It takes me an hour just to get out of New York City, and in Westchester there's highway construction, and in Connecticut there's a traffic jam that looks like it extends all the way to Hartford. This is terrible. I've always been bad at budgeting time, giving myself the smallest margin of error possible. And this time I'm going to pay for it by not showing up at a reading that I organized, where not only will the writers and the audience be unable to figure out what's going on, but at which several writers and editors from the *Boston Globe* whom I personally invited will be on hand to witness the "professionalism" of the new *Paris Review*.

Even worse, this is probably the most stressful reading in the whole series. Robert Pinsky is a man who seems to have made a terrible decision going into poetry, since he is handsome enough to have been a Hollywood leading man and has a voice that sounds either like God himself or a classic rock DJ. (He could have made a fortune intoning movie previews but instead chose to translate *The Inferno*.) As maybe the best-known poet in America, he will bring a crowd that I fear will overwhelm the bookstore.

And then there is Jamaica Kincaid. Kincaid is the sort of writer who unsettles people—me in particular—maybe because she once wrote about giving herself coffee enemas, or maybe because she famously quit a staff writer's job at the *New Yorker* because she thought Tina Brown, the magazine's outrageously successful editor, had sold its soul, or maybe because of the stories about her walking around Manhattan in a hospital gown and other outrageous garb. (Her best friend, the writer Ian Frazier, once wrote about the difficulties of getting a cab when accompanied by "a six-foot-tall black woman in pajamas.") Quite possibly it's because in the cozy little social world of writers and editors, she's a true outsider, a writer from a poor country (Antigua) who came to New York to be a nanny for an Upper East Side family and worked her way up from there. Maybe it's all of these things. In any case, the only thing I feel more strongly than delight in anticipation of her reading is sheer, abject terror, especially since I hassled her for months about doing the reading and never got a direct reply. She was supposed to be teaching a summer class at Harvard, but when I called her department no one seemed to know if she was in Cambridge or not, and when I tried her in Vermont, where she lives, no one answered the phone, and when I asked for her e-mail address, her department secretary said she didn't use e-mail, so finally I resorted to sending her requests via someone at the *Review* whose brother's Pilates instructor was married to someone who had once taken a creative writing class with her (or something like that), and eventually I got a response via this person's second cousin saying she would come, but as the hour approaches I am anything but confident.

As a result, driving through New England I'm too stressed to eat or listen to music—all I can do is stomp on the accelerator and lean as far forward as I can, as if by doing so I can will the car faster. The state of Connecticut is so tiny that normally I feel as if I can see across it, but today it feels as wide as Kansas. Every ten minutes or so I calculate what speed I need to maintain in order to make it to Cambridge on time (according to the latest computations, two hundred and ten miles per hour), which gives me a horrible feeling— not just the physical sensation of Kay's Honda shuddering like the space shuttle on reentry but the uncertainty, the not knowing, the feeling of *Will I make it? And if not, when will I know? What will I do then? Stop? Give up? Run away?*

Yet as unpleasant as it can be, you can't deny that this sort of seat-of-your-pants existence, which is what George cultivated at the *Review*, has its benefits. From day to day you never really knew how things were going to turn out, and that kept you focused on the task at hand, not next year, next month or even tomorrow. It also kept you alive to the smaller pleasures, like the discovery of a new voice, or holding a brand-new issue in your hands, or even something as prosaic (yet wonderfully satisfying) as proofreading a story. You couldn't be distracted by money because there wasn't any, and there wasn't the zombielike drive of large institutions to exist solely for existence's sake. To escape inertia, the only fuel was inspiration and a kind of back-against-the-wall, holy-crap-I'm-not-qualified-for-this excitement.

In the anthology that the reading series is celebrating, my favorite piece, an excerpt from a story called "Nighthawks" by the Chicago writer Stuart Dybek, captures something of this heady feeling: the apparently mild mannered narrator, a man driving through the Great Plains, stops by a restaurant late at night for a cup of coffee, and there he happens to meet a "gay divorcée," who invites him to follow her home. Things subsequently turn surreal as the man finds himself chasing the woman through the wheat fields, driving faster and faster and barely maintaining control of his car as he wonders how in the world he ended up in such a situation and what he's doing. In a mere two and a half pages, the story manages to build up, store and then release a powerful charge.

That kind of spontaneous, in-the-moment energy is what being an amateur is about, and as I myself drive like a maniac through New England, it occurs to me that frustration with George had steered me into doubt of the amateur ethos, but the store had steered me back. The store, and of course George himself, who'd been so on my case last year, but whom as a result of all that sparring I now finally feel like I understand. I'm not sure if the *Review* can go on the way it did under him, but if I had the choice between being an amateur and being a professional, I know which one I'd pick.

Of course, if I don't get up to Cambridge it won't matter, because I'll have shamed myself out of whatever chance I have of holding on to my job, and unfortunately that's precisely how it looks like things are going to shake out. But then at five-thirty a twelve-lane toll plaza signifying the Massachusetts border comes into view, and I know that I have a chance to make it. Pushing the Honda to the limit of its structural integrity, I blaze a comet trail down the Mass Turnpike and pull into Greater Boston with less than half an hour to go. Things are looking good (who says the work of an editor is stately and boring?) and I know that God wants me to pull this off, because when I get to the bookstore, the unlikeliest of miracles—a legal parking space in the middle of Harvard Square— opens up before me.

Dashing inside wearing a crazed look, I find that crowds have begun to show up in the sizable numbers that I was worried about, and that a woman who in a nervous way looks just as crazy as me is standing by the door, scanning the faces of the crowd.

"Are you the editor from the *Paris Review*?" she says.

"Yes, I'm here!" I announce triumphantly. "I made it."

Her expression shows that she couldn't care less. "I'm the readings coordinator for the bookstore," she says. Then, a bit snappishly (but with good reason): "Where are your authors?"

"What?!" I gasp. "They're not here?" This is even worse than I had feared. Jamaica Kincaid I was nervous about, but Robert Pinsky I'd confirmed with by telephone the day before. "When does the reading start?"

"Five minutes," the readings coordinator says. "I'm going to go look outside—you check the aisles and see if they came in without my realizing."

So I start inspecting the aisles: poetry, fiction, cookbooks, dictionaries. The store is like the inside of a car that's been in a hot parking lot all day. There's no air-conditioning, and people are taking off their clothes and fanning themselves with the books they've brought for Jamaica Kincaid and Robert Pinsky to autograph.

And then I see her in the classics section, sitting on the floor, almost as if she were hiding. She isn't wearing a hospital gown. But she does seem to be wearing at least six dresses, along with a pair of baby blue running sneakers. I almost trip over her long, pretty legs.

"Ms. Kincaid," I practically shout, "you're here!"

Her face does not exactly respond with equal delight. She looks as if she has been sitting on the floor for a long time and would prefer to go on doing just that.

"It's hot in here," she says. "Did you notice?" In her hands is a copy of *The Iliad*.

"I don't think the air-conditioning is working. I'll see if I can get someone to open a window. In the meantime, I don't know if you want to come over to the part of the bookstore where you'll be, uh . . . where you'll be . . ."

Jamaica Kincaid is looking at me suspiciously. And who can blame her, given how demented I look? Then she starts taking off her shoes.

"Yes?" she says somewhat quizzically.

"You know, where you'll be, uh . . ." I suddenly feel lightheaded. As if the heat in the bookstore and driving for four hours straight like a pizza deliveryman and not eating all day weren't enough, I missed my afternoon coffee. Nevertheless, I manage to squeeze out that final word, "reading," though more in the manner of a petrified rodent than the way I normally would.

"Reading?" says Jamaica Kincaid, causing a terrifying series of questions to flash across my mind: *Does she know she's reading? Or did I just happen to find her here in the Harvard Bookstore? What if my message never got through?* Anything seems possible— anything but things turning out the way I had planned.

"Yes, well, I . . . You are going to read, right? That's what all these people . . . the audience . . ." I look around: the store is practically rippling in the heat, like a desert mirage. Is it a dream, I wonder, and, if so, how much will I remember when I wake up? What does it all mean—*The Iliad,* the baby blue sneakers and Dwayne pulling out his own tooth?

"Yes, of course!" Kincaid suddenly says with the utmost good cheer, while putting her shoes back on. "Is the audience here? Where do you want me to go? Should I sign books afterward?"

Intense relief. I feel like kissing her toes. But then as we're walking over to the podium, the readings coordinator hisses at me, "Where's Robert Pinsky?"

"I don't know!"

"We have to start without him." She goes up to the podium to begin.

The audience is seated in a part of the store that fits about eighty chairs—not nearly enough. The aisles are packed. Scanning the crowd, I see, among several familiar faces, the people from the *Globe* I invited. Jamaica Kincaid and I are standing in an area just slightly out of everyone's view. The readings coordinator gives a short speech, apologizing for the temperature, and then out comes Jamaica Kincaid—who casually takes off her shoes.

"Well," she says, frowning at the microphone, which appears to be dead. Then she picks up a copy of the anthology, which I had carefully opened to the page where her story began, and, holding it as if it were something from another planet, she turns to me and says in a skeptical voice, "Is this the book?"

Offstage, where no one can see me, I nod frantically. Something doesn't feel right.

"It has my piece? That's what you want me to read?"

I nod again. I had assumed, of course, that she would read her own piece, a kind of fever dream called "What I Have Been Doing Lately." And somewhat reluctantly she does. But then the story, being short and recited in a hurry, is over almost as soon as it began, and the bookstore is filled by awkward silence.

"Hmm . . . should I read something else?" Jamaica Kincaid says. She starts scanning the nearby bookshelves, while the crowd shifts uncomfortably. We're in the atlas section, with cookbooks nearby. Through my sweat-soaked shirt you can almost see my heart jumping.

"Well?" Jamaica Kincaid says, looking directly at me.

No time to think. I come out onstage, take the anthology from her hands and open to "Nighthawks."

Now, "Nighthawks" is perfect because it's readable and fast, with almost no dialogue. She starts reading:

"The moon, still cooling off from last night, back in the sky—a bulb insects can't circle."

The crowd is spellbound. No one, including the reader, knows where this story is headed. And come to think of it, I'm a bit unsure myself. It's been a few months since I read "Nighthawks." However, there's no time to stop. The story picks up momentum quickly, and we're already flying along. Then Kincaid gets to a part where the narrator meets the "gay divorcée" and starts necking with her in the parking lot. She stops.

Panic! I had forgotten that part of what gives "Nighthawks" its momentum is a good deal of sexual energy. *Oh my God,* I think, *have I asked Jamaica Kincaid to read a sex scene?*

"What is this . . ." she starts to say in my direction, looking more puzzled than annoyed. I have the urge to run out and take the book away, but it's too late: I can't breathe, can't swallow, can't move. My fists are two hand grenades. Is the piece lewd? Does it have any nudity? Why can't I remember anything? It's only two and half pages long, for God's sake!

"You intend to sit out here all night like teenagers," the gay divorcée says, when the narrator starts trying to get under her shirt, "or do you want to follow me home?"

This is going to be the worst day of my life. The car chase through the wheat fields is obvious. Everyone knows what it means. But does the piece ever cross the line? Jamaica Kincaid is now coming to the end, where the piece gets really frantic, and I swear to God if she doesn't finish soon I'm going to run out of oxygen and pass out at those feet I wanted to kiss. Please finish, please . . .

"She kept driving faster, and I could imagine the toe of her high heel pressing down on the workboot-sized gas pedal of her truck . . . By the time we hit the dirt roads she was driving like a maniac, bouncing over railroad crossings and the humps of drainage pipes, dust swirling behind her so that her taillights were only red pinpoints, and I wondered what radio station she must be listening to, wondered if she was drunker than I'd realized and she thought we were racing, or if she'd had a sudden change of heart and was trying to lose me on those back-roads, and I wondered if I ought to let her."

And then it's over. We made it. The piece is done. The audience is clapping and Jamaica Kincaid is wearing a somewhat dazed expression.

"Now that," she says, "is writing."

Which means I can breathe again. And then as I peek around the corner I see the handsomest man in poetry, Robert Pinsky, striding into the bookstore just in time.

CLOSING TIME

"YOU MUST ALWAYS KNOW WHEN TO PULL OUT," SAYS THE merchant Nazruddin in V. S. Naipaul's *A Bend in the River,* one of the many excellent novels about running a store. "A businessman is someone who buys at ten and is happy to get out at twelve. The other kind of man buys at ten, sees it rise to eighteen and does nothing. He is waiting for it to get to twenty." Shopkeepers make good narrators because they're passive and steady, and they tend to want relatively small things, while the world keeps taking more from them than it gives back. Plus, in the end something awful always happens to them, whether it's the anarchic revolution that sweeps away the postcolonial African nation that Naipaul's shopkeeper has patiently worked to build up, or the equally pointless churn-and-burn of New York commerce that ruins Morris Bober, the Jewish shopkeeper hero of Bernard Malamud's *The Assistant.*

How do you know when to get out? For Bober, one of the signals he hears but is too stubborn to act upon is the arrival of energetic and ruthless competitors. (Malamud's parents were in fact Brooklyn deli owners, part of the last generation of Jewish immigrants to ply the trade.) "The chain store kills the small man," he remarks abstractly. The world changes on him, and he does nothing to protect himself. Like a lot of shopkeepers, he lives in Plato's cave, a hermetically sealed world where the only evidence of a reality outside are the shadows dancing on a cold wall. "Everything will be fine as long as I manage my affairs *in here,*" he thinks, while outside, beyond his awareness, things change and contingencies grow, nowhere as fast as they do in New York.

Brooklyn is changing. Just down the street from where I had my Sesame Street epiphany a few years ago, developers from Cleveland have signed an agreement with the government to build one of the largest properties to come to New York in a generation. Skyscrapers, a hotel, a sports stadium and, amid it all, many different "cultural spaces"—this new development, called Atlantic Yards, is going to be so big that its impact will be felt for miles in every direction. Traffic will have to be rerouted, buildings demolished, their tenants relocated. Purely in terms of size and ambition, it seems like the antithesis of the people's borough. It seems more like . . . Manhattan.

Maybe, though, Atlantic Yards will turn out to be a good thing for us, by raising the value of our lease. Maybe it will provide the sort of foot traffic, tourism and round-the-clock sales that shopkeepers dream about. Maybe we'll get that Manhattan-style store we once thought of going for after all. But we won't have to wait the five or six years that the construction will likely take to find out, for even closer than where Atlantic Yards will be, the landscape is already erupting in a most un-Brooklyn way, sprouting sunlight-hogging apartment complexes with cubicle-sized dwellings wrapped in unfriendly mirrored glass.

You have to try not to be sentimental about it. It makes as little sense to argue against progress and change when it comes to cities as it does with literary magazines. And so one day in 2004, when I open the newspaper and read that a Manhattan real estate developer has bought a parking lot a block away from us and plans to build two hundred apartments and twenty-seven single-family homes there in the coming year, I look on the bright side.

"Think of all the potential customers!," I exclaim to Gab. "When it's finished, we'll be their closest convenience store."

Gab takes the newspaper from me and reads to the part where I left off. Then she says, "But did you see this?" Right after the part about the two hundred apartments it says that the developer intends to line the block with retail space, "perhaps including a supermarket."

We look at each and wait for the other to say what we're both thinking. *Is it time?* After failing to close the store when Kay got out of the hospital, Gab and her mother have been uncharacteristically indecisive. Given that the store was open, we decided we might as well not tie our hands behind our backs and brought back the cigarettes. Sales then quickly returned to a somewhat normal level, first for wintertime and now by the standards of the spring. The problem is that when you're not fighting for survival, it's easy to stop making decisions and fall into the trap of thinking you don't have to. Ambivalence is a luxury; thinking you can have it both ways is virtually synonymous with being spoiled. That's why the do-or-die condition that new immigrants find themselves in is a good one for shopkeepers, because it forces you to be a ruthless decision maker, like Kay and Gab are. Or used to be.

Given the need for clarity and decisiveness, we're again seeing the danger of a family-owned business. On some days Kay will feel depressed and want to close the store, but then she'll get embarrassed for not being stronger and resolve to tough it out. She vacillates, Gab vacillates, and I vacillate, and as a result nothing happens. What it means is that closing down will take as much will and effort as opening did.

AT THE END of the spring, five months after we bring back tobacco, we get caught in another sting. This time it's a Dutch Master cigar sold to a minor while Emo is running the store, and we face the maximum penalties just in time for what should be the busiest part of the year, summer. We should take this as our cue to surrender, but there's no way we're going out on someone else's terms— especially not the city's. Shopkeeping may be a passive trade, but shopkeepers are hardheaded masochists and always try to do things their own way.

Unfortunately, our best hope depends on us persuading the city to give us leniency, which means swallowing our pride and losing some of the adversarial fervor. There's a stipulation in the city's administrative code that says that a tobacco vendor can be absolved of an employee's mistake if he or she can convince a magistrate that the vendor did everything possible to prevent such errors. It's a long shot, but occasionally plaintiffs do find sympathy, and so after scheduling a hearing, Gab and I march in to John Street in lower Manhattan, where the Adjudication Division of Consumer Affairs occupies a Kafkaesque warren of dim, windowless court-rooms on the eleventh floor of a black marble building.

It is the DMV from hell. Twenty or so grown men—schlubs in their puffy vests and hooded sweatshirts—rock in their chairs neurotically, mumbling to themselves in Urdu, Spanish or Korean while waiting to be summoned to a doughnut-sized hole in a Plexiglas window. We sit like a herd of frightened animals in the center of the room, bunched tightly, surrounded on all sides but one by that humiliating Plexiglas wall. A potbellied security guard with a walkie-talkie the size of a nightstick circles us like a starved cat, looking for new reasons to punish us. "NO TALKING!" he screams when someone's cell phone goes off, and "NO EATING!" when someone takes half a bagel out of his pocket. Meanwhile, the clerks behind the Plexiglas gorge themselves on enormous foil-wrapped breakfasts obtained from delis down on Wall Street.

I try to maintain an upright pose in my chair, but the seat is made of the same kind of hard slippery plastic as bus-station chairs. After a few hours I give up and slouch like a pouty teenager. Soon half the day is gone, and it takes constant effort not to slide into sleep. As lunchtime ends I approach the doughnut hole in the Plexiglas and ask, "We were supposed to be seen at nine A.M. Why is this taking so long?"

"Some of our judges are *very* busy," says a voice behind the glass. "Now go back and sit down."

We wait another hour, until finally an unsmiling man with a Haitian-sounding name (Patrice or something like that) and the smell of someone who just emerged from a steamy locker room and daubed himself with talcum powder calls us into a windowless office.

"So," he says eagerly, licking his lips as he opens his briefcase, "what have you done to mitigate your circumstances?"

Gab opens her own briefcase and presents an affidavit certifying that we have terminated Emo's employment. It's an absurd document—*This is to certify that I have fired my own aunt*—but the city insists upon it if a violator has any hope of leniency.

"Are you representing the deli owner?" Patrice or whatever his name is asks Gab.

"I am the deli owner," Gab says.

This causes Patrice or whatever his name is to raise his eyebrows, a sign that things might be working in our favor. Gab and I had anticipated that the Adjudication Division of Consumer Affairs rarely saw actual lawyers accustomed to courtroom argument. *Well, today for once they'll get a real fight,* we vowed, for Gab has prepared not just affidavits but taken pictures of the store and gathered documents showing that as shopkeepers we have taken every possible measure to prevent underage sales. She's pored over Consumer Affairs' own regulations, highlighting passages in neon pink the way she did with homework assignments in college, then assembled her evidence into a dossier the size and weight of a phone book. And to top it all off she's put on her most fearsome lawyer's outfit, a truly sharklike skirt-and-jacket combo, which more than makes her stick out from those grease-stained schlubs in their puffy jackets.

But Patrice or whatever his name is no pushover. After Gab presents her case, he attempts to show that we could have done more. "Is that sign really visible?" he asks, jabbing his finger at one of Gab's pictures. "Did you give clear instructions to your employees?" Gab, however, is able to parry each thrust, and after half an hour or so she seems to gain the upper hand. Patrice stops probing, leans back in his chair, and smiles for the first time.

"This is very impressive," he says, lifting up the dossier. "I've been here a few years, and I can say I've never seen anything like it." He says that strictly speaking, the tobacco license has to be surrendered whenever there are two violations; however, because of our strenuous efforts to be responsible storeowners, he can see the case for leniency. He promises to inform us of his decision in a few weeks.

On the way home Gab and I can't help but gloat a little. Patrice's reassuring demeanor as he shuttled us out left us feeling no doubt that things will turn out as we hoped. To celebrate, we buy a couple of beers at a deli (wrapped in brown paper bags, of course, as per New York City Administrative Code, section 10-125, "consumption of alcohol in public": "No person shall drink or consume an alcoholic beverage, or possess, with intent to drink or consume, an open container containing an alcoholic beverage in any public place except at a block party, feast or similar function for which a permit has been obtained . . .) and drink them in the company of pigeons and seagulls on the Brooklyn-facing side of the Staten Island Ferry as it makes a glorious midday crossing of New York Harbor.

WHEN THE LETTER arrives, I can almost taste the beer on the ferry coming back up, and wish that the pigeons were around so that I could kick or at least yell at one of them. The city, as Patrice had led us to believe, had given us credit for the measures we had taken to prevent underage tobacco sales, including the firing of Emo. However, says the letter, there was one measure we didn't take: we didn't fire the person who originally got us in trouble for selling tobacco to a minor—that is, me. Apparently the city thought that I should fire myself (something I would have been all too happy to do at the time, if it were possible) or maybe it wanted Gab to, which would have required what? Us to get a divorce and split up our assets? Hide the fact that we co-owned the store? *Sell the business to a relative, just as the deli owner at Habib's suggested?* Regardless, it's too late now, and the city is denying our request for leniency. We must forfeit our licenses or face criminal charges and a fine of one hundred dollars a day.

AT ANY JOB the best part of the day is going home, and our deli is no exception. The last hour of the night is invariably the most miserable, taken up by gruesome tasks like fishing fingernails out of the cash till and wiping down the slicer. At that hour you also get the worst customers of the evening, the drunks, the skeeves and the people who seem to seek out helpless deli workers and other innocent victims who have no choice but to hear about their cat's digestive problems or a scene-by-scene rundown of the latest Pauly Shore movie. (Salim once said when we asked him why he didn't keep the store open past one o'clock, "Trust me, you don't want the kind of customers who come in after one.") If you stay open even one minute later, you can be sure someone will start banging on the window and begging you to unlock the door, reopen the register and sell them a quart of milk. And if it's a regular customer, you probably will.

After that you're free, and not only are you liberated from the store and difficult customers, but at one o'clock in the morning you are physically free to do almost anything you want: drive on the sidewalk, window-shop naked, land an airplane on Atlantic Avenue. New York may be a twenty-four-hour city, but after midnight there is still a big difference between Manhattan and Brooklyn, and at first the stillness is disorienting, if not a little spooky.

However, the drive on the Brooklyn-Queens Expressway is nothing if not pleasurable. The police don't even bother patrolling, and you can drive at speeds that on an elevated highway like the BQE truly feel like flying. Of course, at that time of night most of the drivers are exhausted late-shift workers trying to get home before their eyes involuntarily shut, and you often see the remnants of terrible, fiery accidents that close the highway for hours, but at least until you hit one of those driving the BQE at night is fun, and the ride over the Verrazano Bridge at one-thirty A.M. is like jetting silently into space, the perfect way to end the night.

One stifling August evening I stop by the store on my way home from the *Review* to check on Dwayne and Kevin (the college kid who's still working at the store), have a sandwich for dinner and listen to a few of Dwayne's stories. At eight o'clock the temperature still feels like noon. When a hot day ends and relief doesn't come, you feel cheated, like you're being toyed with, and in the bad old days of New York, you would turn on the ten o'clock news on a night like tonight, and the first six stories would be about murder or armed robbery, half of which would take place at Domingo's Mini-Super in Washington Heights or the New Steve Deli on Avenue C. A grim-faced newscaster would hand off to an even grimmer-faced reporter standing outside a doorway barricaded in police tape, with candles burning on the sidewalk and family members bawling nearby. And then they would show The Video, the grainy, silent, eight-shots-per-minute film from the overhead security cam that would make everything look like it happened in slow motion inside an elevator. "Man, I could have dodged that baseball bat!" you would think. Sometimes since the store opened I've wondered how I'll look in silent, grainy super-slo-mo on the ten o'clock news, and then I remember: *Oh, yeah, we don't have a security camera.* It's one of those decisions we've postponed as we waffle back and forth on the deli's future.

Tonight, though, the city seems peaceful, almost like a small town. On my way home I can feel the barometer finally dropping and see the lightning on the horizon, and after drinking half a beer in front of the TV I fall asleep before midnight for the first time since we bought the store.

The phone rings an hour later, at one A.M. sharp. Lunging across Gab's sleeping body, I end up half on the floor, pressing the receiver to my ear.

"Hello?" I sputter. "Hello? Hello?"

The caller ID number belongs to the store, but no one is at the other end of the line.

"Who is it?" says Gab.

"The store," I say, as if the store itself has called to give us a warning. Then in the background I hear a loud crash and shouting.

"Dwayne, is that you? Who's there? What's happening?"

Finally, I hear Dwayne's labored breath—he's panting, practically wheezing—and he tells me in an awful voice that there's been an incident, some kind of robbery or mugging, and I better come over quickly because there's "blood all over the place." Then he drops the phone and I can hear another crash and a shout, as if the incident's still going on.

"What's happening?" Gab asks. "Did we get robbed?"

"I don't know," I say, getting dressed. "I'm going there now. Call 911."

Soon I'm racing in the opposite direction on the same roads I traveled barely three hours ago, now slick with rain. I keep dialing the store with my cell phone, but no one answers. I want information, details, updates—is everyone still alive? have the cops come?—and I can't wait the twenty minutes it takes to get there. The blood Dwayne mentioned, the blood. Was it his or someone else's? Is Kevin okay? Who was at the store and who is there now?

Then I remember Dwayne's gun and feel sick to my stomach. I should have done something. I should have frisked him every day and checked his backpack, and then as a family we should have done everything in our power to make the store a safer place. For instance, why couldn't we at least have bought one of those fake security cameras that you attach behind the register to make people think they're being recorded? If Dwayne hurt somebody, what does that mean for us? The more I think about this, the more I need to get there, and then because I am thinking in this selfish way, I feel even sicker.

It's time to get out. The gong has sounded, and this time everyone in the family will hear it at the same time.

At Atlantic Avenue and Hoyt Street sirens are flashing, and a police car has parked awkwardly on the sidewalk. And yet the scene looks weirdly peaceful, as if whatever happened took place hours and hours ago. I see the police tape cordoning off a section of side-walk near where we put out the trash, but not the candles or the wailing relatives or the reporters and their cameramen. It seems like nothing all too serious could have happened here tonight.

And then I see the puddle of blood, two feet long and a foot wide, glimmering on the sidewalk. At its center sits an expensive embroidered Yankees cap that was probably bone white an hour ago and now has the same color as the blackening pool.

Turns out it's the robber's cap. At closing time, he and his accomplice—both teenagers from Bay Ridge, a middle-class white community in South Brooklyn—walked into the store. Kevin, who was shutting down the register at the time, appeared, from their point of view, to be the only person on duty. Dwayne had gone back to the stockroom to fill a bucket with mop water, and as the plume beat noisily against the plastic, his hearing was blocked. The teenager in the Yankees cap pointed a gun at Kevin and told him to give him the contents of the register. Kevin, thankfully, didn't hes-itate to comply. He put the entire drawer of cash on the counter next to an aluminum tray of biscotti, and the teens started stuffing their pockets. But then Dwayne turned off the water, and one of the teenagers accidentally knocked over the biscotti.

"Everything okay?" shouted Dwayne.

The robbers bolted, and Dwayne, after sticking his head out of the stockroom and seeing the look on Kevin's face, started running too.

"No, Dwayne!" Kevin shouted. "They've got a gun!"

Dwayne kept going, however, and found the robbers fleeing down Hoyt Street *on bicycles*. The one with the cash had already got-ten away. The one with the gun was struggling, though, and when he realized what was coming after him, he must have wanted to die. After a flying leap, Dwayne tackled the slower robber and crashed with him to the sidewalk, both of them landing on the bike. At that point the robber still had his gun, which during the tussle ended up pointed near Dwayne's face. He pulled the trigger, and what came out of the muzzle—a BB, not a bullet—bounced harmlessly down the street.

Dwayne then began beating the robber to a pulp, until luckily for both of them, a customer happened by and convinced Dwayne to let up. The robber, in addition to having a broken jaw, would later need fifty-two stitches to close up a single arc-shaped gash running from his temple to his chin. Thus the pool of blood.

("They jumped me," the robber would later tell police. "I was just out riding my bike, and this guy came out of the deli and knocked me down for no reason." He and his friend, whom the police will pick up a few days later, will both turn out to have criminal records.)

Armed robbers on bicycles wielding BB guns. It would be a joke if not for that hideous puddle. For days afterward I keep thinking about the blood and wondering how so much of it poured out of somebody who managed not to die. Fifty-two stitches doesn't seem like enough. It makes me wish that I had seen the robber, who has been handcuffed and is already on his way to the hospital when I arrive. I ask Dwayne to describe the incident, expecting the usual amount of exuberant detail, but that is the most surprising part of the evening: Dwayne seems shaken, as if he's as unaccustomed to violence as, well, me. When I come into the store he acts as if nothing had happened by continuing the mopping, but then I notice that he's forgotten to put cleaning detergent in the water, and I say, "Dwayne, why don't you go home. I'll finish up." Initially, he refuses to even look at me, but I won't take no for an answer—something I've never done before with him—and finally he stops resisting. Outside, after forcing him to accept a case of Heineken, I watch him shamble down the street toward the projects without the usual swagger, his head hung low for once.

* * *

THE NEXT DAY at the dinner table Gab says, "I'm calling the Korean newspaper and placing an ad for the store. Anybody have any objections?" No one does.

It takes less than a month. In what appears to be some sort of ethnic paradigm shift, at first all the potential buyers who visit the store are Bengali Indians—stout, mustachioed men who show up in pairs wearing pin-striped suits. But the first buyer to satisfy Gab's price is a Korean-American family that came to America about ten years after the Paks and has slightly younger children, a pair of boys, who want to purchase the store so they can give it to their parents.

On our last day Kay goes to Consumer Affairs in Manhattan and pays off a thousand dollars in fines that she'd *procrastinated* on (deliberately, but still) for as long as possible. Gab, Kay and I go to Jetro and use our store-owner privileges to buy enough toilet paper to fill up the trunk of the car. Then, for the first time when there isn't a blackout or a blizzard, we close early, and stand there around the cash register, the three of us, silently eating take-out Thai food. Customers bang on the door—"Let us in!" "We need lottery tickets!" "A cup of tea!" "Change for a twenty!" "Where's Preach?" Awkwardly and unconvincingly, we pretend not to hear them.

I AIN'T NEVER LEAVING BROOKLYN

IT'S BEEN SIX YEARS SINCE WE SOLD THE DELI, AND DURING that time I've forgotten a lot of things about it, like the price of a Coors Light tallboy and everything I once knew about how to operate the lottery machine. Occasionally I see a former customer on the subway or at a restaurant, and I stare at them, trying to remember what the connection was. *Did we go to college together? Did I work with her? No, that woman likes roast beef and American cheese on white bread with ketchup—cold.* Sometimes these people stare back, as if they're trying to remember too. But I'm afraid to say that most don't even look twice. In an America that people say is becoming less neighborly and more self-segregated, a convenience store might be one of the last places where you spend significant time with people who aren't "you," so to speak. However, it's by nature an ephemeral, shallow community, and only once did I ever make a friend at the store.

One thing I haven't forgotten, though, is the pleasure of the job itself. Sure, nine-hour shifts are physically and psychically demanding, and doing it every day is arduous, and knowing that you'll likely be doing it forever is as demoralizing as the gulag, but according to at least one prominent definition of a satisfying job—the one laid out by Karl Marx in his *Economic and Philosophical Manuscripts of 1844,* which I must have written at least five papers on in college—running a convenience store isn't half bad for the soul. Marx said that under capitalism workers were not "self-actualized" because they merely worked as the equivalent of bolt tighteners or zipper checkers on an assembly line and never saw the fruits of their labor consumed by a living, breathing community. Even in a neighborhood like Boerum Hill, though, where the old community, the one with roots, was feeling more and more embattled, and the new one was composed mainly of young transients, there was no lack of face-to-face connection, especially on those nights when you felt like you were conducting an informal survey of all the different flavors of halitosis. Yes, we were cogs in a way, not having harvested our own shade-grown coffee or baked our own homemade Twinkies, but never did I feel like a mere soda machine waiting to have someone insert a dollar bill in my mouth. The work was varied and challenging, and it took a certain expertise to get each facet of it right. The challenges evolved. There was never a moment in which I didn't feel mentally stimulated by the tasks at hand. The labor itself even had, dare I say, a transcendent moment or two.

Paradoxically, it was this pleasant and even exciting feeling that ultimately convinced me that I was not cut out for the deli business. While I have certainly become less fearful of the marketplace since we bought the store, Kay was essentially right about me at the beginning: I do not love money. Not enough, anyway. And I probably never will, alas. And while I liked the feistiness that shopkeeping brought to life, I was concerned that it was boosting an already healthy sense of paranoia. At some point "Think for yourself" turns into "Trust no one," and this paranoia goes against the communal part of shopkeeping that I enjoyed.

AT THE *Paris Review* there was no future for the editors who stayed on after George's death. A few eventually quit, disillusioned by changes that were either happening or not happening, and the rest, including me, were let go. The board brought in a new team, most of whom were old enough to have had significant experience elsewhere in the media. The office was moved from its cozy little bubble on East Seventy-second Street to a commercial building downtown, and things like marketing and business (hopefully contracts, too) were handed off to specialists in those fields, I'm sure for the better. I have no idea whether the magazine itself is doing well or not, because I haven't been able to bring myself to read it. I get jealous when I think about the excitement that the new editors, whoever they are, must be experiencing whenever they have *that* moment and a manuscript comes out of the slush with an unlikely return address—Zook, Kansas; Auburn Correctional Facility; Staten Island—and the person holding it feels the rush of The Discovery: first their heart quickens, then they start clenching the pages, then they can't do anything in the world except read (a firework could explode right next to them and they wouldn't turn their head), and then all of a sudden they have to get up and find someone, interrupt them, take the phone out of their hands and hang up, whatever, and say, "Read this." The slush is an affirmation that great literature isn't about anything—not what writing program you attended, not how blessed you are in the cheekbone department, not who your friends are—but words themselves. Strange to say, but somehow I ended up missing the part of the *Review* I dreaded most.

THE ONE FRIEND I made at the store was Dwayne, although as I discovered after we no longer worked together, being friends with Dwayne entailed certain challenges. As a coworker I could count on Dwayne for almost anything; the first time I met him he announced that he was on "Asian-people time, not black-people time," and then went on to never miss a day of work, never show up late (except for the incident with the tooth and the pliers) and always return phone calls promptly. However, as a friend, Dwayne was the opposite. Calls went unreturned for months. When we made plans to get together, sometimes he showed up and sometimes he didn't. When he did finally call, you had to spend hours on the phone with him, hearing about his new side career (he was moonlighting as a bouncer), his new girlfriend (a librarian) and the newest addition to his arsenal (a kind of crossbow that shot explosive multitipped arrows containing nerve poison, or something like that). There was endless detail, of course. But I couldn't help wondering if he was leaving something out.

That's because even though he wouldn't say so, Dwayne's life seemed to be falling apart. After we sold the store, Dwayne stayed on under the new owners, who never seemed comfortable with him and let him go after a few months. He then got a job at a deli closer to the projects, which lasted until the store was shut down for running an illegal numbers game. He was subsequently out of work for a while, hunting for jobs, and at one point I met him at the Ale House, a restaurant on Atlantic Avenue, so we could go over a job recommendation I had written. (I had been drinking for an hour by the time he showed.) He said nothing was panning out, not even the openings for minimum wage jobs, but he tried to put a brave face on it.

"Maybe I'll just go back to what all the rest of them brothers doin', standin' on a corner with some product in my pocket. Go back to the roots, to what got me where I am," he laughed.

"What about the new Applebee's"—Dwayne's favorite restaurant—"that's opening at Atlantic Yards?" I asked.

"Do I look Mexican to you? C'mon."

Dwayne didn't seem troubled, but I was. It didn't seem right that someone so smart and hardworking should have to struggle for employment. In an ideal world, he should have been able to find not just any job, but one that capitalized on his vast talents. But at the very least, he should have been able to find a job in the neighborhood where he'd spent his entire life.

"Dwayne, why don't you open your own deli? You don't need to work for someone else, and if you need a loan or something, people will help you. You could do anything."

But Dwayne's ambitions were different.

"I don't want to be no astronaut," he said. "I just want to work, watch my kids grow up and lay back in peace. You ain't noticed that about me yet? After thirty-six years I ain't in jail or stuck on no drugs, and I ain't dead. I think that's pretty good."

A few weeks later I called Dwayne again and got a message that his phone had been disconnected. I waited another month, then went to Boerum Hill and started asking people if they knew where he was. No one could tell me anything except Alonzo, the now retired plumber.

"He moved," he said. "He living down in Far Rockaway."

"Far Rockaway?" I repeated in disbelief. "Dwayne moved to Queens? *Dwayne left Brooklyn?*" It didn't seem possible. After that, I began to panic. It was the same dynamic as with the gun: if anyone could take care of himself, Dwayne could, but also, if anyone could get himself into trouble . . .

A few weeks later, he called. As soon as I picked up the phone he started talking as if I had seen him yesterday, telling me what he'd eaten for breakfast that morning, how long he'd waited for the A train the previous night, a plot summary of a show apparently called *Extreme Factor,* which he'd watched when he'd gotten home, how he would live his life if he only had one arm, and—

"Dwayne!" I interrupted. "Where have you been? You had us worried sick. Alonzo the plumber said you moved to Queens."

This seemed to offend Dwayne.

"I ain't never leaving Brooklyn!" he barked. However, he admitted it was partially true—he had moved from his longtime apartment on Smith Street. "The landlord raised the rent," he said glumly. "I didn't like that neighborhood no more anyway." Part of the week he was spending with his girlfriend the librarian on Bergen Street.

In general he sounded okay. However, Dwayne *always* sounded okay if you let him get going. My worries about him continued. At the store, Dwayne had worked a staggering number of hours, often more than sixty a week, and now to make the same amount of money he was working part-time jobs all over the place: Coney Island, east midtown, the West Village, even Hempstead, Long Island. The traveling was brutal; at least when he'd worked at the store, his apartment had been three blocks away. Now he spent all his time sleeping and eating on trains, which for someone whose lifestyle habits were already lethal (two six-packs of Heineken a day, one pack of Newports, extreme quantities of fast food that probably made him weigh eighty pounds more than he should) was painful to consider. And there was the work itself. Since leaving the deli world, Dwayne had become something of a professional inflictor of violence. His day job was in security at department stores in midtown, where he scowled at and occasionally tackled robbers the same way he'd done at the deli. At night came the dirtier work as a bouncer at a string of nightclubs in Brooklyn and

Queens. One night I visited him at a bar under the BQE, near Jetro, where he was manning the door and where the clientele consisted mainly of falling-down-drunk Central American migrants. Here Dwayne wasn't so much a deterrent as an in-house brawler taking on all comers. The fighting was guaranteed, and after one of the drunks came at him with a broken bottle, Dwayne would sit on the poor fellow until his friends came and peeled him off the sidewalk. It was bloody, sordid work, and for all the risks involved it didn't pay particularly well. But the dirtiest job of all, according to Dwayne, was what he did on weekends, working as an umpire for Little League baseball in Park Slope.

"The parents are some crazy fuckers," he said, shaking his head. It was so bad that he'd bought himself a pit bull and started taking it with him to games.

But were three jobs enough?

"I ain't never leaving Brooklyn!" he continued to shout at me every time I managed to track him down, even after he'd broken up with the librarian and was calling me from Kingsbridge, up in the Bronx, where he'd "temporarily relocated."

"I ain't never leaving Brooklyn!"

That was what he shouted at me, again, the last time I talked to him. He wasn't sure exactly where he was that time—he'd started out on a train bound for Hempstead and slept past the stop; now he couldn't tell which town he was in.

"I'll call you back," he said wearily.

He never did. We went through our worst period of not communicating after that, a good six months where he didn't call. Finally, Gab went to one of the department stores where he worked and asked a cashier what Dwayne's hours were, so she could come back and find him. The woman covered her mouth and ran away, and Gab knew. When the cashier's supervisor came back holding Dwayne's funeral program, she was already crying.

Dwayne had had an aneurysm just two weeks before. He'd been pingponging around the city more than usual, bouncing from his kids to his jobs to his girlfriend (he was trying to get back together with the librarian), and one night something inside him just gave. He was up in the Bronx when it happened, and a friend who was with him called an ambulance right away, but like everything with Dwayne, the rupture was so massive that he never had a chance.

Everyone said the same thing about his funeral: it was the most varied group of people they'd ever seen—blacks, whites, Asians, Mexicans, old people, young people. Everyone. And nine months later I find myself still thinking that one of these days he's going to call.

THE SAME MONTH as Dwayne's death, Gab and I finally moved out of Kay's basement. Like everyone who moves back into a parental household, we'd gone to that subterranean netherworld thinking our stay would last only a few months, then watched as somehow eight years passed by. During that time almost a dozen of Gab's other relatives came and went too, some of whom also stayed longer than they'd intended. But none stuck around as long as us. We were the champion malingerers, the winners of the homeliness sweepstakes, and after a certain point it began to feel like we would truly never leave.

Not that we ever stopped trying; as soon as we had the financial means—after Gab went back to work, after my own income picked up again, and after the store stopped being such a money suck—we started looking for apartments again, and on more than one occasion came within an inch of signing on the dotted line. Things just got in the way. Fate didn't want us to move. And the more we failed, the more resigned we became. (The more stunted our independence became, you might say—just as my parents had feared.)

It was as if we lacked the mass to escape Kay's gravitational orbit. What we needed was to add weight.

Which should have been easy, because a few months before we sold the store, Gab finally became pregnant, and putting on pounds was not exactly a problem. It had been a year since we'd started trying, and our failure remained as mysterious as ever. (According to the results of the fertility testing, we shouldn't have been struggling, which made me think it really was psychological.) When the biology finally clicked, however, the timing was perfect. We would soon be selling the store and getting back our money, Kay's health was looking up (she'd gone nine months without smoking and had significantly lowered her blood pressure through exercise and treatment), and now we had the perfect excuse to at last get back to our independent lives.

But did we want to get back to independent lives? Were we even the same people we used to be before we'd given those independent lives up? Had the store not changed us? It almost would have been disappointing to think that after so much pain and drama, we could just slip back into our former existences, as if nothing had happened. I certainly wasn't the same person. None of us was.

After we sold the store, Kay went through something of a dark period. For the first time in all the years I've known her, she started talking about taking a break from family.

"I'm old person now," she said. "I'm finish being mother. You clean your own room, do own laundry." If my mother-in-law had learned anything about herself as a result of the store, it was that she had limits (limits that had long been obvious to everyone else). Now that she was aware of them, she would have to make a choice: family or work, but not both if she wanted to remain healthy.

In the fall, she bought a ticket to visit her oldest sister, Kunimo, in Los Angeles. Before she left she told me she might stay there for a while, even past the birth of our child. Kunimo had recently joined a retirement community and wanted Kay to look at some vacancies in her building. Kay was curious.

The trip was not a success, however. Kunimo's friends in the retirement community were of a churchly bent common among Korean-Americans, but not Kay. After two weeks of ladling soup to the homeless and picking trash off the beach, she bolted home, and soon the black mood seemed to pass. She said she had decided not to go back to work, and wanted to know if Gab and I would consider staying in the house so she could help us raise the baby.

But Gab was ready to move out. She'd just spent the two hardest years of her life struggling to be a good daughter and measure up to her mother's example. Whether she'd succeeded or not, she knew that she'd (A) tried and (B) suffered as a result. Therefore, she reasoned, she'd finally earned the luxury of escape and a guilt-free independent life.

And there was another reason to move out: *samchilil.*

Samchilil is the traditional postpartum-care regime mothers undergo in Korea. Like everything in Korean medicine, it has to do with maintaining a sort of yin-and-yang balance between cold and hot. After the fetus leaves the mother's uterus, traditionalists see the mother as dangerously vulnerable to cold; her body needs aggressive warming both from within and without; otherwise, she can suffer "loose bones," soft teeth, and bouts of poor health for the rest of her life. The antidote is to eat nothing but steaming bowls of seaweed soup and several large glasses a day of "deer juice" (powdered deer antler mixed with savory medicinal herbs) for three weeks, during which time she must also remain confined to an overheated bedroom while wearing several suffocating layers of clothes, including a girdle. She isn't allowed to shower, read (which supposedly damages the eyes) or eat anything tougher than baby food.

"It's ridiculous," said Gab, who normally takes an assiduously nonjudgmental view of her mother's medical beliefs. "Hocus-pocus."

I figured she was just cranky because it had been a difficult pregnancy. (By the eighth month she'd put on forty pounds, nearly a 30 percent increase of her body weight.) But when Kay came back from Los Angeles and started ordering things like the girdle (which looked as if it were made for a Barbie doll), the seaweed soup ingredients and the deer juice, Gab put her foot down.

"We have to move before the baby is born," she announced. "There's no way I'm going three weeks without a shower."

This was really a change. For years I'd watched Kay force-feed Gab giant glasses of deer juice, which Gab hated (I couldn't even stand to be in the same room as it, the stuff smelled so awful), and never once did Gab resist or try to run away. Holding her nose, she'd say, "It's easier just to do it and not think about it," an attitude that seemed to capture more than just her feelings toward foul-smelling potions.

But now Gab seemed increasingly of a mind to decide for herself what was best for her. So she told Kay we were leaving, and Kay, though disappointed, reluctantly canceled the order of deer juice and returned the girdle. Soon Gab and I were on the hunt again, prowling the real estate offerings in Bay Ridge and Sunset Park. We were on the verge of signing a contract for an apartment in Bushwick when *wham-o!* The guilt hit her like a sledgehammer.

"I can't," she said dejectedly in a Park Slope Mexican restaurant. She'd been thinking about *samchilil* and worrying that maybe she was being too dismissive. "I'd hate to be wrong."

"You mean, you think if you don't drink deer juice for three weeks you'll have loose bones?" I asked, now a bit exasperated by the whole thing.

"Hey, my mother knows people who had that happen," Gab said defensively.

"And you're willing to spend three weeks dressed like a mummy not to be one of them? Not shower? Pee in a bedpan?"

Gab looked stricken. "You don't understand," she said, lowering her voice. "They're in my head."

"Who?"

"The voices of my mother and Emo." (Emo had been enthusiastically gearing up for *samchilil* too.) "I keep thinking that I know better, but there's nothing I can do to ignore them. And what I keep dwelling on is the baby—if I'm not healthy, then who's going to take care of her? Who's going to provide milk and who's going to sleep with her and . . ." Her voice trailed off.

"And I don't want soft teeth," she added almost pathetically. However, now that this had come out and the choice was clear, I knew that she would be feeling better, the way she always did after she made a decision. And indeed soon she was, at which point her mood became downright peppy. I watched in amazement as she summoned the waiter and ordered yet another appetizer, "something with melted cheese."

"But you realize," I said forcefully, trying to make a stand, "that if we stay in the house past the baby's birth, we won't be able to start looking for apartments again until you're back on your feet, which might take a few months, and then your maternity leave will end and we'll become dependent on your mother for child care, and she'll become emotionally connected to the baby, all of which will embed us in the house more than ever." I leaned across the table and fixed her with the most unwavering, soul-penetrating stare I could muster—and for a moment it seemed to work. Gab looked at me wide-eyed and seemed unable to swallow. But then she returned to her normal expression.

"I know," she said cheerily. She seemed impervious to the point I was making. Her eye was on the waiter, who was bringing her more fried cheese.

"But don't you remember how miserable we've been?" I asked, practically pounding the table. "Don't you remember how stressful living with your family can be, how desperately we've wanted our own space?" I threw the book at her, recounting every painful incident I could think of, until I had run out of breath.

Gab wiped away a little hot oil that had squirted from the fried cheese onto her chin.

"Do you have any evidence for that?" she said. "Because not that I'm questioning your memory or anything, but honestly, I'm having trouble remembering it that way. Did you write any of that down?"

It occurred to me then that Gab and Kay were both doomed. Even after coming to an understanding of themselves, they remained largely powerless to do anything about it. And this I envied them for, as I always had. After we went home Gab told her mother that we had decided to stay, and she could get the things she needed for *samchilil.*

AND THUS WE embarked on the only endeavor more likely to blow up a family than co-managing a business: child rearing. As any parent knows, no issue connected with child rearing is too petty to get into a knock-down, drag-out screaming match over. When kids are involved, everything matters, everything is life or death, everything is *the future.* And the more people who are involved, the more viewpoints there are on what the future should be. Not to mention the fact that in a household like ours, the views tend to be as far apart as, well, Seoul and Boston. In all too familiar ways we were recapitulating the battles over the deli: issues of taste and discernment, high versus low, what's popular versus what's good for you. Television time, sugary snacks, plastic toys—you can all too easily imagine the issues, I'm sure. Once again every decision was a showdown of cosmic significance (for me, anyway), and once again we were in a situation where Kay, perhaps because she wasn't living too much in the future or the past (or perhaps because her only goal at all times seemed to be to make a child grow bigger, bigger and bigger), seemed to know exactly what she wanted.

But now so did I. Inhabiting the body of an immigrant entrepreneur, however temporarily, had thrown my own values into relief, highlighting tendencies and beliefs that, when viewed as a whole, had a certain consistency and cohesion. As a result, when I looked in the mirror, more and more I knew what I saw: a villain from a 1980s ski movie. (Literally. Since the deli had opened I'd noticed myself dressing, not always consciously, like someone named Lance who wore long scarves draped over white turtlenecks and crested blazers.) I accepted that. There was no escaping being a Wasp, but I was okay with that. I'd be a chaperone on the great global field trip into the future, a shusher in the movie theater, a terminally ambivalent, hyperaware, hopelessly inward control freak with a sphincter so tight it threatened to invert on itself and create a black hole, and I'd be content. Call me acquiescent, but if I had learned anything from Kay, Dwayne and George (who, you'd think, should have had nothing in common) it was that (A) they seemed to know exactly who they were, and (B) they cut their own path, venturing (in different ways, of course) from the world they'd been born into, as if self-knowledge gave them the confidence to take on unfamiliar situations. The store hadn't started out that way for me—it wasn't an adventure or even an attempt at self-discovery, but more of an accidental voyage into highly foreign territory. However, for someone lacking the kind of confidence Dwayne, Kay and George had, it was a good—maybe the perfect—way of finding it, for which I feel lucky indeed.

And now I'm going to go eat some Chessmen. Thanks to the store, our new apartment has a lifetime supply.

AUTHOR'S NOTE

Occasionally over the last few years while writing this book I've gone back and interviewed people who might appear in the story. Once, I visited an old Brooklyn character named Carmine Cincotta, who used to sell us produce from his stand on Court Street. When I told Carmine I was writing a memoir, he laughed.

"You bought the deli so you could write a book, didn't you? Admit it."

I had to ask myself, Was he right? Could that have been one of my motives, secret even to myself? However, the truth is when we bought the deli, I was involved in an entirely different kind of writing project (a work of journalism) and way too hardheaded to even think about switching to something as self-selling as a memoir. So I didn't begin keeping serious notes on the deli until we'd been in business for a while, which later complicated the job of writing considerably. I had lots of memories—vivid memories, painful memories—but it wasn't always easy to sort them out or remember things like what happened when. In theory, having access to the memories of family members should have made things easier, except everyone remembers things differently, or not at all.

Ultimately it was the experience I wanted to capture, the feeling, and most of all to be honest about what had changed in me and why. And this occasionally required straying (though only slightly, I believe) from the exact verisimilitude of events. Some of the dialogue is an approximation of what people actually said, and some events appear a touch out of sequence. A few minor characters are composites. Except for family members, public figures, Dwayne and a few others, identities have been scrambled, including those of companies we did business with.

Finally, this book was influenced by many other books, but it could not have been written without *Albion's Seed* by David Hackett Fischer, *Changes and Conflicts: Korean Immigrant Families in New York* by Pyong Gap Min, and above all, Nelson Aldrich's *Old Money*. Eternal thanks to my editor, Gillian Blake; my agent, Heather Schroder; Meredith Finn at New Line; and family members on both sides.

ABOUT THE AUTHOR

Ben Ryder Howe has written for *The New Yorker,* the *Atlantic Monthly* and *Outside,* and his work has been selected for *Best American Travel Writing.* He is a former senior editor of the *Paris Review.* This is his first book.